Northern Plainsmen

Northern Plainsmen

Adaptive Strategy and Agrarian Life

John W. Bennett

Washington University

Foreword by Walter R. Goldschmidt
University of California, Los Angeles

Aldine Publishing Company / Chicago

First published 1969 by
Aldine Publishing Company
529 South Wabash Avenue
Chicago, Illinois 60605

Library of Congress Catalog Card Number 76–75043

SBN 20201090

Designed by Chestnut House

Printed in the United States of America

To I., M., and R.

Foreword

WALTER GOLDSCHMIDT

The Great Plains of North America have been a place of social ferment for nearly half a millenium. First occupied by bands of Indians hunting game on foot, it was invaded by successive elements of Western technology and successive waves of European immigrants. Each change in man's technical apparatus altered the circumstances of life. Anthropologists, notably Frank Secoy and S. C. Oliver, have documented some of the changes brought about by the introduction of the horse and firearms, rendering the Indians mobile and effective warriors who eventually contested the Euro-American invasion. Historians, particularly Walter P. Webb in his classic work *The Great Plains,* have demonstrated how the six-shooter, the windmill, and the barbed wire fence gradually tamed the vast wilderness that extended from the Mississippi-Missouri river to the foothills of the Rockies.

John Bennett brings this story up to date. By the careful examination of a sample region of the Canadian plains he demonstrates the patterns of life as they have emerged and taken shape in the 1960's—less than a century after the great cattle drives that first brought the region under the control of outlanders. His method is socioeconomic rather than historical, for he concentrates on the patterns of today. Yet he knows that today's events are fettered to the past, and he gives a picture of the development of modern life out of its historical roots.

Bennett studies four major social groups in the region he calls Jasper: the remnants of Indian bands eking out a marginal existence on welfare, casual labor, and a few cows on submarginal land; the cattle ranchers maintaining social dominance because they control the traditional values of the White Man in the area; the farmers facing the vicissitudes of a land inhospitable to the cultivation of grain in accord with practices developed in other parts of the world; and the colonies of Hutterite Brethren, who bring to the area the most unusual invention of all, a new kind of social organization. These groups live side by side, they share political and many social institutions, they help and occasionally exploit one another, but essentially they remain distinct cultural units, engaging in separate kinds of economic activities. For each has established its distinct ecological niche through a process of adaptive adjustment, both in its techniques of production and in its institutional arrangements.

These adjustments take place through the medium of culture, which may be seen as man's adaptive mechanism—what has enabled him to establish himself on virtually the whole face of the earth. This process involves not merely the acquisition of the tools and techniques by which he gains his livelihood and protects himself from the elements, but also the social arrangements through which men collaborate with each other in exploiting their habitat. Turning this around, we see that man must build his cultures in such a way that he is enabled, minimally at least, to survive under the conditions his environment creates. This adaptive process, which is a continuous pattern of adjustment to continuously changing circumstances, we call the process of cultural ecology.

This does not mean that environment shapes culture or that necessity is the mother of invention. For it is man that shapes culture, transforming his past behavior in such ways as he finds possible to meet the circumstances of the present. He does this by constant experimentation, limited by his sense of tradition and the boundaries of his imagination.

In the technological sphere, he does this regularly and almost automatically and often as an individual, because failure to make the necessary adjustments may mean hardship or death. In the social sphere such adaptation is more difficult to accomplish. For one thing, the functional relevance of social institutions is not nearly so obvious to the persons involved; there is less clear feedback from action to result. For another, institutions by their very nature require a consensus, an agreement among the several parties involved. Consensus to change the patterns of life is difficult to achieve under any circumstances; it is far more difficult to attain when the advantages of such change remain obscure and uncertain. Furthermore, what may be advantageous to the community as a whole may not be advantageous to some individuals, who then reasonably reject the alteration in their patterns of life. Nevertheless, the study of culture shows that man's institutional arrangements do change as circumstances alter, and that these changes are adaptive in the sense set forth above.

Bennett has described this process of adaptation in Saskatchewan, where the plains environment is specialized and demanding. The adjustment that the Indians achieved was destroyed by the invasion of outsiders who eliminated their major resource —the buffalo—and usurped the land, leaving a hollow remnant of a community in marginal areas. This land was capable of supporting two basic resources: livestock and grains. But bringing cattle and wheat to the area was no simple matter; it required that special strains be developed, it required knowledge of soils and native vegetation, and it required that cultivation practices be adapted to the peculiarities of the soils, climate, and topography of the region. It required also that man learn to order his institutions to meet the requirements of these techniques of cultivation and husbandry.

Each of the four groups in Jasper must take into account the existence of the other three as a significant element in their adaptive process. We have already noted that the Indians were forced to make such an adjustment, while the literature of the plains is replete with discussions of the interaction between farmers and ranchers. A most dramatic pattern of adjustment is currently taking place with the introduction into the region of the theocratic social system of the Hutterites. Grafting the most modern Western technology on an old system of religious community life, supported by an institutional ideology of personal asceticism, they have posed a threat to both forms of traditional European economy that preceded them in the area, a threat the non-Hutterites minimize by other institutional devices.

This fact, that each society must adjust not only to its own internal conditions but also to those set for it by the circumambient community of neighbors, is an element in the ecological adjustment of societies and communities that has been inadequately dealt with in the literature. One of the primary contributions of Secoy's study of Plains tribal history is the demonstration that individual groups had to adjust to the new military potential of their neighbors as they acquired the horse and the gun. Similarly, Webb showed that pressures from the East created a constantly shifting set of local conditions as the cattlemen and farmers successively filled the plains.

Internecine warfare is no longer characteristic of the West; nevertheless, external factors continue to be a major factor in the ecological adjustment of Jasper and similar regions. These external factors take many forms, but two predominate. The farmers and cattlemen of Jasper must take into account the vicissitudes of the national and international markets in wheat and beef as surely as they must the uncertainties of rain and sunshine, for it is the nature of the market that determines whether their productive strategies will in the end pay off. Second, the Canadian government and Canadian society in general provide an institutional framework within which the Jasper community must operate. This not only sets limits to what the local people may do, but also, as Bennett clearly demonstrates, provides further opportunities for adaptive experiments. Jasper people must be alert to these external realities—opportunities and constraints—as well as to those closer to home, and it is a signal virtue of this study that Bennett has included these considerations in his analysis.

Preface

The research reported herein was supported principally by grants from the National Science Foundation, with supplementary financing provided by the Agricultural Development Council of New York, and the Graduate School of Washington University. The writer was the principal field worker, but was given assistance by Seena Kohl, Niels Braroe, Charles Thomas, and Peter Rompler. Among colleagues, David Barkin helped with economic matters, and Norman Whitten on social theory. In earlier stages of the analysis, David Schneider advised on kinship, Roger Walker on methodology, and Joseph Kahl on social structure. Important parts of the manuscript were written at Prof. Kahl's hacienda in Cuernavaca, Morelos. Suzanne Findlay and Beverly Schneider aided in the statistical work, and Dorothy Altheimer was typist and general editor. Important assistance was also provided by residents of the "Jasper" region, many of whom were expert consultants as well as informants.

Other reports on the project, which bore the generic title "Saskatchewan Cultural Ecology Research Program," are a volume on the Hutterian Brethren, published in 1967 by Stanford University Press, and a book on the social organization of the ranch and farm communities, in preparation. The present volume was written as a general review of the entire study, and it avoids technical presentations and detailed data tables. It is directed primarily to that peerless officer, General Reader, and less confidently to the private soldiers in academic and technical ranks.

Names of all persons and places in the "Jasper" region are fictitious, incidents have been altered and disguised, and the Jasper reader is advised that attempts to identify them are hazardous!

Contents

Illustrations, Figures, and Tables

TABLES

The writer wishes to convey his gratitude to NIELS BRAROE and SEENA KOHL for their assistance in field research and analysis.

Introduction

This study of a typical region in Western Canada was designed as an exercise in the analysis of a modern agricultural community from an ecological point of view. "Jasper' is the fictitious name of a secondary service center town, and is used to designate the region as a whole. The region is found in the Province of Saskatchewan, Canada, not far from the United States boundary. We selected this particular region for the following reasons: (1) its topography, natural resources, and economy provided a complete profile of the basic western North American economic-ecological pattern; (2) the human groups that settled the region, or had lived in it from early times, likewise duplicated the ecological pattern typical of most western communities, especially the northern Great Plains; (3) the region had experienced a late Euro-American settlement, and therefore had unusually complete historical documentation (at the same time, the stages of this settlement, and the patterns of economic development, though compressed, were similar to those everywhere in the semiarid West); (4) the region had experienced the drouth-and-depression cycles that affected the entire North American West, and therefore provided an example of change and adaptation.

The original inspiration for this research was provided by Walter Webb's classic work *The Great Plains* (1931). Webb sought to show how the social institutions of the humid eastern United States were modified in the arid and semiarid West. He discussed the pioneer range cattleman and his resemblance to the Plains Indians, the invention of the six-shooter and barbed wire, the rise of the horseman, the development of the doctrine of "prior appropriation" in water laws to replace the old humid-lands concept of riparian rights that was inappropriate for a land where streams ran only part of the year, and many other things. Webb has been accused of overstating his case, since the basic Western institutions of land tenure, the family-owned agricultural enterprise, forms of local government and basic life patterns had preserved their eastern character, but Webb may have been more right than he seemed in the 1930's and '40's. Since the end of World War II, the patterns of many institutions in western North American society have begun to change in efforts to adapt to lowering population densities and the need to distribute resources more equitably. An example of the former is the development of the highly specialized prairie town service center, with shops and other facilities developed far beyond the needs of its own modest population and designed to serve an increasingly wide rural hinterland. An example of the latter is the increase throughout the West in the acreage of various forms of cooperatively and collectively managed tracts of land and irrigation projects.

Our overall objective was to examine some of Webb's major conclusions in a particular local setting. The study of localities —that is, human communities or geographical regions—is an anthropological specialty. Most of the data collected by social anthropologists in the past 75 years of professional field work relate to such human situations. The trouble with localities, however, is that one may have difficulty knowing just how typical his community may be of a larger universe—the nation, or some significant section of the nation. In the past, anthropologists were content with studying tribes or communities as objects in their own right, since these were often isolated and out of contact with the larger societies. But the modern world has changed: communities and social groupings have been pulled into macrocosmic frameworks of politics, economy, and social structure at an increasing rate, and they must be studied with reference to these involvements. Thus our specially selected region in western Canada was studied not as a unique object, but as a specimen of the socioeconomic geography of western North America. Consequently our findings have a certain broad generality within this universe.

They may be even more widely representative, as we shall suggest in our final two chapters. Coping with resources and markets is a worldwide phenomenon as demonstrated by the agrarian sectors of the emerging nations of Africa, Asia, and Latin America in their movement toward entrepreneurial, cash-crop agriculture. There is a growing homogeneity in the world: adaptation to natural and social resources, strategy and manipulation, and the relating of cultural patterns to economic needs are processes visible everywhere in the agrarian societies —whose populations, incidentally, still constitute a majority of the world's people. As these tendencies become evident, comparative research on the nature of agrarian development in all societies becomes easier and also more relevant.

METHODOLOGY

The methods used in this study were eclectic. Since the research continued at intervals for a four-year period, it was possible to explore various types of instruments and approaches. The scope of the project required three major types of data: documentary and statistical; interview and questionnaire data; and participative and observational. The documentary and statistical materials were collected in Jasper, and in government and university offices in the Saskatchewan cities of Regina and Saskatoon during the first two years of work. The most relevant statistical materials were assembled in a mimeographed manual and distributed to all members of the project and to some Jasper residents. Many interview data were acquired with a major instrument called the "Regional Schedule," a lengthy affair containing various types of open-end questions and precoded items on nearly all topics of the research. This instrument was administered to a sample of ranchers and farmers in the region, stratified on the basis of data on the region published in the Canadian agricultural census, and slightly modified on the basis of our own experience. It should be noted that our basic regional sample of people was thus based on economic criteria: the types and sizes of agricultural enterprises. Specialized interview schedules on sociocultural topics were also used on special samples of Jasper people constructed with criteria other than economic. The third type of data—the observational—was acquired by the usual ethnological field techniques involving actual residence with informants, visits to homes, attendance at and participation in various ceremonials, meetings, sports events, farm and ranch labor, and the like. There was a great deal of this, and in the long run it probably constituted our most important body of data.

Analysis of the data was equally eclectic. For certain key topics, principally farm management behavior, family cycle data, and certain demographic variables, we used computer technology. Hand or simple machine tabulation served for most of the attitude data and related variables from the Regional Schedule. Various forms of descriptive-analytic and inspectional methods were used for the remainder. We have avoided technical presentations in this book, so the conclusions derived from various methods of analysis are presented descriptively.

One special problem connected with research of this kind should be noted. While our objectives were anthropological—that is, to some extent to obtain pictures of a series of subcultures—we were convinced, on the basis of good evidence, that the key to the Jasper situation lay in ecological and economic processes. This presented us with a challenge, since it required a great deal of technical agricultural and environmental knowledge. We acquired part of this knowledge at the University of Saskatchewan and a federal government experimental farm not far from Jasper on a series of visits throughout the study. We also learned much from government agricultural experts assigned to Jasper, particularly the Agricultural Representative (in the U.S., called "county agent") and supervisors of the irrigation headquarters of the Prairie Farm Rehabilitation Act. Jasper ranchers, farmers, and Hutterites were also an indispensable source of experienced information. We owe much to all of these people; throughout the study they were as much researchers as researched.

As Ernestine Friedl has noted, doing anthropological research on one's own "culture" entails certain difficulties. The very familiarity of the scene diverts attention from important topics, and biasses judgment. We probably did our best field work with the Indians and Hutterites, both of whom had relatively exotic cultures from the North American viewpoint. Farmers and ranchers, being much more familiar, were perhaps treated less intensively, at least in some sectors of their culture. However, similar socioeconomic data was acquired from all groups, and the concept of *adaptation,* as we note in Chapter 2, unified the entire study. Our basic objective was simply to work out the adaptive posture of each important group in the population with respect to the natural and social resources available to them.

Another problem that confronts the student of a contemporary society is the difficulty of making a really novel contribution. The knowledge that already exists is voluminous—hardly an ethnographic detail seems to have been missed. The North American West is a topic of vast and insistent interest in historical writings, social research, and *belles lettres*—and in not-so-*belles lettres*. We were therefore guided, in part, by what had *not* been done. Rural sociologists have often ignored the time dimension, and important aspects of the intersection of social, economic, and natural phenomena in the development of rural society; we accordingly emphasized these topics. Agricultural management specialists have shown little interest in the role of social factors and local culture in the economic development and entrepreneurial economy of farming, and most geographers still focus on description, while only a few are concerned with ecological process. Emphasizing these relatively neglected topics we believe we may have made a contribution.

THE CANADIAN SETTING

How much difference does the Canadian locus of this research make?

The United States West is abundantly familiar to everyone; the fact that Canada had a western frontier is not so well known. The Canadian West was less "wild" than the U.S. West, though just as rugged, and certainly as romantic. The Royal Northwest Mounted Police arrived there in the 1880's, in time to settle down the Indians and nip any real lawlessness in the bud, and the inpouring of settlers was a relatively calm process as compared with some of the more exhuberant cases in the United States. There were few wagon trains, because the Canadian Pacific Railway was built before the bulk of the homesteaders and settlers arrived.

These are differences, but they are not significant differences from the point of view of settlement patterns or the experiences of the settlers in establishing an economy and society, all of which duplicate those south of the border. The basic social processes of the frontier and its aftermath, the droughts and economic depressions, World Wars and recovery—all these are substantially similar. Canada is not as wealthy as the United States, and her western people have enjoyed less in the way of federal support for their economy; consequently their enterprises are somewhat less well established. Jasper farmers and ranchers often remarked that they were "about 15 years behind the fellers down south of here"—meaning the people across the international boundary.

Another difference—but again, not a really important one— is the strong middle-class outlook which characterizes Canadian culture. A British element, this outlook emphasizes the "Protestant" virtues of thrift, sobriety, concealment of violence and conflict when it exists, and a genial, neutral manner of behavior. (Perhaps Canadians are also less likely to use the western frontier experience as a guide for national culture.) Of course not all Jasper people followed the middle-class behavior pattern —Jasperites are, above all, robust westerners. It was the judgment of the field workers, however, that people in Jasper were somewhat less exuberant and outgoing and more inclined to "play their cards close to the vest," than the folks down in Montana. In a more practical sense, these attitudes appear in the general economic conservatism which we felt was a marked characteristic of the Jasper entrepreneurs. But these are chicken–egg questions. The middle-class nicety and conservatism of Canadians may well be nothing more than a response, whatever its historical origin, to the tighter economic opportunities in the Canadian setting.

BIBLIOGRAPHIC NOTES

The classic study of modern adaptation to Great Plains environment is Walter Webb, *The Great Plains*, Ginn, 1931. The definitive critique of this book is found in Fred A. Shannon, *Critiques of Research in the Social Sciences: W. P. Webb's 'The Great Plains,'* Social Science Research Council, 1940. A recent study of the Nebraska section of the Great Plains, with interesting comparative information, is Howard W. Ottoson, *Land and People in the Northern Plains Transition Area*, University of Nebraska Press, 1966. Webb's ideas and findings were brought up to date by Carl Kraenzel in his *Great Plains in Transition*, University of Oklahoma Press, 1955. A study of adaptation to the Canadian section of the Plains is found in W. A. Mackintosh, *Prairie Settlement: The Geographic Background*, Macmillan (Toronto), 1934, and R. W. Murchie and others, *Agricultural Progress on the Prairie Frontier*, Macmillan (Toronto), 1936. The most recent general work on the Plains is Carle C. Zimmerman and Seth Russell, eds., *Symposium on the Great Plains of North America*, North Dakota State University, 1967.

A definition of the problems of anthropological study of the single community is provided by Conrad M. Arensberg, "The Community as Object and as Sample," in C. M. Arensberg and Solon T. Kimball, *Culture and Community*, Harcourt, Brace 1965.

For a summary of agrarian development from the economic point of view, see Milton M. Snodgrass and L. T. Wallace, *Agriculture, Economics, and Growth,* Appleton-Century-Crofts, 1964. A more general and highly recommended study is Albert O. Hirschmann, *The Strategy of Economic Development*, Yale University Press, 1958. Cultural aspects of economic development in the emerging new nations is treated in George M. Foster, *Traditional Cultures and the Impact of Technological Change*, Harper, 1962. (See also notes for chaps. 9 and 10.)

The fact that we are dealing with a society only three generations from its frontier beginning should be emphasized. A compact and insightful analysis of the significance of the frontier in American history (Canada is no exception) is Ray A. Billington, "The American Frontier," reprinted in P. Bohannon and F. Plog, *Beyond the Frontier*, Natural History Press, 1967. A comparative study of pioneer life on frontiers in various parts of the world and including the Canadian Plains is American Geographical Society, Special Publ. No. 14, *Pioneer Settlement: Twenty-Six Authors,* 1932. See also Josiah Bowman, *The*

Pioneer Fringe, American Geographical Society, Special Publ. No. 13, 1931 (this book also contains an article on the more recent pioneering in the Canadian muskeg and forest country to the north of Jasper). For general studies of Canadian society and social culture, see B. Blishen and others, *Canadian Society*, Free Press, 1962, and John Porter, *The Vertical Mosaic*, University of Toronto Press, 1965.

ONE

Adaptation as a Frame
of Reference

This is a study of the socioeconomic adaptations of several human groups to a typical northern Great Plains region in Canada. We call this region, "Jasper," after our fictitious name for its principal service-center town. One of the groups, a reserve of Plains Cree Indians, has lived in the region from early times as aborigines. The others—ranchers, farmers, and Hutterian Brethren—settled in Jasper during the nineteenth and twentieth centuries. In the 1960's, all but the Indians were engaged in gainful economic activities bound up in the larger national agrarian economy of Canada and North America. Only the Indians did not produce crops or livestock for sale on the national market; they survived largely on welfare and various forms of "panhandling." The amount of economic interchange between the four groups varied, but as in other cases where agriculturalists produce for an outside market, the exchanges focused on informal mutual assistance on labor and supplies. Nevertheless, the four groups participated in a common frame of adaptive processes with respect to their use of the natural and social resources of the region.

The ecological problems of agrarian life in the northern Plains are based on the specialized character of the natural resources and their varying distribution in time and space. In aboriginal times, the Indian hunted bison and other hoofed animals on the Plains, and foraged for a variety of vegetable foods and small game in the forested uplands. The highly variable distribution of these food sources, along with water, wood

9

and other necessities, encouraged a nomadic way of life. Population densities were low and population groups widely dispersed, and the essential activities of life were carried on in different geographic locations: bison were hunted on the open plains, other game in the hills; winter camps were established in the coulees; ceremonials were often conducted at the confluence of two rivers.

The contemporary Euro-American population of the Plains settled the area on the basis of a land survey which fixed tenure and residence in particular locations. But since the area's natural resources are marginal or unevenly distributed, fixed tenure meant that many agricultural settlers were not equally endowed. Some had enough land but too little water; others might have water but sandy soil. Therefore natural hazards and economic difficulties worked differential hardships on the settlers, and considerable population fluctuation was the result. Population mobility had been anticipated and "normal" for the nomadic Indians, but it has been disorganizing and "abnormal" for the Euro-American settlers given their customs of sedentary occupation. New types of agricultural production, settlement patterns, transportation, and social customs have emerged to cope with these conditions.

Difficulties resulting from the specialized natural resources of the Plains were, however, only part of the story. From about 1900 to the end of World War II, farmers in the Great Plains suffered from fluctuating prices and markets for their products. Economic depressions (particularly the Great Depression of the 1930's), and exploitative policies of the railroads and the grain companies made economic stability difficult to achieve—a situation greatly intensified by the population's reliance upon only one or two crops (grain and cattle), and the specialized natural resources of the area and high cost of their development for purposes other than agricultural.

This account of the problems of human settlement and economic development in the northern Great Plains has been given an ecological frame of reference. "Ecology," in this book, has two related meanings. First, it is used in the anthropological sense of "cultural ecology," following Julian Steward and other workers in the field. In essence cultural ecology refers to the study of how human utilization of nature influences and is influenced by social organization and cultural values. In an agricultural society like the one examined in this book, cultural ecology is concerned with the strategies used to convert the natural environment into natural *resources,* and then to use these for subsistence and profit. More specifically, the cultural ecological approach in this book is concerned with the study of the interrelationships between population, culturally styled needs and wants, the division of labor, technology and methods of production, and the ways of dividing natural resources among those who need and use them. We study these matters on a continuum of change stretching over a sixty- or seventy-year period of settlement. This focus on change is particularly appropriate for modern agrarian peoples, whose productive activities are geared to constantly changing national market structures. Cultural ecological studies of relatively isolated tribal or peasant peoples are not often concerned with change, and without detailed written records of economic and social change, are often required to ignore it.

A second meaning of the term ecology emphasizes adaptation or *adaptive behavior.* Here we refer to coping mechanisms or ways of dealing with people and resources in order to attain goals and solve problems. Our emphasis here is not on relationships between institutions, groups, or aggregates of data, but on patterns of behavior: problem-solving, decision-making, consuming or not consuming, inventing, innovating, migrating, staying. All of these behaviors and many others take place in the region we studied under special conditions: over the sixty-odd years of settlement, resources of all kinds have been short of supply, and the people have had to learn how to adapt to these shortages. The general problem of our study of adaptive behavior is thus how people respond to severe constraints, people with cultural goals and expectations that are generally much greater than those they might achieve with the available resources.

When we consider ecology in the context of adaptive behavior, several important considerations arise. The first of these concern the kinds of societies one studies and how this affects the nature of the data and interpretations. Most of the work of anthropologists in the field of agrarian ecology has been done on tribal and

peasant societies, where all or many of the produced commodities are consumed locally, and where little economic aid is
given the local communities by external organizations. On the
other hand, contemporary market agrarian societies are intimately related to these external institutions, since they participate in a market economy of national and even international
scope. Modern agrarians can acquire ready-made adaptive solutions to their problems from agricultural extension agencies;
loans of capital from banks and government; new types of
plants and animals from both private and governmental research sources. They sell their products on the national market,
and their consumption patterns are to a large extent guided by
the national culture and its mass circulation media. In many
respects, the rural communities in these highly-developed societies are microcosmic versions of the larger national society.

This complex involvement with the outside world greatly
complicates the task of the ecological analyst. Between the
modern agrarian and nature lie many intervening institutions
and necessities; adaptation is not simply a matter of extracting
food from the local landscape, but requires a transformation of
local resources on the model, and under the demands, of national standards of consumption, national costs and prices, fads
and fashions of production. Therefore an ecological analysis of
a modern agricultural society must consider these involvements
on their merits; ecology cannot rest with a study of, say, the
relationship of population to methods of raising crops, but must
study how local people react to the informational and financial
"inputs" from external sources.

However, the modern agriculturalist also is required to manipulate the local and the externally-supplied resources in order
to develop a productive regime which permits him to make a
living for himself and his family. He must experiment with the
available procedures, and devise his own set, in order to find a
regime that will be suitable for his particular microenvironment.
Hybrid plant seeds are obtainable from the outside, but their
local use must always be subjected to adaptive trial. The farmer
also must learn to manipulate the external agencies and bureaus,
and his own local social system as well, in order to get the
facilities, help, and encouragement he needs. Agrarian develop-

ment, even under conditions of advanced technology and market economy, obviously requires much local strategic action and experimentation.

Out of these considerations flows another: how does one define or measure adaptation? Adaptive behavior can, as we have already implied, be defined in terms of goal-satisfaction: if coping is successful, the people realize their objectives. In a market agrarian society, these objectives can be defined in terms of quantity of production; income; and consumption wants or needs. However, this is only one dimension of adaptation. A second, and equally important one, is the conservation of resources. An economy that realizes economic gain but does so at the cost of exhausting or abusing its resources, may be adapting in one dimension, but can be said to be maladaptive along the other. All agrarian societies, regardless of technological level, must attempt to balance conservation of resources against economic success if they hope for a permanent or indefinite settlement. Or to put the problem in economizing terms: what price are people willing to pay for gratification of their goals and needs?

How does the adaptational approach differ from other approaches to agrarian development? Cultural geography, agricultural economics, farm management research, and economic development research all deal with related problems. However, each of these fields concerns itself with a particular sector or part of the whole problem of adaptation. The geographers are interested in natural resources and social settlement patterns; the agricultural economists are concerned with consumption expenditures and the factors of production; the farm management people work on rationality and efficiency; the economic developers concentrate on increases in the scale of operations. The essential task of the anthropologist is to attempt to unify these points of view and to see the adaptive process as a whole, in its environmental, economic, and sociocultural facets. By the "whole" we do not mean literally every item of business in these spheres, but enough of each segment in order to present a rounded picture. In this book we will not describe every aspect of social life and economic activity, but only those that are clearly related to economic survival. We believe that of all approaches to the study of society, the ecological makes the most sense out of Great Plains human settlements, due to the specialized nature of the environment. This was the case for the aborigines as well as for the contemporary sedentary peoples.

SOME FURTHER CONSIDERATIONS

In older anthropological and geographic studies of man's relationship to the natural environment, the major goal was to describe—statically—the way the social organization and patterns were suited to the natural resources or the particular economic use of the habitat. But when we focus on adaptation, we imply movement of some kind: we are concerned with the process of coping with resources in order to realize goals—and by so coping, creating new goals or problems to solve. This means that the concept of adaptation itself can be divided into two parts: first, the notion of *adaptive strategies,* or the patterns formed by the many separate adjustments that people devise in order to obtain and use resources and to solve the immediate problems confronting them; second, the idea of *adaptive processes,* or the changes introduced over relatively long periods of time by the repeated use of such strategies or the making of many adjustments. Adaptive strategies are generally at the conscious level in the behavior of the people involved; adaptive processes are formulated by observers and analysts. For example, in the region we describe in this book, an important adaptive process has been the movement of different kinds of agricultural activities into specialized locations depending on the availability of particular natural resources. We call this process, "resources specalization." On the other hand, the people of the region are not aware that a "process" is taking place; from their point of view, they simply get land where it is cheaper or where transportation, soil, or water is better suited to a particular business.

Adaptive or "coping" behavior implies the making of decisions or, more particularly, the choosing between alternatives. Often in environments with marginal resources, the alternatives are few, decisions are difficult, and a general constraint is exercised over human actions. In these situations, one might speak of ecological or economic determinism as an explanation of particular social phenomena, and there are many examples of this type of constraint in this book. But the process is not a simple one of automatic controls over human behavior. Even in ecologically constrained situations, or perhaps especially so in these cases, people are confronted with choices and need to make decisions. In addition, human wants and conceptions of action may or may not conform to reality, and certainly man always conceives of possibilities other than the inevitable or most probable.

Decision-making and the choice of alternative strategies involves the concept of "opportunity costs." In economic analysis, opportunity cost is sometimes defined as the value of a particular resource in its best *alternative* use. However, since our approach in this study is broader than the usual economic analysis, we extend the concept to include the "cost" of current uses of resources as well. Thus we consider that a farmer's present use of resources has an opportunity cost as compared with other possible uses of the resources and their corresponding costs. Resources can be an individual's labor power, his soil or water, his farm, his investments, cash itself, his skills in obtaining favors from politicians, or anything else that can be used to provide income or gain. An opportunity cost can be, and usually is, computed in monetary values, but it need not be. The following remark, made by a Jasper farmer to the writer, "I only stand to gain—that's why we go into politics," is an example of a choice made on the basis of opportunity costs. The speaker was saying that he preferred to influence government to obtain the resources he needed than to spend his own scarce capital to finance development of his enterprise. The former carried no risks; the latter, the risk of financial loss. Thus he estimated that the cost of political manipulation is low, while the cost of agronomic innovation is high.

In any case, the nature of agrarian development in Jasper— or the whole social history of the region—can be written as a series of hard choices between a limited number of alternatives, nearly all of them directly involving ecological and economic factors. The behavior of choice, decision, and coping is adaptive behavior; the particular set of means used once a choice is made are adjustments. When these adjustments become standard, they can be called adaptive strategies.

As time passes, the many separate adjustments that have become patterned as strategies, can also enter into culture; that is, as repetitive patterns of action they can be viewed by the people as traditions—as behavior defended as "right" or "good." Or in the language we use in this book, they form part of a group's *cultural style*. However, the extent to which adaptive strategies become culturally sanctioned varies according to the demands placed on the society by various external factors. If, as is the case with most North American entrepreneurial societies, the external institutions compel continuous change and a high degree of productive efficiency, there will be less tendency for a given strategic regime to become "sacred" or traditional. Jasper agrarians are very practical people because they have to be—the outside forces them to maintain a given level of productive efficiency in order to survive, and the changes in these demands require continual alteration of strategies and experimentation with adjustment devices. Consequently we find that Jasper agrarians, though more conservative and more inclined to give their techniques cultural sanctions than many other North American agriculturalists, are still less inclined in these directions than most of the people called "peasants."

Jasperites are recent settlers, and recency confers both a basic flexibility *and* a need for traditional sanctions. Their institutions operate as a general force for molding behavior, adaptive or otherwise. With respect to traditions, Jasperites have a large number: the reverence of the frontier and the Old Timers and the ruggedly individual way of doing things help to sanction hard work and fortitude, still necessary to survival and success in Jasper agriculture. The rodeos, roping clubs, homemakers' clubs and many other organizations all have their ritual meanings associated with the occupational pursuits, basic values, and the ecology of population and production. However, many of the ritualizing and sanctioning functions of celebrations and organizational activity are also devoted to the basic flexibility and adaptability required of Jasperites by their relationship to the "frontier," and to external organizations.

With respect to the molding effect of existing institutions, we can point to the importance of private tenure and private entrepreneurship in shaping the responses made by Jasper agrarians to change. For example, we found that cooperative mechanisms in agriculture are always modified by these private property values and institutions: a group of Jasper farmers or ranchers will not cooperate on livestock production unless they have, as a group, control over the instruments of production, principally land. Such interlocking relationships between ecology and sociocultural factors are structurally similar to those observed for tribal and peasant societies.

When we view social phenomena as resources that people can use and manipulate in order to gain their ends, a number of complications arise. While natural resources exist outside of social systems, and are passive elements, social resources are dynamic, and exist both outside and inside society. They are "outside" when they appear in the form of government agencies or economic markets out of direct control of the local operator and requiring adaptations of much the same kind as are required in adapting to the weather. Social resources are "inside" when they are one's neighbors, or the rules of the local social system and the local cultural norms. Moreover, social phenomena, or these same phenomena that in some contexts are "resources," also control and shape the strategies of adaptation to other and external resources. For example, social prestige may accumulate around a particular style of economic operation, and those who do not follow it, or who seek to innovate, may earn social discredit.

A distinction which helps to resolve some of these complexities of the socioeconomic resource category was provided by the sociologist Max Weber. This concerns the difference between "formal rationality" and "substantive rationality." By "formal rationality" Weber referred to abstract standards of rational procedure in order to obtain the greatest product at the lowest cost. Such standards can be formulated by the economist in his role as scientist. By "substantive rationality" Weber referred to standards of rational or efficient procedure as adjusted to cultural values and socially defined limits and possibilities of action. In this distinction we find possibilities for control and definition of the economic process: a society of agriculturalists may recognize that certain gains would result if they adhered to formal standards, but in actual practice they may modify such standards so as to honor cultural patterns which might be violated or injured. An example would be the Jasper preference for cattle over sheep when sheep would provide a larger product on the same amount of land. Cattle are preferred in Jasper because of custom and tradition, and perhaps ease of management as well. Thus "socioeconomic resources" include the cultural values which define the ends of economic activity, the means to obtain these ends, and the limiting frames in which these means can be exercised.

Since we studied all of the important rural cultural and occupational groups in the region, it was possible to make comparisons of how they used resources and sought their social objectives. Anthropologists have made a number of these "multi-ethnic" studies, with varying goals of comparison. Our objectives concern the differences and similarities of the four groups in handling the resources available to them in a common ecological and economic milieu. The region contains a known quantity and variety of resources, yet these are allocated differently, and used differently, by the different groups. The common economic milieu is the market economy of North America. Thus we have been able to make a study of the alternative ways of functioning within the same general framework of natural and economic resources, or in the language of natural ecology, these alternatives constitute separate "niches." Three of the groups definitely participated in the agricultural market economy; the fourth—the Indians—did not, and had to exploit social resources—local people—for much of its livelihood.

Thus the approach of this book is dynamic in the sense that adaptation is conceived as a process of potential adjustment to existing and changing conditions. This approach differs from the mainstream of work by anthropologists on adaptations of living societies since this mainstream has been concerned primarily with classificatory problems; that is, how various types of economic and technical organization provide determinative frames for particular types of personality, social organization, and cultural patterns. This approach can lead toward cultural evolutionary generalizations if change is viewed as movement toward differing stages or stage-types of adaptation. This approach is useful when dealing with long historical time spans, and also with prehistoric and nonliterate societies, where the available economic and social data are limited and time-depth studies are difficult to make. When dealing with contemporary societies with abundant data of these types, however, a more dynamic approach is possible and necessary.

This point is worth additional emphasis. In a recent book by the anthropologist Marvin Harris, *The Rise of Anthropological Theory,* the concept of adaptation is identified with two things: first, grand-scale evolutionary generalizations about stages of technical-environmental development; and second, the dominance of technical and environmental factors over cultural and valuational factors in shaping society and culture. Harris calls both of these "cultural materialism," or "techno-environmental determinism." It seems to us that Harris has missed the third meaning of adaptation—the meaning emphasized in this book: the problem-solving, creative, or coping element in human behavior that permits a dynamic approach to environment. Without doubt, an element of techno-environmental determinism may be at work in most human situations, and we acknowledge a considerable degree in the case studied in this book. Climate, the national economy, the demands of the enterprise, the influence of occupation on cultural style—all of these matters are well within the purview of Harris' "cultural materialism." But these matters are "givens," in our analysis. We define and accept them, but go on from there to analyze how Jasper people manipulate the environment for purposes of survival and also of change.

Men *do* manipulate their environment; they are not merely determined by it. This manipulation, as we have suggested, can have various results. It can lead to a more secure economy, but it can also lead to the exhaustion of resources. Man, for better or for worse, is constantly using his environment for his own purposes; constantly transforming nature into natural resources. This book is concerned with a small slice of this effort of the ages.

SOME CULTURAL IMPLICATIONS

Readers accustomed to accounts of cultures with more exotic or historically imposing patterns might well ask, "What is there to learn from the brief history of a three-generation society? Why study a society still in the process of formation, with relatively limited experience at its own tasks, and still endeavoring to solve its relationship to the natural and human environments which influence its identity? Why study a dominantly utilitarian culture, with few aesthetic interests or values, and with few traditions of its own save those of the recent frontier life?"

The most obvious answer is a technical one: a society of this kind can tell us much about the problems of agrarian frontiers and the establishment of a viable agrarian economy. Significant portions of the earth's surface remain in wilderness, or in arrested half-growths which will be moving toward full agricultural development in the next generation. The experiences on the North American frontier are not entirely unrelated to these new pioneering ventures, because like the newer ones, the North American was a largely planned, engineered settlement, occurring in an era of high technology and government subsidy.

A less obvious answer concerns the human values of such a society. If this is indeed a utilitarian culture because the tasks of settlement and economic establishment left no time for anything else, then it is also a society in which a particularly appealing variety of human being was forged. Men and women who could postpone their comforts but never abandon hope; who could continue to visualize the future from the depths of misery and discomfort; who could settle their quarrels with calm and tact; and who could endure loneliness without the loss of humor and warmth. Few of these qualities are common among urbanites; the city environment seems to lack the sustaining qualities of the frontier, or the post-frontier society, still in its adaptive phase. There is less to do of a satisfying nature for the greatest number, and a scarcity of those experiences which permit a man to know who he is and measure what he has done.

North American social scientists have provided few studies in depth of these societies, and there are several reasons for their neglect of them. First, the urban intellectual bias of a majority of social scientists has not equipped them to perceive value in utilitarian experience; there is a tendency to measure cultural validity by the depth of historical tradition or the extent of aesthetic-literary development. Second, most of the research on rural North America has been guided by the conventions of rural sociology, a discipline largely molded by certain practical concerns in agricultural extension work. Third, the sense of familiarity, of immersion in a *known* social world, has made these rural societies appear unexotic and uninteresting. Fourth, humanistic interests have been largely ruled out of social science on the grounds that they interfere with "objectivity"—and it is humanistic meaning which is about all these post-frontier societies have to offer to the social scientist interested primarily in the cultural fabric. (Of people with this interest, the novelist has done a much better job than the social scientist.)

The humanistic element is simply this: a man and a woman standing in front of a sod shack or a log hut looking out over the fields they have broken or fenced, over the herd they slowly assembled, toward the village they have fostered and where their children go to school—looking at the *place* they have somehow created to support a human family. Or it is their son, who knows the father's dreams of adding land or improving the breed or building a better house and who manages to do all that in *his* generation, hoping that his own son, in turn, will improve on what is handed down to him. The humanistic element is, then, people who, at their best, think in terms of generations, not in the egocentric terms of individual careers; people who know that the old dreams of wealth were largely dreams save for a lucky few, and that building a community and an economy is hard and slow work. The human meaning of the post-frontier society is achievement, but achievement in the sense of work, not of glibness, or of manipulation of "contacts."

This is, of course, the story at its best. There were plenty of exceptions, and the reality was not always as satisfying, the people not always as honest or as capable of effort as in the story at its best. Many of them left after a brief exposure; some of them cheated and manipulated. But even so, there was very little room for out-and-out frauds, and certainly those who stayed contributed to the building of a humanly valid tradition. The reminiscences of the frontier days are often narrow and monotonous, and they have been desperately coarsened by their use in the mass media, but they do have an authentic meaning. They tell of an age of individualism, and while the value of individualism has been cheapened by many, including self-serving politicians who use the word repeatedly while scarcely knowing its meaning, it remains an important value. On the frontier a man could do something on his own, if he had the strength and the skill.

Perhaps that age will never come again; it seems fairly certain that the requirements of socialization and interdependency in a mass society lead away from it. But for just that reason, that age must not be forgotten.

BIBLIOGRAPHIC NOTES

There is a large literature on ecology, but the portions of it pertaining to man, or human ecology, are scattered and divided among many academic disciplines. There is no unified field of human ecology: the term is applied to a series of very different topics by sociologists, medical researchers, conservationists, and anthropologists. For this reason we have minimized use of the term in this book, preferring to speak of adaptation and adaptive behavior.

The following works have been of particular influence in formulating the point of view developed in this chapter: (1) General ecology: Paul B. Sears, "Human Ecology: A Problem in Synthesis," *Science,* No. 120 (Dec. 10, 1954), pp. 959–63; Robert W. Kates, "Stimulus and Symbol: The View from the Bridge," *Journal of Social Issues,* Vol. 22 (1966), pp. 21–8. (2) Plant and animal ecology (some of whose concepts underlie our approach): E. P. Odum, *Fundamentals of Ecology,* Saunders, 1962. (3) The biological basis of adaptation and its relevance for human behavior: Rene Dubos, *Man Adapting,* Yale University Press, 1965, and Alexander Alland, *Evolution and Human Behavior,* Natural History Press, 1967, especially Chaps. 7 and 10, and Marvin Harris, "Adaptation in Biological and Cultural Science," *Transactions of the New York Academy of Sciences,* Ser. II. Vol. 23 (1960), pp. 59–65. (4) In anthropology the general approach called "cultural ecology" has produced a large number of works in both theory and research, but the best theoretical introduction to the field remains the pioneer statement: Julian Steward, *The Theory of Cultural Change,* University of Illinois Press, 1955. A summary of current developments in the field of cultural ecology is found in Andrew P. Vayda, "Ecology: Cultural and Non-Cultural," in James R. Clifton (ed.), *Introduction to Cultural Anthropology,* Houghton Mifflin Co., 1968. An anthology: Andrew P. Vayda, ed., *Environment and Cultural Behavior: Ecological Studies in Cultural Anthropology,* American Museum of Natural History Press, New York, 1969. A useful review of primate ecology, presenting models from nonhuman to human, is Richard A. and Patty J. Watson, *Man and Nature: An Anthropological Essay in Human Ecology,* Harcourt, Brace & World, 1969.

Near the end of the chapter we refer to a recent work by Marvin Harris (*The Rise of Anthropological Theory,* Crowell, 1968). Harris makes a case for what he calls "cultural materialism," a view that emphasizes the determining role of technical and environmental factors in human affairs. Consistent with Harris' determinism is his preference for a concept from natural ecology: *ecosystem.* This concept illustrates a problem faced by human ecologists: whether or not to use concepts developed in plant and animal ecological science. The problem is not easily solved, since there is no doubt that all natural ecological concepts have a *degree* of applicability to the human situation. At the same time, none of them have universal applicability. *Ecosystem* s a case in point. As used by most natural ecologists, ecosystem implies a balanced state—or a state continually returning to balance—achieved by organisms in a given environment.The concept emphasizes a mutual sharing of food resources, including each other, so that all populations, plant and animal, survive at a more or less constant size. If competition for food sources develops, compensating mechanisms soon return the system to its former state. Now, this type of process can be observed in some human situations: for example, a particular form of agriculture practiced by a tribal society for a long time can achieve local balance with natural resources so that the natural species, the cultigens, and the human population form a relatively balanced ecosystem—a system that will be drastically disturbed, however, if the tribal people are induced to develop cash-crop agriculture, which may require increased use of available resources, or if they introduce practices that disturb the achieved balance. The difficulty with man is that he is constantly changing his needs and policies and disturbing existing "ecosystems"; thus in many instances it is doubtful if the concept applies at all. This greater activity in remolding natural environments is particularly characteristic of modern societies like the ones examined in this book. For these reasons we have been extremly cautious in the use of concepts derived from natural ecological science.

The concept of "opportunity costs," which is of particular importance for the adaptational viewpoint developed in this book, is explained in David Barkin, "Economic Anthropology at the Crossroads," forthcoming, *Current Anthropology*. One of the few studies of a peasant economy using opportunity costs as a tool of analysis is Sydney Mintz, "The Employment of Capital by Market Women in Haiti," in R. Firth and B. S. Yamey, eds., *Capital, Saving and Credit in Peasant Societies*, Aldine, 1964.

The concepts of formal and substantive rationality noted in this chapter are discussed in Max Weber, *The Theory of Social and Economic Organization*, Oxford University Press, 1947, pp. 35 ff.

The work of anthropologists on ecological and economic aspects of tribal and peasant societies is exemplified by Manning Nash, *Primitive and Economic Systems*, Chandler, 1966; Raymond Firth and B. S. Yamey, eds., *Capital, Credit and Saving in Peasant Societies*, Aldine, 1964; George Dalton, ed., *Tribal and Peasant Economies*, Natural History Press, 1967; Robert McC. Netting, *Hill Farmers of Nigeria*, University of Washington Press, 1968. Economic approaches are treated in: Clifton R. Wharton, Jr., ed., *Subsistence Agriculture and Economic Development*, Aldine Publ. Co., 1970.

Studies by anthropologists of modern agrarian societies in various countries are exemplified by Horace Miner, *Culture and Agriculture: An Anthropological Study of a Corn-Belt County*, University of Michigan Press, 1949; E. Z. Vogt, *Modern Homesteaders*, Harvard University Press, 1955; E. H. Bell, *The Culture of A Comtemporary Rural Community: Sublette, Kansas*, Bureau of Agricultural Economics, U.S.D.A., 1942; Julian Pitt-Rivers, *Mediterranean Countrymen*, Mouton, 1963; Clifford Geertz, *Agricultural Involution: The Processes of Ecological Change in Indonesia*, University of California Press, 1963. The pioneer anthropological study of change and development in American agricultural communities is Walter Goldschmidt's *As You Sow*, Harcourt, Brace, 1947. Some studies of American rural communities of particular relevance to the present volume are the following: James West, *Plainville USA*, Columbia University Press, 1945; Art Gallaher, *Plainville Fifteen Years Later*, Columbia University Press, 1961; Angie Debo, *Prairie City*, Knopf, 1944; Joseph P. Lyford, *The Talk in Vandalia*, Harper & Row, 1964. Ronald Frankenburg, *Communities in Britain*, Pelican & Penguin Books, 1966 is a useful comparative treatise.

TWO

The Jasper Region
of Western Canada

In defining an approach for this study we had available the following academic research traditions: human or cultural geography, with its descriptive emphasis on cultural-environmental correlations; economic development, with its concern for the ways agrarian populations use resources to forge a viable economy; or cultural ecology, with its emphasis on the important role played by economic and technological adaptations in shaping social institutions. None of these approaches by itself seemed to provide a suitable format for the synthesis of a large quantity of data from a particular geographical and human region. The basic topic of the research project was, in fact, this *region:* a geographical area having historical unity. Jasper was not unified geographically; its parts could easily be divided among several contiguous geographical sections: the Cypress Hills, the Sandhill country, the prairie. Its unity came from its human associations: the fact that a strategically located town on the railroad was the chief port of entry for the Euro-American population and that a section of the Cypress Hills across the central portion of the region had been a focus for the earlier Indian habitation.

Consequently we were concerned with what Carl Sauer calls "the complex reality of areal association." Our initial task was to define this areal association of natural resources, economy, and society over a historical period extending from the Indian occupation through the three generations of Euro-American agrarian settlement. This chapter summarizes the results of that initial project. It is descriptive and integrative in the classical sense of cultural geography or geographical ethnology, and as such it provides an introduction to the study of adaptive process that formed the more important part of the study.

We selected a region instead of the usual nucleated community studied by anthropologists and sociologists because of the way human activities are distributed in the Great Plains. Since resources are unevenly distributed, people who depend entirely on livestock production will occupy different portions of the region than those who depend on grain crops. Indians are confined to marginal "bush" areas of the hills. Some towns will have many services, others are highly specialized. In the "Jasper" region there are small hamlets whose sole functions are to receive grain or livestock for shipment, or to distribute supplies needed in farming, or to provide education to the young in centralized schools. Thus the only way we could study all of the occupational and ethnic groups typical of northern Plains society was to select a large geographical region containing all or most of the variants.

In selecting this region we had a number of criteria in mind: We wanted an area with a variety of habitats typical of the northern Plains, a variety of modes of economic utilization of these habitats; and a variety of cultural traditions. We were interested in an area with historical unity in the sense of a single geographical focus of settlement. We were concerned also with a society which, despite its ethnic and economic variability, possessed an overall tradition or sense of cultural unity. The choice of the Province of Saskatchewan was a "given" in the study insofar as we were interested in the effects of the many experiments in economic and social organization of an adaptive nature introduced by governments of that province. The Canadian locus was another given insofar as we were concerned with control over historical data; the relative recency of the settlement of the Canadian Plains provided this control—first-generation Euro-American pioneers were still available as informants.

After visits to several possible sites, we selected an area in the southwestern portion of the Canadian Province of Saskatchewan, the central of the three provinces of Canada whose southern portions occupy the Canadian section of the northern Great Plains (see Fig. 2.1.) The region is a long rectangle about

90 miles north and south and 54 miles east and west, or about 4,800 square miles. The conditions of settlement permitted the use of surveyed boundary lines as our approximate regional boundaries; most of the people living within the rectangle represented by Figure 2.2 had more social and economic intercourse with each other than with anyone outside of the boundary lines. Nearly all of the families in the regional population had entered the area through the railroad and service-center town of "Jasper," in the north-central part of the rectangle. The "Jasper region," therefore, gets its name from our fictitious name for the town. In 1962, when our study began, the population of the region was 7,360 people, or about six persons per square mile. About 35 per cent of these people lived in the town of Jasper and two or three hamlets; the rest in the country, on ranches and farms. Therefore the *country* population density was a little over one person per square mile. Our study was concerned primarily with the country or agricultural population. However, since most of the population residing in the towns and hamlets consisted of country people who had retired from farms and ranches, our research really stretched along a continuum from country to town. (What we did *not* study intensively was the social systems and everyday life of the town communities, although we did not ignore these, and have included descriptions of town culture in this book.)

WEST-CENTRAL CANADA

The Jasper region and the province in which it is found is part of what geographers call west-central Canada (Fig. 2.1). The inhabited portion of this region is contained in the Great Plains. Population thins out toward the north, and eventually conifer forests and swampy muskeg country take over to form the great northern wilderness. West-central Canada constitutes 40 per cent of the land area of the Dominion, hence the Great Plains environment constitutes a larger portion of Canada than it does of the United States. The agricultural potential of the Plains—"prairie" in Canadian usage—is therefore very important for Canada's economy, and sales of wheat from this area to foreign countries in recent years have formed a major portion of Canada's national income.

The land area of west-central Canada slopes from west to east at an average grade of 5 feet per mile, which is relatively steep and causes very rapid flow of the major river system, the North and South Saskatchewan. These rivers are deeply entrenched due to their steep fall and also to the eroding effect of the large volumes of water they carried only 10,000 years ago, when the last continental glacier melted. It is therefore very difficult to use their water for agricultural purposes. The first dam on the Saskatchewan River, on its southern branch in the Province of Saskatchewan, was in final stages of construction when this book was written.

The climate of this portion of the Great Plains is similar to Plains climates farther south except that the northerly location means longer winters and shorter summers. Precipitation is uncertain and highly variable, and occurs when dry, cold arctic air collides with moist, warm southern air. This condition is often prevented when northern cross-winds turn the warm air eastward, causing it to miss the northern plains, or when dry, warm winds coming down from the Rockies (called "chinooks") blow eastward across the plains. The variability of precipitation is created by the irregular and unpredictable interferences with normal frontal contacts, and this variability is accentuated by the relatively flat topography, which tends to encourage highly localized rainfall in the form of severe thunderstorms and hailstorms, which can ruin crops. Northern air can introduce severe cold in any month of the year; blizzards are monumental events; southern winds, on the other hand, can raise the temperature to an exceedingly dry 100 degrees during the summer. Luckily for crops, there is a tendency for rainfall to concentrate in the May-June–July period, when it is needed for seed germination. Moreover, the long periods of sunlight, due to the high latitude, hasten plant growth.

Wheat, barley, rye, and some other crops really grow best under subhumid or even semiarid conditions, but there should be a consistent minimum amount of moisture. In Jasper the variability of precipitation—the fact that some years are dry and desert-like, and others may actually have too much moisture,

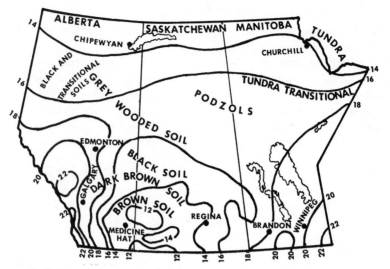

a. Soil Types

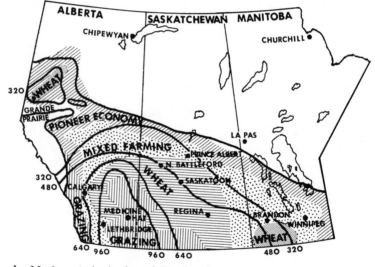

b. Modes of Agricultural Production

Figure 2.1. West-Central Canada

Sources: *Atlas of Canada,* Dept. of Mines and Technical Surveys, Ottawa, 1957; and Donald F. Putnam and others, *Canadian Regions,* New York, 1952

which makes the crops head out too soon—results in extremely variable yields. So far as livestock are concerned, the natural plains grasses provide good fodder since they cure in the fall, hence are nutritious the year around. Chinook winds in the winter can strip snow and ice from the pasture and warm the cattle. However, extreme cold and blizzard conditions, or extreme drought, can cause difficulties for the stockman.

In general, *average* conditions in the northern Plains are suitable for crops and livestock, but the variability of resources introduces great uncertainty. Risks are therefore high. The severity of climate also requires human fortitude and endurance —Ole Rölvaag's famous novel *Giants in the Earth* graphically describes the effects of drought and blizzards on the settlers in North Dakota.

The natural environment of west-central Canada forms a series of bands which slope from northwest to southeast (for soils, see Fig. 2.1., a). Precipitation, temperature, soils, and natural vegetation all follow these sloping bands. Agricultural production has followed this pattern, as can be seen on Figure 2.1, b. The "Pioneer Economy" follows the line of conifer forest and sub-boreal climate; "Mixed Farming" occupies the parkland strip, with its subhumid climate; "Wheat" the subhumid-semiarid mid-grass prairie; and "Grazing," the semiarid short-grass "true Plains" area. Thus, as one goes north from the "Grazing" area straddling the Alberta-Saskatchewan border, precipitation increases slightly, and soils have greater humus content. The Jasper region, in the southwestern portion of Saskatchewan, is in the semiarid "Grazing" area, but the presence of the Hills means that more moisture is available for irrigation. Actually crops were grown in various places in Jasper, but to an increasing extent the regional agriculture was emphasizing cattle. This is a reversion to the original pattern: the first settlers were ranchers, and the farmers came in late, as homesteaders, and subsequently found straight grain agriculture difficult to sustain.

In a few locations in west-central Canada there are hills which rise one or two thousand feet above the level of the plains. The Jasper region is one of these places. In these locations the higher elevations attract more moisture and have greater rain and snowfalls. The latter are particularly important for livestock raising, since the snow melts in the spring and can be impounded in reservoirs which then furnish water for irrigating fields of hay and other forage crops. Two such systems, one to the north and one to the south of the Cypress Hills, can be seen on Figure 2.2. The combination of plains and hills forms a classic topographic pattern described by John Wesley Powell for the arid West in 1878; the crests of the hills can be used for forestry and some grazing; the watershed slopes provide watered grasslands for livestock production and reservoirs; the plains provide the flat land for crops.

The Jasper Region

The Jasper region has a great, sweeping, northern plains landscape: endless stretches of undulating grassland, with little lines of trees here and there marking the sites of the farms with their belts of tree windbreaks. Low places collect rainwater during the spring rainy season, and in a humid year these may remain as ponds all summer long—although farmers are draining them and reclaiming their heavy clay soil, which is good for crops because of its moisture-retentive qualities. In the spring and early summer, the great prairie is a bright green; by late summer, the color changes to a dull yellow as the grain crops mature and die and the native grass cures with its nutriments intact, ready for fall and winter grazing.

The Cypress Hills are a dark green line across the horizon all year round—due to the thick growths of trees on their crests. The trees follow the creek coulees down the slope, and out onto the plains, where they diminish finally into brushy and weedy channels. From June to August the Hills display a constantly changing panorama of wild flowers—all the familiar Rocky Mountain and prairie species can be found there: the magenta fireweed, purple bergamot, the blue lupine and harebells, lavender fleabane, orange paintbrush, yellow gaillardia, and many others. On the slopes the forest thins out into neat, manicured clumps of aspen, with its cream-colored bark, interspersed among native grass prairie—a lovely and inviting sight.

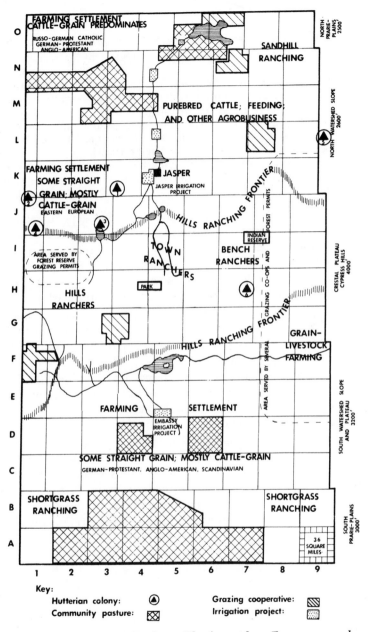

Figure 2.2. Jasper Region: Physiography, Economy and Ethnicity

The vistas, the spaciousness, formed the primary point of departure for perspectives on the Jasper region by its residents:

I couldn't stand to live hemmed in by all those mountains [speaking of British Columbia and the need for migrants from Jasper to move there in search of jobs].
I liked the sea and the cliffs, but most prairie folk don't— they miss the open space and the sky. I was glad to get back here [speaking of a vacation to the Pacific coast].
It's the sky I miss when I went back East—the trees get in the way and you can't see it [an elderly man talking about his trip to his birthplace in Ontario].

Wild animals and birds are common, but are kept in careful control lest they disturb agricultural activities. Herds of antelope roam the lower slopes of the Hills, and in the winter congregate around the ranchers' feed stacks of hay. Deer live in the forest and follow the wooded coulees down onto the plains. A herd of elk is maintained by conservation officers in the park section of the Hills. Porcupine, badger, and many other small animals live in the hills and coulees. A rare coyote family will inhabit a rancher's grazing land, but because they hunt barnyard fowl few are permitted to live.

.The climatic parameters of the Jasper region (shown in Fig. 2.3) are such that (1) the longest frost-free growing seasons are experienced in the north and south prairie-plains areas; (2) the most abundant precipitation (rain plus snow) is found in the hills; (3) the greatest variation in precipitation (suggested by the "minimum annual" line compared with the "mean annual" figures) is found in the prairie-plains. Thus while temperature and topography are most suited to grain crops in the prairie-plains, the moisture conditions there are far inferior to those in the hills, where the growing season is too short for anything but certain forage crops.

Figure 2.4 illustrates variability of rainfall. Swift Current and Jasper are about 70 miles apart—a "short" distance as distances are judged in the northern Plains. While the years of rainfall shortages are grouped similarly, the actual amounts and the precise patterns are different, showing the variability in space. In addition, the variability through time has no clear pattern other than the reasonable expectation of some dry years each decade.

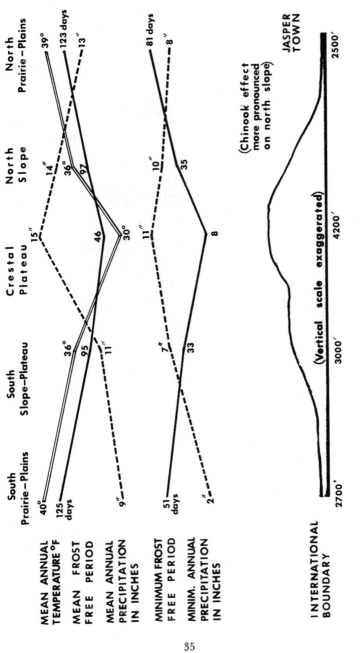

Figure 2.3. Climatic Parameters for Jasper Region

35

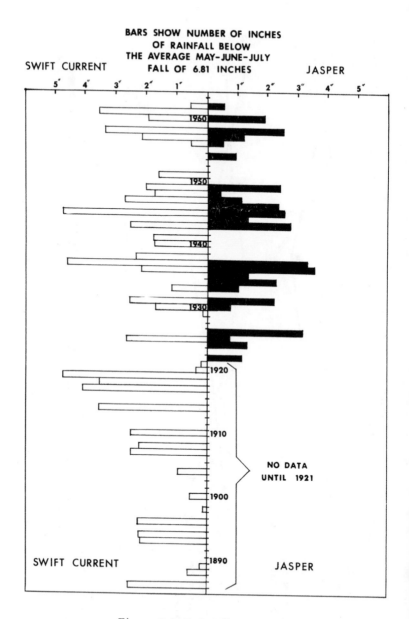

BARS SHOW NUMBER OF INCHES
OF RAINFALL BELOW
THE AVERAGE MAY-JUNE-JULY
FALL OF 6.81 INCHES

Figure 2.4. Rainfall Variability
(Swift Current is a small city about 70 miles from Jasper.)

The soils of the region also vary greatly. The heaviest soils (which are best for grain, since they hold moisture) unfortunately are often found in the hills, or in the prairie-plains at the bottoms of sloughs or old lake beds which are often hard to drain. These basins collect salt minerals from the drainage off the hills, or from the saline-bearing marine clays and shales not far from the surface of the soil in the plains. Over most of the prairie-plains, soils are light and stony, and crops often do not grow well in them, but cultivated pasture grasses do very well. Along the base of the slopes are areas of mixed soils (produced by alluvial action) where there may be as many as five distinct soil types (as classified by agronomists) in a single 160-acre tract of land. Each of these types will have differing agricultural potentials.

The higher or sheltered portions of the crestal plateau of the Cypress Hills are covered with a forest of aspen, lodgepole pine, and spruce. These trees provide a small income for a few Jasper region families from forestry, but the tree growth is not sufficient to supply all local needs for lumber. Fenceposts cut from the aspen are the main product. In addition to the Hills' watershed function, their other principal economic value is as a recreation area. The Provincial Park (Figs. 2.2, 2.10) has a lake, streams, store and restaurant, a dancehall, and a large number of cabins most of which are owned or rented by local people. The general appearance of the Hills is similar to that of the rolling Rocky Mountain "foothill" country of Alberta 300 miles to the west, and the Hills have become a mecca for naturalists interested in this curious island of Rocky Mountain flora and fauna in the midst of the shortgrass Plains.

Human intervention in the natural ecology of the Jasper region has been extensive, but probably not critical. The native sod of the plains has been disturbed for cultivation in about 90 per cent of the level areas, but the rougher areas remain in natural grass or have returned to an approximation of natural cover. Soil loss due to blowing of the cultivated fields has been a recurrent problem, but was not as severe as in portions of the central Great Plains, largely because Jasper farmers had learned to handle their fallow land more carefully. Early irrigation projects were poorly leveled, and there has been some salinization. Water erosion has been serious, but is under control. New plant species have been introduced, many or most from Siberian loci: crested wheat grass and Russian wild rye, and strains of alfalfa (for forage crops) and the ubiquitous caragana, a leguminous shrub, and the Chinese elm (both used for ornamental plantings) are all from Siberia—Siberia having been minimally glaciated and therefore having retained a larger number of cold-and-drought-adapted plants, than the North American northern Plains, which lost most of this type of flora during the severe glacial epochs.

In the early 1960's ranching (straight livestock-raising) was confined to the Hills and to the very dry, sandy, shortgrass Plains areas in the northeast corner of the region and across the very dry southern boundary (one of the dryest and most climatically variable portions of the entire northern Plains area of Canada and the U.S.) (Fig. 2.2). Mixed farming of various types, but usually with livestock emphasis, occurred on the flattest areas of the prairie-plains areas north and south of the slopes, and the beginning of grain-emphasis agriculture can be seen along the eastern edge of the map (Fig. 2.2), from whence it continued eastward. On the thin alluvial soils east and north of Jasper town, various types of agribusinesses, such as cattle feeding or finishing, have developed.

POPULATION

The human populations—as well as natural grazing species like the bison—of semiarid-variable grasslands generally fluctuate. For example, after the Plains Indian tribes got horses from Spanish herds in the Southwest during the seventeenth century, and were able to kill more bison, the Indian population increased. Fluctuation has been the lot of the modern Plains human populations as well. In the 1930's, after a decade of serious drought, Frederic E. Clements noted that Great Plains populations had fluctuated in accordance with moisture conditions: the first homestead settlers entered the U.S. Plains during and after the Civil War, and this contingent was reduced by half when the drought and grasshopper plague of the early

1870's developed; then improved moisture conditions in the late 1870's encouraged another wave of settlement, only to end in partial withdrawal during the drought of the late 1880's and '90's. More recently, the first decade of the twentieth century had good rainfall, with a new wave of settlers, followed by the droughts of the 1920's and '30's, which caused another out-migration.

Jasper missed the nineteenth-century fluctuations since substantial farmer settlement did not begin until the 1905–10 period. We have graphed the population of each township for the Jasper region over the 60 years of reliable census reports in Figure 2.5. These curves show a number of cultural-ecological relationships. The following are the highlights:

1. Areas that had livestock for the entire 60-year period of reliable census reports (in these same areas incomplete census data go back to the 1880's), also had small, slightly fluctuating human populations (e.g., the townships in the 1 to 5 E-W range, in rows I, H, G, F, E, D, B, A, and 7, 8, and 9, in rows O, N, M, and L). The small number of ranches operated by single families, with regular out-migration of most of the children, accounted for these low, gently undulating curves in the Hills.

2. Areas that were homesteaded had, on the whole, a characteristic high-peaked curve (e.g., E5) which rapidly declined in the 1930's and '40's, reflecting not only regular out-migration of children, but also considerable loss of population due to entire families leaving their farms when droughts and economic depression made it impossible to survive. Many of these townships also display population curves which fluctuate drastically (e.g., D5) showing the effects of the boom-and-bust character of the economy: the alternation of good years and bad, of hope and frustration. Replacement by new families of the out-migrating homesteaders was common in many districts down through the 1920's.

3. The effects on population of resources-development projects sponsored by the government can be seen in several townships near the community pastures, grazing co-ops, and irrigation projects shown in Figure 2.2 (note townships E4, C6, N5, J9, and others). In these townships the curves indicate that slightly more population was being retained in the 1950's and '60's than in

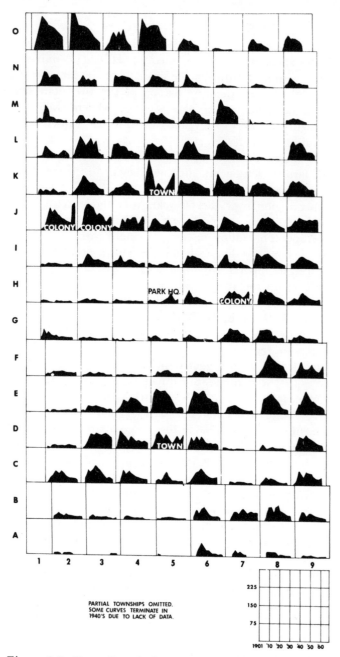

Figure 2.5. Gross Population Curve for Each Jasper Township: 1900-1906. (Some townships, as indicated, contain population units causing modifications of the typical "country" curve shapes.)

40

townships more distant from these new agricultural facilities; we calculated about 5 per cent, on the average. That is, if the farmers had pasture and irrigation facilities available—and the majority of patrons of these facilities were usually living in the vicinity—they would be less likely to sell their farms and move away. In addition, we found that many of them would be inclined to keep older children on the farm for a longer period. While these curves imply a resources-potential for support of a larger population, it should be remembered that this does not mean an actual increase in the number of farm enterprises—only a higher retention rate of the existing enterprises.

On the other hand, in some districts population has been *reduced* as an indirect effect of man's utilization of natural resources (e.g., N6). Some farm population was eliminated by commercial pastures. Some of the irrigation projects constructed in the 1930's were poorly graded, with the result that salts were brought to the surface from underlying marine sediments. Such land cannot be cultivated. While only about 5,000 acres were involved, many cows can be fed on the feed raised on very small irrigated plots; consequently the crop loss is reflected in the human population, which suffers a reduced income. These lands can be reclaimed, but at considerable cost.

4. Rapid increase in population can be seen in two groups of townships: (a) due to the in-migration in the 1950's of whole colonies of Hutterian Brethren: J2, J3, H7; and (b) due to the growth of services and population of two towns: K5 and D5.

5. On Figure 2.6 it can be seen that the pattern of population density has changed significantly over the period of time represented by the curves (1900–1960). From 1900 to the late 1920's, the greatest population density occurs along the railroad lines to the north and south of the Hills. Between 1930 and 1960, the density of this region becomes much lower, but the density of the areas away from the rail lines does not change appreciably. Thus, by the 1960's, population is dispersed fairly evenly throughout the region—only the highest parts of the Hills have an appreciably lower population; and the townships with towns and Hutterian colonies significantly larger populations. The effects of a sparse but more evenly distributed population on

trading service areas of the towns and villages will be discussed later.

6. The relationships between the town and country population of the Jasper region were as follows. The overall trend since the year of the first good census, 1900, was toward a build-up of town population and a diminishing of the country population: in 1900 country population was 81.2 of the total regional population, while in 1960, country population was only 55.4 of the total, indicating a proportional gain for the towns. This was due largely to the loss of population in the countryside.

The majority of small towns and villages had either disappeared by the 1960's or were inhabited by a few families only (most towns and villages of the region founded up to 1920 had lost their "incorporated" status by the 1960 census, whether or not they had a few residual families or individuals). However, two towns were rapidly *increasing* in population in the 1960's: Jasper town in the north, and Eldora in the south (see Fig. 2.10). Both of these towns were service centers for their respective districts, though Jasper was by far the more important and of course the major service center for the region as a whole. Jasper town in 1963 had about 2500 persons, or 33 per cent of the total regional population of about 7400. In 1950 Jasper had only 1280 persons, and the region, 6813. As may be noted in Figure 2.5, township K5, which includes Jasper town, experienced a considerable increase in population after 1950, all of this from the town. Township D4, which includes Eldora, does not show a comparable increase, because Eldora did not really begin to increase in population until about 1962, after the 1960 census. In any case, in 1963 Eldora had 200 persons, representing an increase of 100 since 1950, a rapid and decisive growth as towns go in the Northern Plains. While Eldora occupied a position that encouraged its growth as a service center, the town actually did not begin its recent rapid increase in population and commercial buildup until the provincial Department of Education picked the town as a site for a new regional high school—the first high school south of the Hills, one that permitted children in the area to attend a school nearer home instead of having to be bussed into Jasper town.

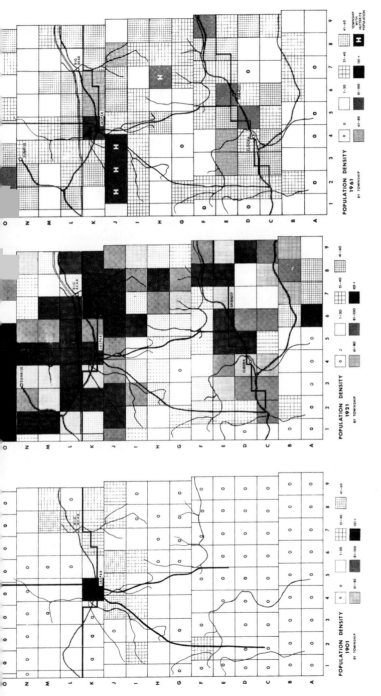

Figure 2.6. Population Densities by Township: 1901, 1921, 1961

Figures 2.5 and 2.6 diagram the economic history of the Jasper region, expressing it as the ecology of settlement and population. The history begins with the in-migration of a few ranchers who live in scattered settlements. This was followed by a substantial movement of farmers into the region who took advantage of the cheap land and established a large number of 160-acre and 320-acre homesteads. As the difficulties of making a living (or a profit) on these relatively small tracts became evident, the great majority of these farmers left, and their land was taken up by the remaining families. In one typical 36-square–mile farming township in Jasper, there were 76 homesteads in 1912, the peak of the homestead period. By 1920 this number had declined to 72; by 1940 to 41; by 1962 to 24. Not all of the 24 were original homesteaders; the dropoff in the earlier days was often partially compensated by new families taking over the abandoned homesteads. In the 1940's and '50's, federal and provincial governments established a series of projects that made scarce or unevenly distributed resources available to a larger number; helping to stabilize both the economy and the population. Even so, another extensive drought or economic depression like those of the 1930's would have very serious consequences: protection against fluctuation is not complete, and will never be.

Therefore, the number of farming enterprises in Jasper has dwindled (Fig. 2.7) and the amount of land held by the remainder has increased (Fig. 2.8). The diagrams show the effects of both environmental and social forces: the homestead settlement peak was reached about 1920; the drought and post-World War I economic depression resulted in extensive abandonment of farms; these farms were taken up by local people and replacement settlers in the 1920's; drought and depression in the disastrous 1930's resulted in another decline, this time longer and deeper, down to and into World War II. Increasing prosperity after the war resulted in a slight gain in number of farms as some land in very poor soil areas went back into cultivation. The trends shown are found for every district in the Great Plains where farming is important. In Saskatchewan as a province, the total number of farms reached a peak in 1936, with 142,472; by 1960 this number had dropped to 93,924, and was declining several thousand a year during the 1960's. The average size of farm holdings in Saskatchewan in 1940 was 432 acres; by 1960 the average had risen to 686 acres and was rising by about two percentage points per year.

Curves of these shapes are not found for ranching districts, since the number of ranches and the number of people supported by ranching have remained nearly stable from the beginning of settlement. The curves of Figures 2.7 and 2.8 therefore say something about the adaptive problems of *farming* in the Great Plains environment, and how the limitations created by natural resources are reinforced in periods of national economic difficulty. Thus ecological process in this typical North American region includes factors which are external to the locality— the region's adaptations are in many ways the reflection of its relationships to the national society.

The interlocking relationships are represented on Figure 2.9, which shows the curves of precipitation in Saskatchewan, the dollar-purchasing power of a bushel of wheat (to suggest fluctuating income), and the population of a typical Jasper homestead-farming district. Moisture fluctuates wildly, with three serious drought periods: the 1890's; the 'teens and around 1920; and the 1930's. Only the latter two periods affected Jasper, since farm homesteaders did not arrive in large numbers until 1910. Their arrival coincided with a rise in precipitation, which encouraged settlement. The value of a bushel of wheat also fluctuates greatly, but has a general downward trend, reaching its lowest point in the 1930's, when, in addition, the drought drastically cut yields.

Thus, in many respects, Jasper society and economy are under the control of moisture gradients. That is, since the key resource in this semiarid land is water, and since man is supported by agriculture, the available moisture determines his fortunes. Figure 2.9 shows this in general terms, but to make the point more concretely we can give data on land sales in the Jasper region. We found that for key municipalities in the region the number of tracts of land changing hands through the years clearly fluctuated in accordance with moisture cycles: in very moist periods, land sales went up noticeably within a year or two after the increased moisture had resulted in good crops, and cash became available for purchasing. On the other hand,

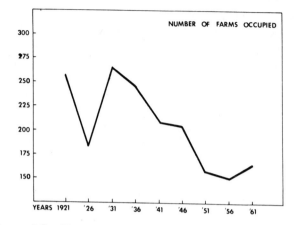

Figure 2.7. Change in Number of Farm Enterprises in a Typical Farming Rural Municipality

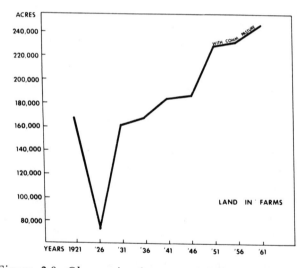

Figure 2.8. Change in Amount of Land in Farm Enterprises in a Typical Farming Rural Municipality. ("With Comm. Pasture" refers to the land counted in the local community pasture as available to farmers for production. If this land were not counted, the curve would be somewhat lower.)

46

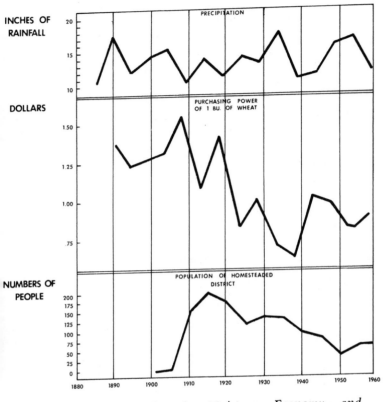

Figure 2.9. Fluctuation in Moisture, Economy, and Population

land sales also went up—but usually not as much—in very dry periods when the drought required sales of farmers' cattle, and this made additional cash available for land purchases.

Social Ecology

Figures 2.10 and 2.11 show the distribution of some of the principal social phenomena in the Jasper region. Settlement of the region began along the railroad line feeding the town of Jasper. The town was founded as a camp for the railroad

workers in 1882 but was not incorporated until 1905, after
the Province of Saskatchewan was formed out of part of the
old Northwest Territories (which in turn had been taken over
in 1871 by the Canadian government from the Hudson's Bay
Company). The area along the tracks was owned by the Canadian
Pacific Railroad and the first settlers there bought their land
at bargain rates from the company. Rancher pioneers filtered
south into the Cypress Hills from the railhead, but also came
up on horseback from the south, from the United States. This
initial north-south traffic established the major roads of the
Jasper region on a north-south axis, following the irregular
lines of the creeks and passing through the Hills. After the land
was surveyed and the homesteaders began arriving, a rectilinear
grid road system was laid out on the plains areas, which established east-west transportation. However, major traffic was still
north-south, due to the continuing importance of Jasper town
as a service center, and this added to the isolation of the region
from adjacent parts of Canada and from the United States.
(The roads into the United States were very few and all were
in bad condition in the 1960's, and impassable for much of
the winter.) In any case, the two road patterns—north-south,
and the east-west grid system—nicely reflect the different settlement patterns of the major types of modern pioneers: ranchers
and farmers. The former established their homes and grazing
lands where the resources dictated; the farmers were confined to
the checkerboard survey, thus establishing a typical open-country
neighborhood pattern.

The political divisions of the Jasper region mirror the ecology.
The boundaries of the Rural Municipalities (RM) and Local
Improvement Districts (LID) are shown on Figure 2.10. The
former occupy the relatively thickly settled farming areas; the
latter enclose the thinly populated ranching areas in the Hills
and the dry shortgrass prairie areas to the south. The Saskatchewan Rural Municipality is comparable to an American
county, although the RM's are smaller and always consist of
exactly nine townships. Each has a municipal office with a
Secretary who collects the land and school taxes, supervises
road construction, and distributes agricultural chemicals and
other commodities at bargain prices. The two Local Improve-

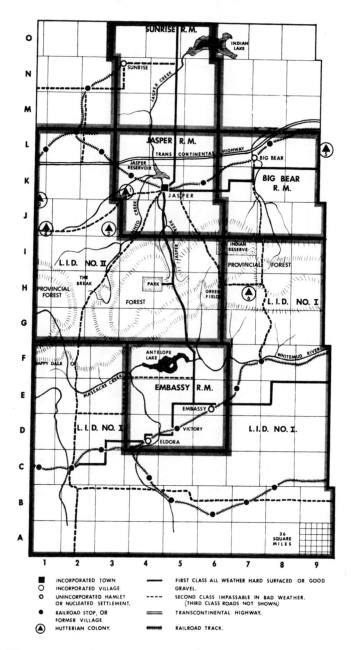

Figure 2.10. Jasper Region: Political Divisions; Major Roads; Places

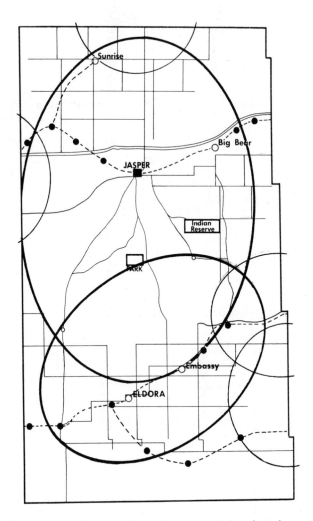

Figure 2.11. Towns, Grid Roads, and Service Areas

This diagram shows the pattern of towns along the railroad lines. The black dots and circles indicate the pattern at its peak, around 1920. The circles and named towns alone show the surviving towns and villages, although a few of the "dots" still retain a tiny population. The named places also represent service centers with a reasonably full range of domestic and business functions, although the Park is quite specialized. The ovoids represent the areas served by these centers, indicating a change from the linear patterns along the rail lines. The major portion of the grid roads serving farming settlements are also shown.

50

ment Districts are supervised from a central office in two towns: Jasper for one LID and the other in the town of "Whitemud," just beyond the southeast boundary of the Jasper region. The LID's are financed almost wholly by the provincial government, since their small populations do not provide sufficient tax moneys to maintain roads and other services. Their chief officer is called an Inspector.

The Rural Municipality and the LID share governmental responsibility with provincial and federal government offices, all located in Jasper town—the Department of Agriculture, with its many extension services is provincial; the Prairie Farm Rehabilitation Agency, with its community pasture and water development services is federal. The Provincial Park in the Hills is run by the Provincial Department of Conservation, and this department also supervises forestry activities in the Hills and the wild game program.

The towns of the region are governed by an elected mayor and council, like their American analogs.

Figure 2.11 shows the position of towns and villages as they were at their peak, about 1920, and as they are today. The earlier pattern was dominated by the railroad; except for a few hinterland villages with single stores, the settlers had to come north or south to the major villages along the rail line for services; consequently settlement tended to cluster in a linear alignment on either side of the rail line. As noted earlier, during this period the population density of the areas along the two railroad lines, north and south, was two to three times what it was in the early 1960's. By the 1960's the population had thinned out and was not particularly greater or denser along the two rail lines than it was in most other parts of the region, with the exception, of course, of the highest parts of the Hills (Fig. 2.6). Most of the villages had disappeared, and the trading areas enclosed between villages had changed shape from elongated, east-west strips, to ovoids, with an important north-south dimension, as suggested by the lines enclosing the existing service-center villages—each around a more populous central small town—Jasper on the north, and Eldora on the south (Fig. 2.11).

The reasons for the change in the pattern of service areas

and centers are to be found in an ecological process common to many thinly populated parts of the world. When resource availability, population, and transportation are relatively evenly distributed across geographical space, the cost of doing business and traveling for services is approximately the same over large areas. Hence, over time, the space between service centers tends to become equal, creating an overall pattern of uniformly shaped service areas; thus surviving towns and villages are arranged in a geometric pattern. Most of southern Saskatchewan and Alberta have these uniformly shaped service or trading areas, each with a major town located near its center, subsidiary smaller towns and villages located around it. If the area mapped is large enough, the service areas tend to become polygonal—often hexagonal—a shape reflecting the actual statistical frequency of people making trips to certain service centers. On the larger service-area map of the general region, the town of Jasper is about equidistant from two major service centers—or "central places," as they are called in the special terminology of settlement location theory—the two small cities east and west of Jasper town mentioned in other contexts. Jasper has therefore developed into, or held its own as, a secondary service center. providing a number of services that people are willing to obtain there withoct going all the way to the small cities. But while Jasper is secondary to the central service centers to the east and west, for the Jasper region it has become the central service place, and a few other hamlets and specialized services depots have persisted or developed around it.

The original linear pattern of villages and towns along the railroad lines was planned by the Canadian Pacific to permit farmers, using horse-drawn vehicles, to bring their produce to market and to receive their necessary services. (Ranchers, of course, had no interest in such a landscape, since they had little need for town services and were willing to drive long distances to Jasper once or twice a year for supplies.) As time passed, roads were built which tended to equalize transportation facilities throughout the region; these and the introduction of resources-development projects helped to equalize access to resources. Thus the linear pattern of villages gave way to an ovoid pattern, resulting in the disappearance of most of the rail-line villages. In the course of this process—which took only about 30 years—most of the small hinterland hamlets (many of them a single postoffice and store) also disappeared, although a few lasted on the periphery of the service areas.

A few of the rail-line villages were retained as shipping points for agricultural products or for specialized services, and one of the common sights on the Saskatchewan prairie is the forest of tall grain elevators—from a distance resembling a metropolis, but actually a tiny settlement containing only a few families of agents who tend the elevators and occasional farm equipment distribution agencies. Of all the towns in the Jasper region, only Jasper town and Eldora, south of the Hills, had survived as really viable, multi-purpose communities (Fig. 2.10), although a few villages were hanging on because of their useful retail services.

The preceding discussion may have given the impression that these changes in population and commercial significance of towns and villages are "natural" processes, somehow out of man's control, operating automatically on the basis of the cost of distance and similar economic factors. To some extent this is the case, of course. The processes can be controlled, however, and the fate of the small towns to some extent can be determined, providing enough information is available to use constructively. We noted earlier how Eldora began its revival after the government decided to locate a new high school there. This choice was not entirely random, but was made on the basis of studies of the changing patterns of service centers, which had indicated that a service center was needed, or could exist, in the approximate location of Eldora. Political consideration also counted.

In the 1950's a similar decision was made with regard to the location of the region's Union Hospital. Saskatchewan has remarkably progressive health programs, and the first of these consisted of the construction of regional hospitals and clinics located in various areas so as to service population units and communities equally. Jasper town was selected as the obvious site because of its transportation facilities and importance as a secondary service center. The hospital attracted many visitors and some new residents to town, and patronage of town businesses increased.

The ethnic composition of the Jasper region mirrored the history of settlement (Table 2.1). The earliest stratum was, of course, the Indians, reduced by 1960 to a small group of about one hundred people living on a reserve in the Hills. An even smaller number of people—about twenty five—were descendents of the *Métis:* French-Indian or English-Indian "breeds" who came to Jasper with the Mounted Police. A few Chinese, proprietors of the restaurants, lived in Jasper and two other smaller villages. The rancher pioneers were almost entirely Anglo-Americans from the United States, eastern Canada, or the British Isles. The farmers were more varied in ethnic composition, but the various nationalities (Fig. 2.2) arrived at different times. The earliest group were Anglo-Americans, closely followed by northern and central Europeans, with eastern Europeans coming last— and therefore getting the poorer land. The differential access to resources meant that the Anglo-Americans and northern-central Europeans, with the best ranches and farms, formed a kind of ethnic elite.

The population of Jasper town is a mixture of all these nationalities. The town is a surprisingly cosmopolitan place: one can hobnob with retired Ukrainians, local ranchers, British doctors, nurses from Jamaica, farmers from the U.S. Midwest, mounted policemen from Toronto, Indians from the immemorial hills and plains, Chinese restaurateurs, or Hutterites from Alberta who are originally from sixteenth-century Moravia. The atmosphere of the old polyglot frontier is still very much alive.

The composition of Jasper's regional population, as revealed by census data, displays its recent frontier settlement character. In 1920 only 2 per cent of the ranchers had been born in Europe, but 50 per cent of the farmers; in 1960 the rancher figure remains the same, but the percentage for farmers has fallen to 23 per cent. The ratio of males to 100 females in 1920 was 132; by 1960 this had fallen to 113. The earlier figure reflects the relatively large early settlement of single men. In 1960 the age group with the greatest preponderance of males—in same cases double the number of females—was from 65 to 79 (about 90 per cent of the sex disparity was found in this age group). We found in our social organizational study that in the contemporary period the concentrated excess of males is due almost entirely to the custom of aging women, whose husbands have died, leaving the region to live with a son or daughter who has migrated.

Table 2.1. Population of Ethnic Groups, Jasper, 1960's	
Anglo-American (Canada, U.S., British Isles) *	3500
Central and Northern European *	2000
Eastern European *	1000
Hutterian Brethren	550
American Indians	125
Chinese *	35

* Note: *Ethnic status is defined in terms of the place of origin of the first generation of settlers.*

About two-thirds of the wives of Jasper men were born outside of the region (for both ranchers and farmers); this reflects the tendency of the majority of Jasper girls to migrate when they become adults. The number of divorced people in the Jasper population was extremely low—only about ten males and six females for the entire population of 7360. Marriage is the "normal" state of life: it is extremely difficult for a man to operate an agricultural enterprise without a wife and children. And of course a divorced woman has no established economic role in the society since women do not, except in very rare circumstances, take over farms or ranches.

The distribution of age in the Jasper regional population has a number of interesting facets. Taking the population as a whole, it is "young"; 60 per cent were age 15 or younger. The distribution of ages in sections of this population, however, was remarkably uneven. The young people were concentrated in (1) the six Hutterian colonies, with their very large families, and (2) in the town of Jasper, with its relatively large number of young families of workers in the town businesses and government services such as road construction crews. The oldest populations were found in the country districts of ranchers and farmers, and in the villages. The town of Jasper also had a markedly "bipolar" age distribution, with a large number of both young people and very old (retired) persons, with a slump in the intermediate (ages 30 to 50) ranges. In the ranching townships, people age 15 or younger constituted only about 35 per cent of the population; in farming townships, only about 25 per cent, the results of heavy out-migration of young people from the country neighborhoods.

From the standpoint of social control, the Jasper region, while having many young people, was dominated by the older folks, since they were in control of the agricultural sector of the economy, and also the town businesses and government. As we will note in Chapter 3, this is a source of complaints by the young people that Jasper is an "old folks'" community, one that reflects the cautious policies of an adapted population that has suffered considerably during droughts and depressions.

Since the Jasper population was controlled primarily by migration, and not fertility, we made a special study of the patterns and circumstances of migration. Details of the process will be given at various points in following chapters; here we may summarize the basic patterns. For young men we found that about 60 per cent of all ranch men would leave the region between ages of 18 and 25, but that about 30 per cent of them would eventually return. For farm men 75 per cent leave and only 25 per cent return. These data reflect the fact that the ranch boys are more culturally bound to the region and its ranching style, and also that they have better opportunities to succeed to a ranch than farm sons have to take over a farm. But the difference reflects even more the higher educational levels of the farm boys, and their better preparation for jobs on the outside. As for young women, 85 per cent of both the ranch and farm girls leave the region and very few come back.

The older age groups retire from the farms and ranches. Nearly all of the aged ranch people retired to Jasper town or one of the other villages of the region, but only about one-third of the farm people did, the majority leaving the region to retire to British Columbia or one of the larger cities of Alberta or Saskatchewan.

In addition there is in Jasper a "floating" group of men in the age group 30-45 who come and go, seeking enterprises and jobs where they can. Usually inadequately prepared educationally and experientially, these men never "make it," as the local people put it. They can be found in farm and ranch labor jobs, manual labor positions, truck driving, and comparable occupations in Jasper town or elsewhere.

The Hutterian Brethren were the last substantial migration into the Jasper region. Their first colony was established in 1951, and the other five visible on Fig. 2.2 came between that date and 1960. The Brethren bought land in districts where failing farms were up for sale and where resources were so variable or marginal that small-scale individual agriculture was not viable. The Hutterites in 1963 had a population of about 559, or 7 per cent of the regional population, and occupied about 4 per cent of the total land area in private tenure used for agriculture. Only about one Hutterite out of one hundred would leave his colony permanently and only one woman left in a decade—a very stable population.

The significant sociocultural groupings of the contemporary Jasper population consist of the permanent town-dwellers in business; two country occupational groups, ranchers and farmers; one ethnic sectarian group, the Hutterites; and an ethnic minority, the Indians. This classification reflects the process of socioeconomic and ecological development: the European ethnic strains that went to make up the farming settlement in its first generation were no longer significant in terms of cultural differences. If ethnic identity had any role to play, it was an indirect one in terms of economic opportunity. The eastern Europeans received the poorer tracts of land, and many of them also practiced division of their land among the sons at the end of the first generation, further reducing the viability of the enterprises. Except for the Indians, the Great Plains were a remarkable case of the "melting pot": the ecological constraints required relatively uniform adaptations and in Jasper the ethnic cultures survived only by conscious policy (the Hutterites); as a consequence of exclusion and discrimination (the Indians); or in a special sense for a group of German Catholics, noted in Chapter 3.

In the three human generations of Euro-American settlement in Jasper, the region moved from a raw frontier with none of the facilities of civilization to a settled, developed northern Plains agricultural society. The transition was not an easy one, and it was marked by a series of mistakes and experiments. Ranching was and is the occupation best suited to the region's semiarid and variable resources, and the general drift back into livestock production attests to this fact. The farming frontier was developed on the basis of a rectilinear grid survey which located farms without regard for the variability of resources, and this meant considerable out-migration and also the necessary development of projects to enhance existing resources and make them available to farmers who lacked them. Increasing recognition of micro-habitat differences led to the development of new business, such as cattle finishing, purebred cattle raising, and others which can make a profit on small and submarginal tracts of land. The automobile outmoded the many small towns dependent on rail transportation.

On the whole, then, present-day Jasper farmers and ranchers represent a settled, adapted fraction of the original pioneers— a population that has accommodated to the natural hazards of the environment and found ways to cope with the uncertainties of making a living from its variable resources. We asked the sample of ranchers and farmers used in our Regional Schedule if they would like to move elsewhere, and the great majority expressed pride in their ability to cope, firmly dismissing any inclination to leave. These attitudes had been influenced by government efforts to assist them (described in Chapter 5), but with or without such aids, Jasper agriculturalists are determined to stay. In an entrepreneurial society, however, economic development and consumption needs are never static, and as they rise, increasing pressures on the resources, as well as an increasing tendency to become dissatisfied with the returns on one's investment, are bound to occur. Man's relationship to nature in Jasper, while currently in a state of adjustment, can be expected to change.

BIBLIOGRAPHIC NOTES

For a discussion of "region," "landscape," and other geographical concepts relevant to this study, see Carl O. Sauer, *Land and Life: A Selection of the Writings of Carl Ortwin Sauer,* University of California Press, 1963. For an anthropological definition of "region," see Alexander Spoehr, "The Part and the Whole: Reflections on the Study of a Region," *American Anthropologist,* 68 (1966), pp. 629–40.

Accounts of the Canadian West and its economic and geographical development appear in Donald F. Putnam and others, *Canadian Regions: A Geography of Canada,* Crowell, 1952. Pages 347–55 contain additional maps of the distribution of environmental and cultural features of Western Canada. For the relationship of climate and other environmental features to the agricultural development of the West, see A. W. Currie, *Economic Geography of Canada,* Macmillan (Toronto), 1945. An informal history of agriculture in Western Canada is found in Grant MacEwan, *From the Red to the Rockies,* University of Toronto Press, 1952.

Just off the map of the Jasper region, to the southeast, lies the village of "Whitemud," featured in Wallace Stegner's memoir, *Wolf Willow,* Viking, 1962. Stegner's book contains the best historical account of the Cypress Hills area, but largely ignores the town of Jasper and environs. Jasper was the earliest and remains the most important community in the region.

A description of the Cypress Hills as a natural curiosity is found in Wilfred Eggleston, "The Cypress Hills," *Canadian Geographical Journal,* Vol. 53, No. 2 (1951).

For accounts of John Wesley Powell's interesting career as explorer and founder of the U.S. Geological Survey, and his attempts to convince the United States government to consider the natural environment more carefully in planning settlement in the West, see Wallace Stegner, *Beyond the Hundreth Meridian,* Houghton Mifflin, 1962. Powell's original report, a pioneer study in human ecology, is available in Wallace Stegner, ed., *Report on the Arid Region of the United States, by John Wesley Powell,* Belknap Press, 1962. Canada had no really comparable figure, although the explorations and writings of John Macoun, a Toronto geologist and botanist who later became the first Director of the Canadian Geological Survey, bear comparison. Macoun accompanied the Sanford Fleming party in its survey of the Northwest Territories during the 1860's and provided an early report on the agricultural potential and problems of the Jasper region. See Sir Sanford Fleming, *Progress Report on the Canadian Pacific Railway Exploratory Survey,* Queen's Printer (Ottawa), 1872, and other reports issued in 1874, 1877, 1878, 1879, 1880. A readable popular account is George M. Grant, *Ocean to Ocean: Sanford Fleming's Expedition,* Charles A. Tuttle Co., 1967. Macoun was preceded by the explorer John Palliser, who provided the first descriptions of the Jasper region (J. Palliser, *Journals, Reports, and Observations Relative to Palliser's Exploration of British North America.* Parliamentary Blue Book, 1863). The best early accounts of the agricultural potential of the region were provided by Henry Y. Hind (H. H. Hind, *Report on the Assiniboine and Saskatchewan Exploring Expedition of 1858,* By the Authority of the Legislative Assembly, Toronto, 1859).

For histories of settlement in western Canada, see Arthur S. Morton, *History of Prairie Settlement,* Macmillan (Toronto), 1938, and James B. Hedges, *Building the Canadian West: The Land and Colonization Policies of the Canadian Pacific Railroad,* Macmillan (New York), 1939.

A study of the fluctuations in population in Saskatchewan caused by natural and economic difficulties is found in S. W. Alty, "The Influence of Climate and other Geographic Factors on the Growth and Distribution of Population in Saskatchewan," *Geography* (British), Vol. 24 (1939), pp. 10–33. For the Great Plains in general, see F. E. Clements, "Climatic Cycles and Human Populations in the Great Plains," *Scientific Monthly* (Sept. 1938), pp. 193–210. The cycles of population in the Great Plains seem to have characterized the aboriginal Indian populations as well (see Waldo Wedel, "Environment and Native Subsistence Economies in the Great Plains," *Smithsonian Miscellaneous Collections,* Vol. 101, No. 3, 1941, and "Some Aspects of Human Ecology in the Central Great Plains," *American Anthropologist,* Vol. 55 (1953), pp. 499–514. Whatever the level of economic or technical development, the variability of resources in the Plains have imposed constraints on population growth. The Indians avoided drastic depopulation by moving from the dry Plains to the more humid margins; the modern populations did precisely the same thing—both the aboriginal and the modern populations have been controlled by migration to a considerable extent. On the other hand, the Indians, with their hunting economy, were far more free to move than the agricultural settlers. From the Indian point of view, migration was "normal" since they were migratory people; from the point of view of the white settlers, migration is "abnormal"—an undesirable condition to which one must adjust, but never tolerate.

For a detailed comparative study of drought and its consequences in South Dakota, see Delbert C. Myrick, *Climate the Limiting Factor,* U. S. Dept. of Agriculture, Bureau of Agricultural Economics, 1941. Thomas Saarinen describes an attitude survey in *Perception of Drouth Hazard on the Great Plains,* University of Chicago Press, 1966. A valuable account of the Great Plains and its human occupance is James C. Malin, "The Grassland of North America: Its Occupance and the Challenge of Continuous Reappraisals," in W. L. Thomas, ed., *Man's Role in Changing the Face of the Earth,* University of Chicago Press, 1956.

The study of settlement pattern and the location of towns and economic service areas is a highly specialized topic, carried on mainly by social and economic geographers. B. J. Garner reviews methods and theories in "Models of Urban Geography and Settlement Location," in R. J. Chorley and P. Haggett, eds., *Models in Geography,* Methuen, 1967. Less technical treatment can be found in Michael Chisholm, *Rural Settlement and Land Use,* Wiley, 1967. A technical treatment of some of the basic theories is given by A. Lösch, *The Economics of Location,* Yale University Press, 1954. On towns and villages, see H. A. Stafford, Jr., "The Functional Bases of Small Towns," *Economic Geography,* 39 (1963), pp. 165–75, and for a definitive study of settlement patterns and service areas in southern Saskatchewan, based on the theories referred to in the above works, see Royal Commission on Agriculture and Rural Life, Province of Saskatchewan, Report No. 12: *Service Centers,* Queen's Printer, (Regina, Sask.), 1956. An anthropological approach to the problem of community patterning is found in Richard K. Beardsley and others, "Functional and Evolutionary Implications of Community Patterning," in P. L. Wagner and M. W. Mikesell, *Readings in Cultural Geography,* University of Chicago Press, 1962. A treatment of settlement from the standpoint of its effect on the landscape of western Canada is found in: J. G. Nelson, "Man and Landscape in the Western Plains of Canada," *Canadian Geographer,* 11 (1967), pp. 251–64.

For a study of the rapid fusion of European ethnic groups in the Canadian Great Plains, and loss of Old Country identity, see Marlene Stefanow, "Changing Bi- and Multi-Culturalism in the Canadian Prairie Provinces," in C. C. Zimmerman and S. Russell, *Symposium on the Great Plains of North America,* North Dakota State University, 1967. This symposium volume contains many other articles of direct relevance to the present book, including one by the author on the Jasper region.

THREE

Jasper Culture

This chapter offers a perspective on the patterns of Jasper agrarian life, and their relationships to the natural environment of the region, with emphasis on the styles of life of the majority population of the Jasper region: the ranching and farming communities. It begins with a review of the relationships between the significant geographical areas of the region, economies, and cultural styles, and continues with descriptions of life in town and country, festivals and ceremonials of regional significance, and attitudes toward nature and animals. The cultural patterns of the Indians and the Hutterites are described in Chapters 5 and 8, and additional details on ranching and farming styles of life are provided in Chapters 6 and 7.

Throughout this book we handle the phenomena of culture in two ways: (1) as descriptive material denoting particular styles of living and thinking; and (2) as standards or guides for action. We are also concerned with the extent to which these standards, in the form of traditions, have become involved in processes of adaptation. Since all Jasperites except the Indians entered the region in recent times, they appeared in the region with cultural patterns that had evolved in different natural and social environments: Europe, eastern Canada, the U.S. Midwest. While in many respects these backgrounds provided suitable guides to life in western Canada, in other respects they did not, and changes had to occur.

Environment, Economy, and Culture

One approach to human ecology is the mapping of correspond-
ences between natural features, technoeconomic patterns, and
particular styles of life or cultures. Much anthropological and
geographical research on human ecology took this form down to
the 1950's, when a more dynamic approach, "cultural ecology,"
emerged. The earlier approach, called "cultural area" by its
practitioners, dealt with tribal societies, and since historical
data on evolving and changing relations to natural resources
was usually absent, little more than correlations between geography and specific culture traits could be demonstrated. Nevertheless the areal approach has utility in providing a descriptive
background for the study of adaptive strategy and process.

One of the first tasks of our research project was to map the
distribution of the contemporary modes of economic production
and cultural styles to determine their relationship to the natural
landscape. In doing this mapping, we were aware that we had
historical data on the changes and development of these patterns,
and that the present distribution was by no means the first or
permanent one. We were chiefly interested in an elementary
problem: the extent to which cultural style coincided with the
technoeconomic modes of using natural resources. The historical
aspect of this problem concerned the extent to which the
cultural traits of the settlers had changed in the course of their
adaptation to the Jasper environment, and to the larger environment of North America and Canadian society and economy.

It was obvious from our first mapping of technoeconomic
modes that broad correlations between these and the other
factors existed. Four groups emerged immediately: the ranchers
in the hills and on the watershed slopes; the farmers on the
prairie-plains; the Hutterites on the prairie-plains; the Indians
in the hills. The first two groups were defined by their occupations; the latter two on the basis of ethnic cultural traditions.
These categories cut across the environmental divisions, however,
since the ranchers and Indians inhabited the hills, and the
farmers and the Hutterites the plains. This told us that relationships between cultural style and the physical environment

were mediated by both economy (mode of production) and ethnicity; there was no simple causal relationship.

Our accumulating historical data refined these conclusions still further. We found that the ranchers inhabited the hills and slopes not necessarily because this area was ideally suited to livestock production, but because the land survey and the homesteading laws had driven them off the plains. That is, they ranched in the higher and more rugged areas because these areas had been judged to be unsuited to crop farming. Secondly, we found that the Indians had their reserve in the hills mainly because the government had located it there, in a tree-covered, unproductive part of the region where they would not compete with the settlers for land. These facts told us, among other things, that external forces such as government laws and decisions also affected the relationships between nature, economy, and culture.

We next considered the cultural patterns the various groups of the Jasper population brought to the region. The relevant facts are described elsewhere in the book, but we can summarize them here. There was a definite difference between the outlook and habits of the early ranchers and the homestead farmers. The ranching pioneers and settlers were generally more mobile, adventurous types, few of them with families, and with long and varied work and job records in many parts of North America. Most of them eventually married, but even in the 1960's there was a goodly sprinkling of bachelors. The homestead farmers were, on the other hand, small-town or country people from stable communities who came to the West to make a new start. A majority had families or acquired them almost immediately, since it was difficult to farm without a wife and children to help in the tasks, and because marriage and children were viewed as normal and necessary. Most ranchers were ambivalent about town life and organized social relations; the farmers insisted on both.

The Hutterites have a distinctive ethnoreligious culture, one sanctioned by powerful sacred values that define not only religious beliefs but also economy and social organization. This differs importantly from the rancher-farmer culture in its insistence on communal property and decision-making. It is symbolized by distinctive costumes and customs, and self-imposed exclusion from the majority culture. When talking about Hutterites, ranchers and farmers feel an identity between themselves; when discussing each other, ranchers and farmers make careful distinctions:

> Them Hutterites—they are a kind of foreign group, they do everything different from us ranchers and farmers. They don't really belong. (farmer, age 50)
> Now these ranchers—they're a different breed, it seems like. They keep to themselves, awful clannish bunch. (same farmer, different interview)

The Cree Indians were originally plains buffalo hunters who also hunted in the forested hills on occasion. Nomadic people without a permanent residence, their traditions of open-handedness and loose social networks were ill-suited to sedentary life, and the smallness of their reserve made it virtually impossible to live on it. Little change occurred in their basic way of life after they were settled forcibly—they simply carried on their mobile, roaming ways, using jalopies instead of horses. From the point of view of all the other groups, the Indians were a pathetic and very divergent group. Ranchers and farmers would even show a degree of identity with the Hutterites when the Indians were the topic of conversation:

> When you come down to it, the Hutterites are really our kind of people. It's the Indians who are different around here. Still savages, I guess. (rancher, age 40)

These perceptions of identity and of similarity and difference have a relationship to real variation in style and in social solidarity. Ranchers and farmers usually marry within their own groups, and rarely across them; Hutterites, of course, are completely exclusive; and the Indians have no chance to develop intimate social relations with the white population. Therefore the Jasperite's perception of four relatively distinct groups in the population mirrors the social and cultural reality to a considerable extent.

Problems arise when we attempt to distinguish between styles within each of these groups and major subcultures. Jasperites make their own marginal distinctions, but since the differences between subgroups is often economic, and to point out these differences would question the belief in equal ability, they frequently deny such differences or are inconsistent in their descriptions of them. Moreover, these subcultural differences often do not necessarily correlate with social exclusiveness. Sometimes the subcultural differences were closely related to geographical location or the historical circumstances of settlement of a particular group; in other cases they were primarily created by level of income or mode of production.

The following descriptions constitute the summarized results of our efforts to map and define subcultural differences within the two majority groups of ranchers and farmers.

For the *ranchers,* we found four principal district groups. Each was located in a different part of the region, and these differing locations reflected certain patterns and times of pioneer settlement. These four groups are named on Figure 2.2; they are: (1) the *Town Ranchers* on the north slope; (2) the affluent *Hills Ranchers* south and southwest of the town; (3) the *Bench Ranchers* on the "Bench" or high plateau of the hills; and (4) the *Sandhill* and *Shortgrass* ranching areas in the northwest corner and the far south—the last two more remotely connected with the region's heartland and really out of the regional status and kinship system. The first three, though ranked to some extent by prestige status, were intermarried, and formed a single kin network.

The *Town Ranchers* are people of mostly British and eastern Canadian origins who came to the region to make a living any way that seemed convenient or congenial. Some had hoped to be farmers; others wanted adventure. Some of these families were involved in town businesses from the beginning, with ranching as a sideline. Large-scale range cattle raising was not their forte, and most of them acquired small- and medium-sized ranches. The group contained a high proportion of efficient, innovation-minded operators. The proximity to the town meant that their domestic life was considerably urbanized; the old rough-and-ready traditions had been replaced by well-furnished homes and a flair for horsemanship and decorative Western costumes. Urbanization in their case meant both participation in town social affairs and adherence to mass media-reinforced Western hobbies and styles of life. These people were conscious of the high prestige of ranching in the region

as a whole, and especially in the district around Jasper town—
"The Old Cow Town," as it labels itself with self-conscious
pride in its Western heritage on the sign one sees on the highway. The Town Ranchers also constituted a particularly well-
organized social or district grouping, with many kin ties and
patterns of interaction.

The *Hills Ranchers* represent the oldest stratum of the
ranching population. A mixture of people of British-Canadian
and (mostly) American origins, they established the first ranches
in the vicinity of the Mounted Police fort in the Cypress Hills,
then spread out along the south slope. Acreages of these ranches
were always large, and the robust traditions of the range cattle
and horse industry were still visible in the attitudes and behavior
of their owners. Their interest in horsemanship and other
features of the Western style of life was more variable and less
infused with status-seeking or status-maintaining than in the
case of the Town Ranchers. The Hills Ranchers valued their
isolation and some of them, by choice, lacked telephones and
good roads into the ranch headquarters. Their physical isolation from the town helped to sustain their more individualized
or more generalized cultural pattern. At the same time, the
very largest and most affluent ranchers were in this group, and
these people also possessed the largest number of offspring with
higher education and histories of residence in cities and even
foreign countries. While the Town Ranchers were conscious
of elite status, or sought it, most of the Hills Ranchers lived it,
with the ease and individualism of a rustic Western aristocracy.
Hills Ranchers were less of a discrete social group than the
Town Ranchers. They were as inclined to marry out of the area
as within it, and to develop ties of friendship and economic
exchange with ranchers anywhere.

The *Bench Ranchers* were sometimes called the "real" ranchers
by local people, meaning by this that they adhered to the rough
old frontier tradition. They were mostly British-Canadians, with
a few Americans, living on small or medium ranches of doubtful productivity. A few were of Central European origin, former
farmers. Some, but not all, had casual interest in Western hobbies and styles of life; their clothes were usually nondescript;
all their horses were the standard cowpony breed (the Town
and Hills Ranchers always had a few Arabians and standard-

breds); their roping and rodeo clubs were casual and exuberant. They lacked the intense seriousness and devotion to skill characteristic of the Town Ranchers and a few of the Hills group, and did not participate much in the English-style riding display held annually in Jasper town patronized by the other more sophisticated ranchers. The Bench Ranchers also represented, besides the Hutterian Brethren colony in the area, the only Euro-American settler population remaining in this section of the hills. Bench Ranchers had been a district social community at one time, but in recent years this disintegrated as many of them migrated or changed their locations.

Sandhill and Shortgrass ranching were specialized forms with very large acreages on very low-productivity land. The cultural style of these people resembled that of the Bench and the Hills groups, depending on family backgrounds and general affluence. In some districts a "Texas" or "Montana" style of life, with large, elaborate ranch houses and expansive behavior, had emerged. This style was looked at askance by nearly all of the ranchers in the vicinity of Jasper town and the Hills. A few of the latter had enough money to permit them to participate in this pattern, but the tradition of consumption restraint, still important in Jasper culture, held them back. The Sandhill and Shortgrass people interacted with groups outside the Jasper region and had few kin ties with the dominant Town and Hills groups.

Farmers were more homogeneous than ranchers in their styles of life, largely because of the relatively greater homogeneity of income and resources. What differences we found, however, were almost entirely due to income, and these subcultural styles did not constitute social solidarity groups. We distinguished two subcultures: the *Prairie Homestead* style was confined to the smallest and most marginal farms, and usually to those in the dryest or roughest localities. Relative poverty and less interest in "modern conveniences" meant a very simple mode of life, one resembling the original pioneer homestead period. Their houses were simple, two or three-room wood shacks, a few with dirt floors. Clothing was scarce and old; furniture even scarcer and older; decoration primitive or nonexistent. All had electricity and usually a refrigerator, but many had wood stoves and no plumbing. The simplicity and casualness of their life resembled that of the Bench Ranchers. At the same time, most of these "Prairie Homesteaders" did not differ appreciably from their more affluent neighbors from the standpoint of education —their style was due largely to relative poverty.

The style of the more affluent farmers we called *Prairie Farm*. Here the rural middle-class pattern of life characteristic of the entire Great Plains was fully represented. Their houses were sturdily built, enlarged versions of the homestead shack, or newly built, some of them contemporary semifabricated bungalows, with screened porches and tree shelter belts enclosing the yards. Interior furnishings emphasized bright, overstuffed furniture mixed with shabby old heirloom pieces, plastic flowers, miscellaneous knickknacks, family photos, and mementos of the 4H club or the trips to the coast or possibly the sunny South.

Both of these styles also varied by ethnic origin of the family. Marginal survivals or acknowledgment of ethnic-religious elements occasionally appeared: portraits of Jesus in the Catholic families; old clothes chests from the Ukraine; details of German or Scandinavian cuisine. Another source of variation was the amount of cattle owned by a farmer. Often the acquirement of cattle was accompanied by a drift toward ranching attitudes, costumes, and pastimes.

As previously noted, these two farm subcultures were mainly a matter of income and did not constitute distinct social groupings, in contrast to some of the ranching subgroups. Social groups among farmers, as we shall note in greater detail in Chapter 7, were primarily a matter of neighborhood or district based on the original homestead settlement pattern and the early school districts. Many such districts would have representatives of both the Prairie Homestead and Prairie Farm subcultural style, and intermarriages would have occurred between families whose way of life could be classified in each of the styles.

What these facts suggest is that social and cultural differences among ranchers and farmers are really not very great, particularly when relative incomes are matched. These people have a broadly similar Euro-American heritage; they are all second- or third-generation residents of Western North America; they are all engaged in producing for the national agricultural market. These facts tend to push their cultures together; what differences exist are due to income, or to marginal survivals of original ethnic differences, or to the special pushes exerted by occupations: ranching emphasizing individualism and conservative economic ideals and decorative Western dress and sports; farming emphasizing agrarian politics and down-to-earth ways of living.

. At the same time, the Jasper region as a region has its own cultural norms, most of them associated with the ranching culture, since this was the earliest and remains, on the whole, the most prestigeful. Farmers take to it—as a hobby, or as a rather natural result of accepting cattle in their farming regime. Associated with it is Jasper's nostalgic attitude toward the past, its reverence for the pioneer ways, and a pride in an independent and individualistic spirit. These emphases overlie subcultural and occupational cultural differences, and help to blur the distinctions.

While ranching and ranchers constitute a kind of cultural and social elite in the region, the farmers hold the reins of power when it comes to dealing with the provincial government. There is, in fact, a kind of "moiety system" in Jasper: within the region, the ranchers have a monopoly on prestige and can bask in the security derived from knowing their symbols are, by and large, the regional symbols. But the farmers, while acknowledging the prestige of the rancher, and even borrowing it, nevertheless derive security from their conviction of power in numbers and in their ability to influence the provincial government to do things for them. Ranchers have the "country" culture, with no elements of small-town character; farmers have rural versions of town life, and can look down on the ranchers as provincials, rustics, when elevating their own style to a position of dignity or superiority, as they sometimes do. As cattle production becomes the regional economic mainstay, ranchers and farmers are also in postures of real competition for land and water.

Neither ranchers nor farmers were especially interested in art and literature or other pursuits in what is known as high culture. While illiteracy was rare (only a few older men who grew up in districts lacking schools), Jasperites were not "readers." The typical home took the Canadian farm papers, the *Jasper Weekly News*, an urban paper, and a national magazine. Books appeared in the more literate families.

Wallace Stegner, in the Epilog to his book on southwestern Saskatchewan, *Wolf Willow,* regrets the shallow development of high culture and notes that the farmers were more interested in art, literature, and intellectual interests in the pioneer period than they are today. The original homesteader contingent had a respectable number of people who could play musical instruments, write poetry, or stage amateur dramatics—all skills acquired in small Eastern and Midwestern towns. The mimeographed pioneer reminiscences prepared for Saskatchewan's 50-year Jubilee in 1955 are full of accounts of songfests, plays, sewing and embroidery competitions, essay-writing contests, and the like. The Jasper town Agricultural Society, in its heyday between 1900 and 1930, held an annual regional "show" in which penmanship, paintings, recitations, tableaux, and musical performances were featured on an equal plane with displays of livestock, grain, and garden produce. But though the show was still held in the 1960's most of these cultural activities were gone, and the displays were confined to garden flowers, grain sheaves, and 4H club projects.

This loss of high-cultural or aesthetic interests and skills was associated with the privations and difficulties of the hard life on the prairies, the lack of diversified education, and the special difficulties of the drought-and-depression years. People who must do hard manual labor every day of the year, and who for years receive very little return on this labor, have little energy and time for the "finer things of life," and certainly little money to permit their professional practitioners to survive. (A few—a very few—Jasper town families drive their children to the small cities 60 or 80 miles away for music lessons.) The adaptive success of Jasper people must be measured in terms of grit and determination, patience and forebearance—not cultural refinement. Another factor is the isolation of Jasper from continental centers of culture. The narrowness of viewpoint of the rural religions and the complacency of Canadian middle-class culture also played their roles.

But there were signs of change: the consolidated town schools, with their enriched provincial curriculum, were reintroducing culture in the 1950's and '60's, and the third generation of Jasperites may display an awakened interest in aesthetics and intellectualia. But this interest will not take hold unless there are correlated changes in leisure, income, and opportunity. Jasper still has a long way to go, and one must not expect too much in this direction of these hard-working people.

SOCIAL STATUS

Jasper society, like other North American rural societies, had several criteria that could define and differentiate personal and family position in the district and in the region. But at the same time, there was no overall status system that would permit us to speak of "social class," that is, a general regional upper-middle-lower rank system.

In this chapter, and in Chapters 4, 6, and 7, we discuss various criteria of status in the particular contexts in which these criteria are operative—which is exactly the way Jasperites think of them. People in Jasper have no general or overall category of "social status" or "class," but consider a person's position differently in different contexts of thought and discussion. If one is speaking of the history of the region, certain names always come up, and their owners are spoken of with admiration as people who "are the real Old Timers, you know, they were the first ones in the district." On the other hand, if the context shifted to farm/ranch management, these same people might be referred to as follows: "those old fellas never did know nothing about raising stuff; they're not much good."

Here we may summarize the list of status-giving criteria we will discuss or define in other contexts: (1) *Social credit,* or a man's or woman's rating as a good human being, manager, homemaker: probably the most important criterion of all. (2) *Ethnic prestige,* or elements of prestige or status associated rather vaguely with the European country of origin. (3) *Occupational prestige,* or the fact that ranching generally carried more prestige than farming, and that *within* these categories people could also be differentiated on the basis of their style of life, or of district-group culture, especially in the case of the ranchers. (4) *Settlement prestige* or status—prestige assigned to an individual or family, based on the date of their arrival in the region (the earlier the arrival, the higher the prestige). This criterion is fairly marginal. (5) *Hardship prestige* or status was applied particularly to farmers, and really was similar to settlement prestige, only greater emphasis was placed on the hardships endured during the drought and Depression of the 1930's. (6) *Economic power* and *political power*. Wealthy people, ranchers especially, exercised considerable power in certain contexts, particularly over issues of town government, investment and capital, and business enterprises. Farmers had weak local power but considerable political power with the provincial government. Many of the locally powerful ranchers had very low social credit ratings, since their power was seen as the result of inheriting a big ranch and not native skill at operating the ranch.

Was there a tendency for some of these criteria to coincide, that is, to pile up for particular groups? We have already answered that negatively on the whole: Jasper had no clearly defined class system. In some cases, however, there were tendencies toward correlation: the most important of these was visible when families of Anglo-American origin also had large, prosperous enterprises, operated them well, and manifested humane, egalitarian manners. Such people could be considered a "social elite" for the region, as we have occasionally noted previously. This elite was poorly integrated, however, and was constantly giving way to other status criteria. Its sphere of power or influence was also in continual flux, as other groups in the towns and the country would move in to swing policy in some desired direction. There was a tendency here toward an "upper" social class, but the strong cultural egalitarianism and relatively weak economic differentiation among Jasperites made it a tendency only. If, then, we can make something of a case for a Jasper regional "upper class" or elite, can we do the same for a "lower" segment? Here the answer is negative, since the lower status groups seem to be strictly local or district in identity, not regional. For example, the town has a poverty and "drifter" group, but these people have little or nothing to do with the country population. There are low-income ranchers who are paternalized by the bigger ranchers, and some of these are eccentric "characters"—but again this is the concern of the ranching community or particular districts. From a strictly economic standpoint, of course, there are "lower" groups for the region as a whole—the ones mentioned above plus the Indians —but it would be misrepresenting the real ambiguity, fluidity, and egalitarianism of the Jasper social system to construct a layer-cake class system for the region as a whole.

The summary above pertains to the ranching-farming society, and neglects the town-dwellers, the Hutterites, and the Indians. For the first, we can say that they may become part of the country status groupings or assignments to the extent that they have kinship or financial connections with country people; if they do not, they work out their own statuses in town society. Hutterites are a withdrawn religious-ethnic group; they have only the most tenuous connections with social networks in the country districts, and none in town. Indians are best understood as a kind of nonpeople, an almost caste-like minority, excluded from intimate participation in all other social groupings and networks.

LIFE IN COUNTRY AND TOWN

The physical isolation of a sparsely-populated countryside is the key to many Jasper cultural patterns. Communication and social contact usually need to be planned; they do not emerge spontaneously when neighbors are miles apart and the urban habit of visiting across the lawn is impossible. Social occasions seem to have been more frequent in pioneer days than today, at least for the farmers, due to the larger population and thicker settlement. The pioneer reminiscences compiled in mimeographed books by each district continually emphasize this fact:

After the Kletzar School was built, everyone enjoyed the card parties and the dances and things held there. It was such good times. It was a real community center. There were lots of young folks around at that time, the Booth family, Concords, Swensons, Haags, Irma and Niels Hansen, Biersachs and Stanhopes to

name a few, and always a school teacher to make a boy sit up
and take notice. John Potts, Bill Concord, George Booth and Wes
Frieser furnished a good share of the music, and Bob Booth
called the squares. No one could do a polka like old timers Jake
Haag or Karl Wilensky, with—God bless them—Mrs. Booth and
Mrs. Kelly as partners. At times that school must of rocked back
and forth on its stony hill!

The automobile has revived many of the old customs, however. Jasper people began intensive use of cars as a means of
social interaction relatively late, modest incomes and bad roads
delaying the process until the 1940's and 50's except for the
families living near the towns. In the 1960's traffic had increased
considerably, and men moved up and down the roads in their
trucks, visiting and often combining their trips with work
exchange. One medium-sized rancher averaged about 550 miles
per week during the summer months on his two vehicles—pickup
truck and passenger car. About 115 of these weekly miles were
used for social purposes (visits, picking up relatives in town,
shopping, trips to the doctor, etc.), the remainder for tasks
connected with ranching. About 150 miles of the latter were
driven on the ranch property itself, inspecting fields, fences,
and cattle.

The women traveled to refurbished old country schoolhouses
or the village hall (often about the last building still in service)
for their many clubs and "circles." This was an improvement
on the "old days," when the only time a woman got to town
was when her husband took her there, and then she had to
spend most of her time in the little shack, usually situated
in a weedy lot, labeled "Ladies Rest Room." In one district each
farm and ranch wife attended one club meeting, card party,
bridal shower, or similar function at least once a week; the men
had comparable mingling schedules, although most of their
social occasions were combined with business. Everyone attended
annual picnics, cooperative brandings, riding and roping clubs,
ball games, curling in the winter, or the regional "ceremonials"
to be described later. Social life was reviving, thanks to the cars,
although Jasperites still nostalgically complained that the old
weekly dances and house parties of the old days were so much
more satisfying and frequent. It is impossible to know whether

they were or not, since Jasperites love to look back wistfully at the good old frontier and use it as a symbol of everything that is sound and rewarding in man and nature.

For the country districts the telephone was a relatively recent innovation in Jasper. A few districts had "barbed wire" telephones as far back as the 1920's (the line was usually the top strand of the fences, lifted over gates by poles), but regular country district exchanges became common only in the 1950's with the coming of electric power. The telephone opened up a new sphere of communication, especially for the women; speed of transmission of news and gossip was extremely rapid over long distances, and secrets were nonexistent. But communication was always relatively good, even before the telephone. Jasperites can produce astonishingly detailed information about family affairs simply by driving by a farm or ranch and glancing at the premises: are the boys helping their father instead of in school? Is the car out of the yard? Are the shades drawn? Light in certain rooms? What is the size of the feed stack for the cattle? All of this information has manifold meanings that escape the visitor from the city.

Life in the *towns* is just plain dull—if we can believe most of the ranchers, some of the farmers, and all of the young people living in them! Jasper town, and one other small town south of the Hills (Eldora), remained the only viable centers in the region by the 1960's. All the rest had disappeared or were reduced to one or two basic services. Jasper town itself, with over half of its population of 2,500 consisting of retired ranchers and farmers, was not a community to inspire much enthusiasm on the part of children, young people, or the handful of town liberals in business and the professions. The majority of business establishments were operated by aging men who seemed more interested in preserving the old customs, making a simple living, and avoiding competition from chain stores than in aggressively building the town's commercial and recreational life. The town had a plethora of churches and organizations: for a population of 2,500, 15 churches and 32 clubs, lodges, and other "voluntary organizations." The relatively few persons with leadership skills were diffused over this array of groups and it was extremely difficult to organize the many separate groups for joint civic efforts. One ancient movie theater, mostly showing old Westerns and musicals, a small swimming pool, a curling rink, and an outdoor horse-show and rodeo stadium were the recreational facilities, and most of these catered to the adults rather than the young. The main street had scarcely changed from the heyday of the community in the first two decades of the twentieth century. The old false-front buildings still gave the town an old-time Western look, and the streets remained dust (or mud) until 1964 when, in a sudden burst of "progress," the town passed a referendum and an assessment and had all the streets paved at once—an action demonstrating that the extreme modesty of the dwellings and businesses sometimes disguised reasonably comfortable bank accounts.

Jasper also had a "shanty" district on the edge of town which was populated by impoverished aged people, manual laborers who drifted from town to town, other low-income families with jobs in town businesses or in construction crews, and a few Indians and Métis people—all of these constituting about 10 per cent of the town's population. A persistent run of petty crimes, drunkenness, automobile disasters, and acts of violence emerged from this segment of the population, which was kept in mild check by the Mounties, who were the town's only police force (on a contract basis). This seamy side of Jasper life was almost always a topic for silence on the part of the town's respectable citizens, but in very relaxed moments the most objective residents made jokes about "Jasper—the town of churches and bums." A few recognized the basic cause: the very slender occupational opportunities and low educational level of the region as a whole.

From the viewpoint of the more objective or cynical Jasper residents in both town and country, the churchgoing proclivities of the people could be considered hypocrisy in view of their neglect of essential services for the young and the aged, and in their convenient ignoring of the seamy side of Jasper life and the sad plight of the Indians. Like other northern, Western, and semi-frontier areas, Jasperites consumed a fair share of alcohol —the provincial government liquor store in Jasper town had one of the largest dollar turnovers of any store in town. Teenagers were certainly less "wild" than many of their big-city counterparts, but there were plenty of incidents of drunken driving, car accidents, minor vandalism, and the like, and all parents, town and country, constantly complained about their inability to discipline the younger generation.

By the stricter standards of rural Midwestern communities in Canada and the U.S., sexual mores were relaxed. Pregnancies before marriage were common enough in many districts so that the women interviewed felt free to admit them, but we have no reliable statistics. Nearly every family in Jasper had a skeleton in some closet, and some of the contemporary "elite" families had horse-thievery or other pecadilloes in their background. The basic equality of social origin and behavior of most Jasper settlers is one of the factors encouraging the persisting eglitarianism of the society despite growing economic differentiation in some spheres. Eccentrics were numerous; as in other small and isolated communities, behavior that might result in institutionalization in urban society was easily tolerated.

As we have hinted, law enforcement in Jasper was informal. The Mounted Police, who were on contract to the town, but who also furnished free law enforcement for the countryside, maintained a policy of interfering as little as possible with affairs of violence or theft. This meant that their activities were confined largely to the town; that is, keeping the marginal population in line. In the country, infractions were usually handled by neighbors: a Hills rancher who knew that a small Bench-rancher was stealing an occasional calf, would simply appear one day on the premises with a long whip and make a few casual remarks about what he would do if he "caught the fella taking my stock." This was usually sufficient to stop the practice.

During the early 1960's, Jasper town people were considerably shaken by a number of crises brought about by some of its residents who campaigned for a more vigorous community policy on commercial expansion, reform in church and club organization, and improvements in recreational facilities. Well ahead of the protests against the "establishment" that blossomed in Canada and the U.S. in the late '60's, these people fought the grip of the old guard of retired elite ranchers and farmers who dominated town organization and government. The rebels were often defeated and frustrated, but the attack was determined and some changes *were* made. By 1967 the town showed some signs of movement. Real estate codes and tax structures were being reexamined to make it easier for outside businesses to locate, and the town elite had been penetrated by a few vigorous younger men and women. But one root cause of conservatism had not changed: the town banks. In Jasper, as elsewhere in Canada, these are all branches of Eastern institutions, follow an extremely conservative policy on financing, and make it difficult to find venture capital.

The important role of Jasper town—and to a lesser extent, its analog, Eldora, on the south slope—lies not only in its schools, hospital, stores, and repair services, but also in its function of binding together the vast and sparsely populated Jasper region.

The *Jasper Weekly News,* published in Jasper town since the early 1900's, and distributed throughout the Jasper region, contains an intimate record of the social affairs, visits, meetings, sports events, blizzards, road conditions, illnesses, and nearly everything else for the five or six main "districts" of the region. Each district has a female correspondent who writes a report to the paper about every other week. These articles are detailed records of the activities of nearly every family in the community —at least of every family that is considered a member, and this is usually at least 90 per cent of the total. In a typical article, 26 names were mentioned, 14 social calls, three ladies' parties, two Western horse events, one baseball game, three automobile trips to nearby small cities for recreation, two people stuck in the mud on the road to town, one sore throat, two people in the hospital, and one thanks delivered to a tractor dealer who opened his agency on Sunday to accommodate a farmer with tractor trouble. The last item is especially typical: much space is devoted to friendliness, neighborliness, and other pioneer affiliative values of which Jasperites are particularly proud. These news notes in the weekly paper serve many functions: calling attention to basic values; communication in a sparsely populated country; confirming or correcting gossip; gentle hints to the authorities.

The paper has a large circulation among former Jasperites elsewhere in North America and the world. The total circulation in 1963 was about 3,000, of which 1,600 was local and about 1,400 to other parts of western Canada, the remainder divided between other U.S. States, Canadian provinces and foreign countries. The paper's correspondence columns frequently print letters from writers living outside the region commenting in detail on particular items of news, the writers giving the impression of having just left. Missing persons are quickly located via the letter columns. The doings of Jasperites thus are circulated and discussed by a wide external network of relatives and former residents covering 23 states and provinces and five foreign countries.

Another important feature of the paper is the long obituaries of "old timers." These were particularly prevalent in the early 1960's because a whole generation of 1910-and-before pioneers began passing away. These obits are often more than simple, objective accounts of the deceased; they are moral tracts emphasizing all the desirable pioneer virtues: fortitude, patience, homespun qualities, humility, strength, humor. Particular attention is given to the ability of the deceased to weather the economic and climatic storms of Jasper agriculture, since, after all, he was one who stayed. They are supplemented by many special articles on local history, all of them consistently stressing nostalgic features of the old frontier, and usually provoking a spate of letters correcting details:

Last week I said old Joe Kelley told us that Jake Freneau cooked for the Massacre Creek roundup outfit in 1912. Herbert Wallace says this is not so, and he will whup the man who says that it is. According to Herb, and he should know, he was there, Jake Freneau cooked his last batch of biscuits for the Pool Roundup on the Whitemud in 1909.

The images Jasper people have of themselves and their country are constantly reinforced by the mass media, who often use Jasper as a typical example of the Old West. A Jasperite could see one of his neighbors riding herd on his cattle in an advertisement for Saskatchewan tourism, produced by the provincial government and disseminated in national magazines in 1963:

Room to breathe—and roads to roam all over! If everything's as new and unspoiled as you'd expect of a new frontier except for the old-fashioned friendliness, if you don't have to charter a plane to get away from it all, if you can order a 72 ounce steak, or see where the Mounties learn to get their man, you're in Saskatchewan for sure.

Other Jasperties participated in a television special about the Cypress Hills, written up as follows in *TV Guide* (and reprinted by the *Jasper News*):

Director Robert Barclay and photographer Roger Morido went to the Cypress Hills last fall at round-up time, and filmed a beautifully evocative color portrait of this fresh and airy expanse, where man and beast know the true meaning of freedom. The commentator is David Haig, a Calgary lawyer and historian who grew up in the Cypress Hills and returns there often to enjoy the soul-nourishing beauty. A ranching wife and mother describes her life and tells why she wouldn't change it. Cowboys talk of the job of rounding up cattle and cutting out their own brands.

Over all these people in their big, wide country is a tremendous feeling of peace, the sort of contentment that comes from abundant space, fresh air, good food, satisfying work with its own brand of pride and independence oddly coupled with a helping hand freely given and received, in a place where there is time for thinking and for strong, uncomplicated friendships, for finding one's own identity, and accepting it.

After viewing the program, one Jasperite wrote as follows to the *News:*

Enjoyed Telescope Thursday night with the Cypress Hills roundup. It came at a good time also, just when a number of us were thinking there must be better places and ways of making a living to see the herd of cattle and real cowboys, Fort Smith, and the beautiful Cypress Hills on TV makes you feel proud to be a part of it.

INTEGRATIVE CEREMONIALS

All societies have gatherings that define the purpose or meaning of life for their members. A tribal society has a single religion, hence the services of this faith serve this function. The Plains

Indian tribes had their famous Sun Dances. A North American society like Jasper, with a plethora of religious sects, must look elsewhere for a focusing ceremonial, and it has been found, in the West, in cooperative work activities and in recreational events like the rodeo. The need for associations that symbolize community integration is also especially acute in a farming population relatively small and widely dispersed but still retaining traditions of an associative, densely populated society.

The Jasper region is not an official political entity: it is rather an informal network of social and economic transactions, held together by broad historical traditions of settlement, channeled through the railhead at Jasper town and maintained by the functions of the town as a service center and retirement home. Its ceremonials are also voluntary affairs. If they become symbolic of the entire region, or much of it, it comes about through informal processes of selection and consensus. Actually each district of Jasper region had its own gatherings: baseball clubs, homemakers' organizations, roping and riding clubs, particular church or neighborhood picnics, some of them descended from the old country school district functions. Most of these were at least two generations old; Jasperites cling to the pioneer past, since it is their only authentic local history.

Through the years only one event has attained the full status of a Jasper regional festival: the annual Greenfields Stampede and Picnic. This amateur rodeo was actually one of the district gatherings, in this case sponsored by the Greenfields Roping Club, an old organization of this district southeast of Jasper town in the hills (Fig. 2.2). Down to the 1940's, the Stampede had been strictly local, but as the Greenfields farming settlement disintegrated, the Stampede continued to be held by the remaining Bench ranchers. By the 1940's it had become the distinctive Jasper regional festival and one of the last true amateur rodeos in the old "Whoop-up Country" of Montana, Saskatchewan, and Alberta. Amateur riders from Jasper, and a few from Montana or Alberta, entered the contests, and spectators came from diverse points. Usually about 1,500 persons could be counted on to attend—a big crowd by Jasper standards. The Club financed the Stampede by collecting attendance fees, entry fees for the riders, and voluntary contributions from and trophies

donated by town merchants. Posters advertising the affair are
distributed to all the villages and hamlets. The North Slope
Homemakers Club, a women's organization, is in charge of the
refreshment booth. All of these women live close to Jasper town,
but many of them had been Greenfields residents in the old days.
Thus their service represents a symbolic return to the old district. After a day of rodeo events, family picnics, and a few simple
carnival "rides" for the kids, the day ends with a dance on a
portable board floor. The following description is quoted from
our field notes:

The setting is important: this is no longer a settled area, but
is now isolated and remote, reached by a rough road up through
the Hills, over 20 miles from town. This remote location, on a
famous old deserted ranch, has a romantic meaning for everyone—it is a kind of symbolic place, the Delphos of Jasper, representing all that is rough and wild in nature, and enduring and
strong in Jasper character. The rodeo and picnic are held in a
large natural amphitheatre, the old corral area of the ranch,
surrounded by gentle slopes crowned with aspen—the whole a
setting of park-like beauty.

One notices immediately the absence of any obvious attempt
to commercialize the event. Aside from the refreshments, and a
few small-scale concessions—a dart game, a miniature ferris
wheel, or a bingo game—there is nothing to buy, and nothing is
advertised. The emphasis is on the rodeo events and the family
picnics, the kin group reunions, and the strolling spectators
making the rounds and greeting old friends.

The corrals and fences are crude and rough, but serviceable.
The rodeo announcer sits in a little ramshackle booth, raised
above the main chute, and carries on a continual patter: calling
out names, making private jokes about leading personalities.
Most of this is pointed at the ranchers, who tend to dominate
the proceedings, but the farmers are not neglected, and the announcer himself is a "mixed farmer," a man with cattle as well
as crops.

Although the initial impression is one of informal mingling,
more careful observation reveals considerable segregation in
seating. The men clustering around the chutes and announcer's
booth are nearly all ranchers, and above them, on the heavy
board fence or wall framing the chutes and the booth, sit the
biggest ranchers and the old-time rancher pioneers. The "old
folks," both ranchers and farmers, sit in state under the trees
well back of the corral fence, where they hold court for relatives and friends. The younger families sit or stand along the

fence. The Indians sit at the very end of the corral in a dusty area away from everyone else, although one or two Indians always compete in the rodeo events.

There are always a few city folks, usually relatives of the country people, who may come from long distances for the kinship reunions and general fun. Occasionally the sheriffs of neighboring towns in Montana show up wearing their six-guns, studiously ignored by the one or two Mounties in mufti, who neglect to enforce the strict Canadian law against carrying sidearms in public. A few stray tourists may materialize and, in latter years, a few hippy-type teenagers. There is little drinking, and an occasional drunk, but alcohol is not a feature of the day, partly because of laws against transporting it in cars, but perhaps more importantly because of the tradition that the Stampede and Picnic is a family affair, and in Jasper one doesn't drink with "family" present, at least not to excess.

The Stampede had its ups and downs—some years the early July date means chilly and wet weather, and many of the younger families couldn't "see the sense in going way up there and get yourself full of dust to see a lot of old timers"; or, "The rodeo is a lot better in town—it's real professional, and up at Greenfields its just all them ranch hands and farm boys." But like the Broadway theater, the Stampede hangs on, sick or hearty, with always enough patronage and interest to guarantee a reasonable crowd. Its symbolism is important: a real country folk festival, the Sun Dance of the settlers, up there near the Indian Reserve in the heart of the old Jasper country. The automobile had a lot to do with the late emergence of the Stampede as a "traditional" ceremonial, since the car made it relatively easy to get to the remote location, even over its difficult roads. So long as Jasperites can get around in automobiles, their festivals will probably thrive, and despite their laments that there was more social life in the old days, there is evidence that they are doing at least as well, if not better, today.

Another celebration with a certain regional significance is the annual Old Timers' Day sponsored by the Old Timers Association of Jasper town. This organization is run by second-generation sons and daughters of the pioneers, but its most honored members are the rapidly vanishing handful of octogenarian ranch and farm people representing the original settler population. Membership in the club is limited to members of families that had been in Jasper before 1903, the date of incorporation of the town, although the thinning ranks of old timers were leading to a revision of the limiting date. People in the region gain a certain status depending on the date of entry of their family—the earlier the higher—but this is a largely honorific prestige and not as significant as what we call "social credit ratings," described in later chapters.

The Old Timer's Day consists of a long parade in the morning, a picnic, a small rodeo and horse show in the Agricultural Society arena on the edge of town, and a dance in the evening. The parade, like every other frontier days celebration throughout the West, features transportation devices: ox wagons, hay wagons, buggies or "Democrats," old automobiles, and steam and early gasoline tractors and threshing outfits. Each float in the parade is a voluntary affair, "got up" by particular families who usually advertise their date of entry as settlers on their float's placards and signs. Interspersed are entries from civic organizations, the usual "queen" float, Sunday school children and their decorated bicycles, and—bringing up the rear—a party of amused Indians in makeshift costumes, with occasionally a horse travois with a very young child swaddled on its triangular platform. The preeminence of transportation vehicles is a convenient mating of the need to symbolize movement out to the frontier and transportation and communication *within* the sparsely populated region—and of course the need for original floats to make up a parade.

ATTITUDES TOWARD NATURE AND ANIMALS

Earlier in this chapter we observed that ranchers and farmers divide a number of cultural elements between each other to produce a kind of moiety system: power differentials, relatively distinct marriage and kin groups, and competition for the natural resources of the region. This division is based ultimately on the differing ecological postures of the two occupations: the extensive use of grass for pasturing animals, on the one hand, and the intensive cultivation of small tracts of soil, on the other. These ecological differences also have their concomitant attitudes toward nature and animals.

Those Jasperites (a majority of the farmers) who came from the humid East found it difficult to understand the significance of aridity and treelessness. While their agricultural methods have accommodated to the harsh realities of the region, their aesthetic preferences often remain centered on the idea of a green and moist land—an ideal kept alive by printed pictures and descriptions of humid lands. Yet while they attempt, in one way or another, to recreate symbols of greenery and water in their gardens and tree belts, they have also adapted attitudinally to the vistas and distance of the Plains. We noted earlier their feelings of being "hemmed in" by the narrow horizons and dense vegetation and architecture of the East—but at the same time they still strive to grow gardens and lawns, especially in town, after retirement.

There is a vast lore about the prairie, the Hills, roads, rain, hail, the chinooks and other spectacular items of weather and the skies, of how to avoid grasshoppers and how to fertilize and water flowers and shelter them from the drying wind and the bitter winter cold. This lore is a mixture of sardonic gallows humor, genuine pride, and enthusiastic experimentation. Running through it all is a thread of determination:

Geologists tell us that these Cypress Hills withstood the grinding forces of the glaciers. Some of the resistance could have rubbed off over the years on the inhabitants. (Jasper rancher, writing in a district mimeographed book of reminiscence)

And not only determination, but an element of pleasure and enjoyment in the rough, wild weather, and the stern and unending Plains.

The women are less enthusiastic than the men, largely because for years they have fought dust and dryness in their efforts to make old log or board houses into homes, or to grow flowers and fruit in order to realize those middle-class dreams of the ladies' magazines. The first sign of relative prosperity was storm windows and a "modern kitchen"; then followed the Simpson-Sears–furnished parlor. Through the years they struggled with the dust that forced its way into the house despite the stuffing in cracks around the windows, or with the drying winds that parched their flowers before they could bloom. And behind the farmers' drive to get leased grazing land from the ranchers was the bitterness of their wives, who envied the ranch wife in her snug house in the protected coulee, with water and shelter for the garden.

The worst storm we experienced was in 1925 when a hail storm ripped down the lake at ten o'clock at night, tearing a path of destruction half way to Eldora. It took the whole crop, left the pasture like a plowed field, ripped the roof off the house and blew in the windows. (I never found the blinds and curtains.) The cat was killed in the yard, and the stock crawled around for days, all stove up. We repaired the house, but in spite of everything the roof leaked. I remember rigging up an umbrella on a tilt over the bed so the drips would be diverted over the side of the bed into a pail. Not that we were strangers to leaks, for the barns were made of poles and straw and the roofs would drip long after the storm was over. We got off the prairie after that. The following year we bought the old Stenko place on Massacre Creek.

Throughout the Great Plains much interest has been shown in "natural" beauty, always defined as created greenery and water: tree belts, lakes made from dammed streams, and flower gardens protected by hedges. Even the experimental farms in the Plains states and provinces have put considerable emphasis on breeding drought-resistant varieties of plants for ornamental gardens and plantings, and the agricultural extension services publish bulletins devoted to adapted "farm beautification." (Not all such efforts are purely ornamental: tree belts around farmsteads conserve moisture, break the force of winds, and make gardens possible.) These efforts are those of people with humid-land conceptions of nature who persist in their desire to make the arid Plains resemble their homelands—even into the third generation. Jasperites worked hard on these concerns in the early years of settlement, but by the 1960's, many of them had abandoned the effort, postponed it until their retirement years when the shelter and water supply of the town would make it possible. As one farmer put it, "You either raise flowers or crops around here—you can't do both."

These efforts at "symbolic adaptation," as we have called it, have their civic dimension as well. Jasper town takes responsibility for planting trees on the sidewalk strips; in Regina, the capital of Saskatchewan, whole forests and lakes, and extensive English-style formal gardens have been planted in the civic centers. The campus of the University of Saskatchewan in Saskatoon has great stretches of emerald lawns created by stripping off all the soil to a depth of about two feet, building up new soil and gravel in layers to conserve water, and then laying sprinkler pipes and nozzles underneath. Special grass is permitted to grow to a length of six inches, making a deep, carpet-like sward that conserves its own moisture.

But symbolic adaptation is only one aspect of the attitude toward nature. Jasper farmers and ranchers, however much they may seek to beautify, also regard nature as a resource, something to use. An agrarian society with entrepreneurial tendencies must conceive of nature as natural resources to exploit and to use, even if this view is qualified by conservationist tenets. Professional conservationists often misunderstand the farmer's definition of the concept: he practices conservation in order to use nature more efficiently and continuously, not to preserve its wildness.

Within this broadly utilitarian approach to nature, ranchers and farmers displayed some important differences. Ranchers emphasized the conservationist point of view more than farmers. To the rancher, natural resources were part of the unspoiled natural wilderness in which man and his domestic animals lived, using the resources sparingly and tolerating wild species so long as they do not hinder economic pursuits. The "great open spaces" represent an important symbol for ranchers: they will talk with pride about "them antelope I'm always feeding my hay to!" or concerning the yell of the coyote: "I like to hear them out there—it sounds like this country ought to sound." Ranchers like to view farmers as exploiters and spoilers of nature, "soil miners" who tear up the native grass and slaughter the wild animals, destroy the old Indian stone tipi rings, or start the soil blowing away.

Farmers are required to disturb the soil to plant crops, and to kill the animal and insect pests who eat crops—there is no question that farming demands more manipulation and transformation of resources than ranching. However, the Jasper ranchers' attitudes toward the farmers were prejudiced, and were only part of the truth. The Jasper farmer also maintained a profound respect for nature, since he suffered greatly from its unpredictability and ferocity. He knew that winds could blow away his topsoil, and that storms and hail flatten his crops, and drought kills them. He had to husband his moisture supplies and treat his summer-fallow carefully lest it become vulnerable to wind. Planting and harvesting of crops had to be done with great precision because the unpredictable weather could prevent these operations during the very times they should be done. The farmers with cattle—the majority in Jasper—had to treat their limited pasture areas with great care lest they be injured by overgrazing, and those with irrigation plots had learned to handle the water carefully lest it fail to drain properly and bring salts to the surface.

Thus the conservationist attitude characterized farmers as well as ranchers—the difference being that rancher's ideas were based on his minimal disturbance of nature, the farmer's on a more extensive manipulation of resources. The Hutterites' economic regime represented the most comprehensive form of control and manipulation of resources—but at the same time, the most conservationist, as well, since their "economy of scale," as we shall note in Chapter 8, permitted them to withhold land from use if conservation required it. The Indians really had no comparable "attitude" toward nature—they did not use natural resources to make a living and hence simply lived *on* the land, but not *by* it. This situation was paradoxical, since in aboriginal times, the Indians had made full use of animal and plant species.

The impact of Euro-American settlement on nature in the Jasper region was in its early third human generation during the period of our study. Unquestionably farming had contributed to erosion and soil-blowing, the growth of destructive weeds, and other deleterious consequences. Poorly levelled irrigation areas had resulted in salinization of about 5,000 acres of good cropland. Ranching had not perceptibly changed the resource picture, but the steady increase of livestock population in the region was beginning to result in injury to the grass cover, especially in the community pastures. Exhaustion of soil fertility was beginning to become a problem in the older and more intensively homesteaded districts. Still, these effects were not as yet great, and the developing conservationist attitudes of ranchers and farmers were keeping them in control.

Jasper farmers and ranchers differed in their attitudes and values directed toward some animals, but with respect to cattle, members of both occupations regard them as economic objects, without sentimentality or affection. The cow is there to produce calves to sell; bulls are there to service the cows. Cattle are a saleable item, and also a form of property that can be borrowed against. Since the end of most cattle is the slaughterhouse, little affection comes their way; they are herded, not petted; they are manipulated en masse, not treated as individual animals. The collective treatment is important; sentiment and affection toward animals in any society develop when relationships emerge between men and single animals, and it is significant that in Jasper when affection does emerge toward cattle it is always toward one particular animal: "That old cow there, she's a nice old girl."

These utilitarian attitudes toward livestock are accompanied by a good deal of indifference to pain, illness, and decreptitude. By the lover of animals this is often interpreted as cruelty, or by the veterinarian who treats animals as individuals as callous indifference to suffering. Little compassion is shown by their owners to a sick cow, a heifer having difficulties with parturition, or an animal dying of old age. The prevailing utilitarianism carries over into reluctance, on the part of many, to summon a veterinarian and pay the fee for putting the animal out of its misery—yet the owner often will not himself put the animal out of its misery on the chance it may recover. Animals are sold or shipped without attempts to treat injuries or decrepitude; cattle may be put through the auction sale ring in Jasper town with such blemishes and not draw a murmur of protest or sympathy.

At the same time, the owner does not neglect modern methods of preserving health: routine injections and special feed supplements. These methods have been spreading as Jasper farmers and ranchers realize their practicality: the healthier the animal, the greater its value. Ranchers and farmers boast of the health of their stock and criticize that of their neighbor's. In this context livestock become objects of prestige as well as utilitarian possessions. Cattle can become a symbol of an owner's separate and exceptional mode of operation; the rancher may boast gently of his superior methods of wintering his animals, or of handling them in the chutes during the branding and inoculation ritual. Such boasting is usually devoid of sympathy—it is basically utilitarian and prestigeful. Pronouns are not generally used when speaking of livestock: "that bull," or "that cow over there" are more frequent than "him" or "her."

To some extent, these attitudes are traceable to the absence of laws that punish owners for "cruelty." Such laws exist in the British Isles and in Australia, and informants from these countries felt that ranchers and farmers in the American and Canadian West were much less solicitous of their animals than their counterparts in the other countries. But sympathy and affection aside, Jasper cattle are well known to buyers for their vigor and health, and this is evidence that purely utilitarian attitudes can serve the same ends as love.

One attitude encountered frequently among ranchers (but never among farmers) is the mystical appreciation of the psychology and behavior of cattle. Upon first encounter it is easy to confuse this with genuine affection. Ranchers often pride themselves on their ability to "think cow," to know what the animal will do next, to anticipate movements and sudden decisions, likes and dislikes, so that the herd can be managed with efficiency. This efficiency factor distinguishes the attitude from affection. To "think cow" is to be able to outwit them, to get them to do what you want them to do. Man can attain power over the animal by reaching into the mentality of the animal; thus the attitude is basically one of mastery and ascendance—a familiar element in the psychology of all pastoralists. The art of "thinking cow" is also a frequent focus of criticism by the rancher of farmer methods of handling cattle. The farmers, in the view of ranchers, lack the art and ability of penetrating the mentality of the animals. There is considerable truth in this; farmers have not had as much experience with cattle. A grain farmer who sometimes raised small lots of cattle when he had hailed-out or surplus grain to use for feed remarked, "I'm a farmer, I don't like cattle, that's all there is to it. I put up with 'em, but I just can't stand to think of 'em wandering around loose out there, getting into the fences and so on."

The horse, for the rancher, or for the farmer who has learned to like them, is an object of prestige, a device to demonstrate skill in training and riding, and of course a utilitarian object, particularly for the rancher. When used exclusively for hobby purposes, a horse costs more to raise and feed than he returns in money. The horse is also a recreational device, and the recent modest revival of horse-breeding in Jasper is associated with this function as well as the prestigeful and nostalgic meaning of the horse as a symbol of the old frontier.

Riding is considered the basic skill of the rancher—and, to a certain extent, of ranch women as well. One of the unique features of North American Western pastoralism, as compared with Asian and Middle Eastern styles, is the incorporation of the woman in many of the activities concerning horses. The leading Jasper 4H club featured horsemanship skills and one of the important annual festivals was the competition and show of this club held in the Agricultural Society arena in Jasper town. There was strong emphasis on children's horsemanship; learning to ride a horse was, for many children, an important part of their socialization.

The skills of horsemanship in Jasper were principally those of the breaker and rider; that is, the emphasis was placed on the human component of the team. The objective of Western horse breeding is a sturdy, obedient animal, not especially intelligent and flexible. The effort runs toward showing what the rider can make the horse do, and this contrasts with one other major tradition of Euro-American horsemanship, the equestrian, where there is greater emphasis on the horse and its abilities. This difference stems from the basically utilitarian origins of Western horsemanship, where the animal was an indispensable means of transportation and handling of cattle. (There are some exceptions: the classic behavior of the cow pony during branding and cutting can attract approval for the animal itself.) One of the critical differences in these patterns is the nature of the basic training routine: whether a horse is trained to respond primarily to bit, rein, and spur, or whether he is trained like a dog or other show animal, to respond to auditory and visual cues. The rein and bit pattern is uppermost in Western horse training.

Thus there is a similarity in attitude toward cow and horse at one point: mastery by man is the important element. But there are differences because the horse is ridden and the cow is simply manipulated. In the case of the saddle bronc, or his wilder partner, the unbroken horse, the attitude reaches its clearest expression: the skill is the rider's—his skill in forcing the horse to do what he demands—a pattern similar to the decorating and bulldogging of steers. But again one must contrast this with the trained cow pony—here the man and horse form a partnership in order to dominate the brutish steer or calf.

Another difference in attitudes toward horses and cattle lies in the greater tendency to display sentimentality toward the former. This should be distinguished from love or affection. The horse, as a symbol of the frontier and as an animal with which the man or woman can develop a paired attachment, can attract a kind of nostalgic sentiment associated with long rides across the prairie or the valiant service of bringing the rider home through a killing blizzard. This means as well that the horse owner is likely to be kinder toward his horses than to his cattle. Horses are not, after all, important sources of financial profit and economic survival. One form of hostile gossip in Jasper concerned men who were known, or suspected, to be "cruel" toward horses—something one never heard in regard to cattle.

Wild animals attract a variety of attitudes. To the farmer, wild species are pests, on the whole, since they eat grain, tear up fields, raid the chickens. The farmer does his best to eradicate them, and resents the hunters who come each year for the deer and antelope seasons. To the rancher, wild animals are symbols of the old wilderness and are objects of sentimentality and nostalgia. The rancher is proud of the antelope that eat from his haystacks in the winter—although he may complain to the game wardens if they eat too much! The rancher loves the howl of the coyote, but will not hesitate to shoot one if it steals chickens. Ranchers tolerate wild animals so long as they do not get out of hand; farmers are more forthright: the things are simply varmints. Ranchers often go hunting; farmers rarely.

Animals figure in Jasper legendry. The Cypress Hills once had a grizzly bear population, and the Old Timers' Museum in town has a skull or two, proudly displayed. A family of trumpeter swans has lived in a hidden lagoon in the Hills Park, and a scandal developed in 1962 when some local boy wounded one of the young birds with a .22 rifle. There are endless stories of the abundant game in the Hills in the old days, its decimation by Indians and early settlers, and its recovery under modern management.

The tendency of ranchers to view wild animals with somewhat greater tolerance than farmers is part of the differences between the two occupations in their attitudes toward nature as a whole. We came to regard the rancher as having a concept of the *wild;* whereas the farmer thinks of nature as *wilderness.* The difference is as we have defined it earlier: the rancher sees himself as a part of "unspoiled" nature, a partner with the coyote, the grass, the coulees, and the open spaces—however much he may in practice have to modify this approach. The farmer, on the other hand, sees nature as a wilderness ready for and in need of taming—something to compete with. Yet the farmer, like the rancher, must be careful in his dealings with nature, and both show far more awareness of the need for conservation and "sustained yield" principles of resource management today than they did in frontier days.

BIBLIOGRAPHIC NOTES

For some discussion of the culture concept in its professional anthropological context, see James A. Clifton, "Cultural Anthropology: Aspirations and Approaches," in J. A. Clifton, ed., *Introduction to Cultural Anthropology,* Houghton Mifflin Co., 1968; A. L. Kroeber and Clyde Kluckhohn, *Culture: A Critical Review of Concepts and Definitions,* Papers of the Peabody Museum of Archeology and Anthropology,

Harvard University, Vol. 47, No. 1 (1952; also published by Random House in a 1953 edition); Pertti J. Pelto, *The Study of Anthropology,* Merrill, 1965, especially Chap. 5.

The single most impressive study of the culture area concept and its application to the American Indian is A. L. Kroeber's *Cultural and Natural Areas of Native North America,* University of California Publications in *American Archeology & Ethnology,* Vol. 38 (1939). Some other studies and discussions bearing on culture areas are Clark Wissler, *The Relation of Man to Nature in Aboriginal America,* Appleton, 1926; R. B. Dixon, *The Building of Cultures,* Scribners, 1928; John J. Honigmann, *Understanding Culture,* Harper & Row, 1963, pp. 320–21, which includes a map of world culture areas and a bibliography.

Some anthropologists have used the concept of "niche" to describe the particular activity performed by a human group in a particular environment or microenvironment. The concept is borrowed from plant and animal ecology. Thus in Jasper the ranchers and Indians both inhabit the Hills, but are in different "niches," since one raises livestock and the other raises nothing. Likewise, the Hutterites and farmers inhabit the Plains, but one inhabits a "niche" consisting of intensive and diversified use of all resources, the other limits use to fewer resources. For a study of the ecology of pastoral peoples, using the niche concept, see Frederick Barth, "Ecologic Relationships of Ethnic Groups in Swat, North Pakistan," *American Anthropologist,* Vol. 58 (1956), pp. 1079–89.

A study of high culture on the American frontier is found in Louis B. Wright, *Culture on the Moving Frontier,* Indiana University Press, 1955 (also published in Harper Torchbook series, 1961). The material in this book is also applicable to the Canadian scene.

Many novels have dealt with the alleged dullness of life in the Canadian prairie towns. A classic is Sinclair Ross, *As for Me and My House,* McClelland & Stewart, 1957.

There is a large anthropological literature on religion and ceremonial. Some classic and informative statements are William J. Goode, *Religion among the Primitives,* Free Press, 1951; Charles Leslie, ed., *The Anthropology of Folk Religion,* Random House, Vintage Books, 1960; Ruth Benedict, "Religion," in Franz Boas, ed., *General Anthropology,* Heath, 1938; Murray Wax, "Religion and Magic," in James R. Clifton, ed., *Introduction to Cultural Anthropology,* 1968.

For accounts of the efforts at "beautification" of the bare Great Plains landscape and manscape, the reader can consult the book edited by Carle C. Zimmerman and Seth Russell, *Symposium on the Great*

Plains, North Dakota Institute for Regional Studies, North Dakota State University, 1967. The relevant articles are by J. H. Stoekeler, J. B. Leicester, Harry Graves, and Thomas A. Gwynn.

The human impact on nature is actually imperfectly known, despite considerable concern and preoccupation in recent years as man's destructive proclivities become obvious to the eye. Some studies of the consequences for natural resources and for man himself of agrarian development are Paul B. Sears, "Changing Man's Habitat," in W. L. Thomas, Jr., *Man's Role in Changing the Face of the Earth,* University of Chicago Press, 1956, and other articles in that same volume; J. G. D. Clark, "Farmers and Forests in Neolithic Europe," *Antiquity,* Vol. 19, No. 74 (1945), pp. 57–71; Nyke C. Brady, ed., *Agriculture and the Quality of our Environment,* American Association for the Advancement of Science, Publ. No. 85 (1967); J. T. Middleton, "Control of Environment: Economic and Technological Prospects," in *Environmental Improvement: Air, Water and Soil,* The Graduate School Press, U.S. Dept. of Agriculture, 1966.

Relationships of man and his domestic animals and wild species are summarized in Anthony Leeds, ed., *Man, Culture and Animals,* American Association for the Advancement of Science, Publ. No. 78 (1965); F. E. Zeuner, *A History of Domesticated Animals,* Harper & Row, 1963.

Much has been written on the Western horse and the arts of breaking and training him. The following is representative: J. Frank Dobie, *The Mustangs,* Curtis, 1952. The history of the Western horse is also treated in this book, and a bibliography is provided. The most important genetic ingredient in the Western horse is the semi-wild and tamed stock emanating from Spanish herds in the Southwest, taken over by the Plains Indians (see Walker D. Wyman, *The Wild Horse of the West,* 1962 University of Nebraska Press; Robert M. Denhardt, "The Horse in New Spain and the Borderland," *Agricultural History,* Vol. 25 (1951), pp. 145–50.

e town of Jasper, with a portion of the Jasper Irrigation Project,
ut 1960. The crop is alfalfa (Photo courtesy PFRA).

The Jasper prairie, with the usual grain elevators and semi-abandoned town on the horizon, seen across the gate of a farm yard now used as a wheat field.

The Cypress Hills Park in winter. This scene is just twenty minutes by automobile from the upper picture.

A pioneer log ranch house. The rancher pioneers built these little cabins in the wooded coulees. As the family grew, additional rooms were added.

A modern ranch house. The main house is a remodeled version of the home built by the present operator's father. The log barn was built by his grandfather, the aluminum shed by the present operator. Hence, three generations of proprietors are represented.

A homesteader's shack on the prairie, about 1912. The dirt banked up against the rear (northwest) side of the building is for winter protection.

A modern farmhouse. Most Jasper farmhouses were built in the 192? like this one. Also note the caragana hedge-windbreak, and the dy? ash in the front yard.

A typical Jasper Hutterian colony.

…e Jasper Indian Reserve in the Cypress Hills. The plywood houses,
…ally unused during the summer while the Indians roam the roads
…live in town, are glimpsed through the remains of a dance lodge.

Roundup of farmer cattle on a Jasper community pasture. The Cypress Hills are a dim line on the horizon (Photo courtesy PFRA).

Stacking hay bales on a Jasper ranch. These handling systems are gradually becoming mechanized.

*ief technician of a Jasper Hutterian colony repairing the electric
at saw. The community refrigeration storeroom is at the right.*

*Hutterian children's cart. The cart is homemade and is a standard
Hutterian child's toy. Note contrast of the homemade clothes and cart
with the shiny equipment above.*

Hutterian women at work. The task is noodle-making, using a machine improved and rebuilt by colony technicians. The women do this about once a month.

Hutterian men at work. The task is shingling a quonset grain storage building. Colonies are moving rapidly toward the use of metal buildings.

A traditional Jasper festival: the Greenfields Stampede, one of the last true amateur rodeos in the Northern Plains.

A typical family float in the annual Jasper Pioneers Day. Note the emphasis on date of arrival in the region.

Jasper farmers. The adult faces are Ukrainian, Scottish, Norwegian, British-Canadian.

Jasper farmer and wife.

Jasper rancher and son.

Jasper Hutterian father and son.

Leaders of the Jasper Indian community.

A pioneer Jasper ranche

FOUR

Jasper Economy

In this chapter we shall describe the economy and occupational structure of the Jasper region and the processes influencing their development from pioneer days. The story is concerned almost exclusively with agriculture: 95 per cent of all income in the region is provided by agrarian activity or by businesses supplying agriculture with its tools and commodities. This economic pattern developed out of the settlement processes of a Western frontier; it began with the cattle and horse raisers on the unfenced and unsurveyed range and ended with the influx of farmers once the land was surveyed and opened for homesteading. The dominance of agriculture also means that occupational opportunities for young people have decreased steadily, since rising costs of operation and the need for mechanized efficiency have led to consolidation of agricultural enterprises into fewer hands. At all times Jasper agricultural economy has been influenced by the conditions of the national and continental economy for which it must produce: the market is a major factor in the total ecological system of the Jasper region. We begin with a general description of the relationship of Jasper, and Great Plains economy, to the national picture.

GENERAL CHARACTERISTICS OF NORTHERN PLAINS ECONOMY

One Jasper farmer sized up the homesteading period as follows:

They say that when the politicians saw all the cattle die off in the bad winters of 1906-07 in this country, they decided they

97

could stock the land with people instead, because they could carry themselves through the winter. So they went ahead and put on a lot more people than the land could stand, figuring that the people could thin themselves out. And then the CPR made money hauling them in, and then made money again hauling them out.

The economic development of the Canadian prairies, like that of the Great Plains of the United States, was based on investment opportunity for Eastern bankers and manufacturers —the main goal was not to develop an agricultural civilization. The ranchers, farmers, and townspeople who settled the area believed they were doing the latter, however, and they did so, often under great hardship. Homestead policy, formulated by financial and political interests, ignored the variability and marginality of the available resources. The tendency to rely on only one or two major crops, and the manipulations of the economy by financial interests, led to fluctuation of prices and costs which left the farmer at a severe disadvantage, and he responded by organizing a number of political and economic reform movements. In the Great Plains as a whole, these movements took the general form of *populism,* a political doctrine that advocated cooperative ownership of resources and marketing facilities, and pooled prices for farm products—but in the framework of privately owned agricultural enterprises. Thus the farmers' movements had something in common with socialism but did not go as far as orthodox socialist doctrine would require. In Saskatchewan effective agrarian radicalism began as a more radical socialist group, but it eventually emerged as a populist movement called the Cooperative Commonwealth Federation (CCF), and as a political party it governed the province from 1944 to 1963.

In contrast to other geographical sections of North America, the proportion of population supported by agriculture is large in the Great Plains, although, as elsewhere, this proportion has been declining. Such a lack of diversification of income sources means that Great Plains economy is vulnerable to even slight changes in prices and costs affecting its special products. It also means that the economy has relatively few opportunities for its young people, since nonfarm jobs are scarce and the available land is taken up by existing farm and ranch enterprises.

A related characteristic of Great Plains economy is its sensitivity to changes in national and continental economic conditions. Thus when the national economy declines slightly, Great Plains economy declines greatly; and vice versa for rises. The Province of Saskatchewan furnishes a classic example of boom-and-bust: in the 1930's it had the lowest per capita income in Canada; in 1965 it had the second highest (caused by a bumper crop in a wet year and large sales of grain abroad). Thus fluctuation has been the norm: wheat sold for 75¢ a bushel in 1921; went down to 25¢ in the 1930's; then up to 53¢ in 1941, and $1.60 in 1962. For a period during the Depression, calves were selling for $25; in the 1960's, for $125.

A third characteristic of Great Plains economy is its relatively low productivity—if we measure productivity by the amount of dollars a man can earn by his labor. A farmer or factory worker in the U.S. Midwest or Ontario can earn more gross income per man-hour of work than his counterpart in the Plains: the Plainsman works more hours for less money. If a man, knowing this, chooses to stay in the Plains and make his living from agriculture, he either invests in land and machinery in an effort to boost his productivity, or he simply likes the Plains and his work and is willing to take less in order to stay there—or both! In other words, an agriculturalist buys himself the "right" to stay in agriculture. In the language of economics, his "labor opportunity costs" are high—which means in this case that he could earn more by his labor doing something other than farming.

It might be argued that there are compensations in the form of lower food costs (due to home gardens) and the joy of living in the country. But Great Plains agriculturalists measure their returns to an increasing extent by national consumption and income standards, and there is no question that the small businessman in the city, or the farmer in the Midwest, can provide his family with a more comfortable life on the same amount of invested capital than can be the agriculturalist in the Plains. In other words, the Great Plains agriculturalist must recognize certain deprivations when or if he compares his situation with that of others. If he does this, and decides to remain in farming, he is obviously making a choice on the basis of his preferences for rural life and its compensations, for relatively low income. That is, his subjective evaluation of opportunity costs makes them "low," not high. Jasper farmers, when we discussed this issue with them, invariably responded by pointing out that despite the hardships and uncertainties, they preferred farming "because out here a man is his own boss. If something drives him he can always say that it comes from inside him, if you know what I mean there." Objectively this answer is ambiguous, since the major forces that "drive" men come from the external society and economy, but in the subjective view of the matter, the farmer does set his own preferences and pace. At least he does not need to punch a time clock, and it is this "freedom" that he values highly.

During the 1960's, Jasper income provided a very modest living for the great majority of the region's residents. There was a minority of well-off ranchers, three or four affluent Hutterian colonies, and a very small number of reasonably prosperous farmers. On the other hand, there was an equally small number of genuine poverty cases among farmers and ranchers. One or two Hutterian colonies were having a struggle (although mainly because they were in the beginning stage), and the region's small group of Indians were the truly impoverished segment of the population.

Income figures can be deceptive, especially in a situation where many indirect and concealed benefits and considerable fluctuation exist. We determined on the basis of Canadian census data, corrected by our own sample surveys, that the distribution of income for farmers and ranchers differed considerably, both in amounts and range. Table 4.1 summarizes the results.

Table 4.1 shows that the majority of Jaspers farmers fell into the middle range of gross income, while the majority of ranchers had incomes toward the high range. A farm income of around $8,000 gross would permit a family between $3,000 and $2,000 net income after expenses of production were paid. (In 1960 the average net income of all Saskatchewan farmers was about $2,500.) This would be enough to provide for the family's

Table 4.1. Farm and Ranch Gross Income, Jasper, Early 1960's

	High Income	Middle Income	Low Income
Farms	$20,000–$15,000	$15,000–$8,000	Less than $8,000
	16%	62%	22%
Ranches	$30,000–$20,000	$20,000–$8,000	Less than $8,000
	43%	38%	27%
	(one or two		
	around $100,000)		

modest level of living, but not enough to provide for very many vacations or expensive college educations. And part of this net income would have to be used from time to time for farm investments. Occasionally a bumper crop or a good livestock sale would bring more—even double the previous year's "take," and these windfalls, though unpredictable, help greatly and probably permit a large number of farmers to survive and afford occasional luxuries.

A standard method of comparing enterprises from the standpoint of their economic soundness and profitability is to compute their rates of return on investment. Usually this is done by computing the percentage of the total investment represented by the annual gross income after an amount equivalent to the "wages" of the operator and his family members working in the agricultural enterprise have been deducted. This rule has to be modified, or the results qualified at least, depending upon various cultural factors. In many cases agriculturalists do not regard their own labor as a cost—certainly most Jasper ranchers and Hutterites did not, although farmers were beginning to view their labor as a cost factor simply because they recognized that they had to work very hard for rather low returns. Another difficulty in computing rates of return is brought about by extreme fluctuation of annual income—the situation in Jasper. Long-term averages have to be taken, and these often obscure short-term conditions.

In any case, we found in some experimental computations that Hutterites and ranchers had the highest average rates of return on their investment, the latter probaly higher than the former. Ranching requires very low overhead and since grazing lease rentals were very low during the period of our study, cattle could be produced at considerable profit. The rates of return on their investment, the latter probably higher than the the highest rates (around 10 per cent) were being received by well-developed medium-sized ranches, with most of their costs of development paid off. The very small and the very large ranches received lower rates, but still high compared to farmers. Hutterites were receiving high rates of return, especially those at the peak of their development (around 9 per cent). Farmers were uniformly low—around 3 per cent on the average, though a few large farms were close to 6 per cent.

As economic and natural disasters affected the Jasper economy, the number of operators diminished and there was more land available for the remainder. This had the effect of raising per capita income, which means that the relatively modest financial position of the majority of Jasper agriculturalists was obtained in part by a reduction in their number. This position can be maintained only if there is a regular rate of migration of young people out of the community, since opportunities other than succession to or purchase of a ranch or farm have been almost nonexistent.

LAND TENURE

Populating the Canadian plains was not a slow and silent drift of people westward, but an organized and promoted event taking place over a relatively short period of time (from about 1895 to 1915, with the peak in 1910). Up to the mid-1890's Canadian attempts to settle the Northwest Territories had met with little success, due largely to the opening of the American frontier to the south. The relatively unfavorable environmental conditions north of the border discouraged prospective settlers who could choose the apparently warmer U.S. plains and mountain areas.

Efforts to attract settlers made in the 1880's by the Dominion Government had been less than energetic, but a measure of self-government granted to the Northwest Territories in the 1890's provided an opportunity for a fresh attempt. Clifford

Sifton, a young Minister of the Interior and the first Westerner to hold a cabinet post in the Dominion, undertook this new colonization experiment aided by the Canadian Pacific, which wanted to divest itself of its extensive holdings. Sifton's campaign used all the old methods and invented some new ones: newspaper and magazine advertising, medicine-show solicitations at county fairs, organized tours for newspaper editors and farmers—almost every conceivable technique was used, with expense no object. Since the effort coincided with a period of economic distress among tenant farmers, small farmers, and farm laborers in the U.S. Midwest, the Canadian campaign received an immediate favorable response from the Americans. Its effects continued down through the 1910–1915 period.

At the same time efforts were made to attract Europeans by government and railroad agents. A special effort was made in those portions of Europe with environments like the West (e.g., the Ukraine), or where on the basis of the American experience one would be likely to find exceptionally good farmers (e.g., Germany and Scandinavia). The response from Europe was good, but the majority of settlers continued to come from eastern Canada and the United States.

The settlement of the Jasper region actually began before the land was surveyed. The Royal Northwest Mounted Police opened a post in the Cypress Hills to control the Indians, and also the whiskey trade from the United States, and on their heels came the railroad and the pioneer adventurer-ranchers. These men ran horses and cattle on the open, unfenced range, and cooperated on roundups and brandings. The land surveyors followed the railroad and by 1910 all of the land in the region had been surveyed on the standard Anglo-American system of a one-mile section grid, corrected at intervals for the curvature of the earth (see Fig. 2.5). With the land surveyed, the area could be opened for homesteading, and this brought the farmers.

The basic conception which guided the land survey was that of the relatively small, self-contained agricultural enterprise owned and operated by a single family. In order to operate a farm or ranch of this type efficiently, especially with the limited power and machinery of the late nineteenth and early twentieth century, all of the land and ground water resources would have to be found within the perimeter of the land area of the enterprise. (This is no longer true, since with automotive transportation and powered machines a farmer can profitably have his land in scattered plots. In 1910, with horse-drawn reapers, it took 20 man-hours to plant and harvest an acre of wheat; by 1960, with powered combines, the job took 2 hours or less.)

Since the resources of the Jasper region were unevenly distributed, the survey-and-homestead system meant that many of the new farms would be without good soil, water, suitable topography, or sufficiently lengthy growing seasons. Suggestions had been made in the nineteenth century for a different type of survey, one which would have laid out farms irregularly with concern for resource boundaries (e.g., along drainage patterns), but these were never taken seriously by planners and politicians in either Canada or the United States. The financial and political pressures to get the settlers out in a hurry, and to tie the land survey of the West into the national grid, were too strong. Sheer ignorance was also a factor: few Easterners had any real understanding of Western resources.

The history of the Canadian homestead laws, like those of the United States, is long and complex. The Canadians in the 1860's followed the American practice of providing free 160-acre homesteads from the first, but throughout the history of Canadian laws there was greater liberality with the "pre-emption": an additional amount of land purchasable for reasonable prices, in varying locations. While the pre-emption system was revised often and sometimes withdrawn, its final version, in 1908, provided for an amount of 160 acres, at $3 per acre, adjoining the free homestead.

Even so, the 160-plus-320-acre allotments were really too small for the environmental conditions. These amounts were set by Eastern planners who based their decisions on the amount of land one man and a team of horses could farm without extra labor. This was a valid criterion for the humid East, with its diversity of crops. In the Plains, however, the farmer was limited to grain and a few livestock, and if drought hit, there was no grain. Even at the lower price levels of the time, the land simply was not productive enough to permit a decent living for the homesteading family and also to supply needed capital for further development of the farm—a vital consideration as the North American economy developed and prices increased.

While in the 1910–15 period a homesteader could break his 320 acres of land, build his modest buildings, and finance his simple horse-drawn machines for about $1,400, a low figure and within the capacity of most serious homesteaders, it required considerably more to increase the productivity of the land in order to bring it to a level that would provide enough income in good years to cushion the bad. This extra capital was precisely what the majority of homesteaders did not have. (Incidentally, it has been calculated by economists that to put 320 virgin acres into routine cultivation in the 1960's a farmer would need about $40,000!—which is an index of the increasing values in agriculture, a matter that we will discuss in later chapters in relation to succession of sons to the fathers' enterprises.)

Before intensive homesteading began, land tenure in the Jasper region was a complex patchwork quilt of public and private ownership. The Canadian Pacific Railway and the Hudson's Bay Co. still held substantial tracts. The provincial government controlled the leased grazing land, and there still remained some "open range" land, only vaguely titled to the government. In every township land was reserved for the school districts to provide a tax base of school support. Incoming homesteaders were rapidly taking up land into private, "deeded" title, but were also abandoning it, in which case it reverted to government. Before long the Railway and Hudson's Bay lands were all sold off, the school lands gradually were sold to private owners, and the great majority of land was in the hands of private agrarian entrepreneurs. However, reversions to government control began in the 1930's, a process that will be described with the help of Table 4.2.

With the land survey and the coming of the homesteaders, the cattlemen had to take out definite tracts of pasture land on a government lease. This introduced fenced ranching, which required many cattlemen to begin a more intensive development

*Table 4.2. Change in Tenure Categories of Agricultural Land
for Jasper Region, 1900–60's (in acres)*

Deeded to Individuals and to Hutterian Colonies	Period 1906–12	% of Total	1960's	% of Total
	1,350,890	52	1,186,890	46
Titled Held by Government	1,248,329	48	1,412,329	54
Total	2,599,219		2,599,219	
a) Leased or in the process of being leased to individuals for grazing (open range in 1900)	1,011,193	39	935,017	36
b) Community pastures	None		335,239	13
c) Leased to grazing cooperatives	None		76,176	3
d) Irrigation projects	None		14,000	Less than 1
e) Provincial forest and park, most under grazing permit	Not completely organized; acreage vague		51,897 (organized as cooperatives after 1950)	2
f) Open to individual use for grazing without lease or permit (various owners)	237,136	9	None	
Increase in government acreage collectively used or managed, 1900–63 (b + c + d + e)			477,312 acres (18% of total, 2,599,219)	

Note: *Our data for periods between the two shown on this table are incomplete, due to omissions in the official records. However, it is relatively easy to reconstruct the events. (1) The 14,000 acres of irrigation land were almost entirely in private hands in the earlier period, and were acquired after desertion by former homesteaders. (2) deserted land, or land on which taxes were not paid, reverted to municipal tenure. In many cases such land was transferred to the Land Utilization Board, and made into PFRA pastures (about 150,000 acres). The balance had not been homesteaded, but was not definitely lease land in the earlier period, being open range. Some had not yet been surveyed. (3) Forest and park land was open range in the earlier period ,and the first step in the region toward controlled collective use of land was made when permits were required for grazing in these areas. (4) The 1960's figure for leased land is about 50,000 acres higher than it was in 1930, representing reappropriation by the government for leases. (5) The categories 'c," "d," and "e" came into existence between 1939 and 1941, although one community pasture was established in the early 1950's.*

and care of their resources. The leases were of different sizes, adjusted in most cases to the existing resources, so that the "ranches" which emerged after 1910 in Jasper were usually more fortunately endowed than the average farm. Through the years most of the inequities in the size of leases or their location with respect to water were adjusted, so that on the whole the ranching economy was a more rationally planned endeavor than the farming.

As shown in Table 4.2, by the 1960's the tenure pattern had changed in terms of how the land was used and who had ultimate tenure rights. The amount of land held by private individuals in freehold tenure had dropped slightly, representing a transfer of some land to government tenure. Most of this land was formerly homesteaded, but was located in the very dryest or coldest districts. The amount of land leased to individuals had also dropped slightly. These amounts, plus some other land not developed in the earlier period, had in the 1960's become part of community pastures, grazing cooperatives, and irrigation projects. These latter institutions—constituting 18 per cent of the total land area—were used collectively or cooperatively, and constituted a basic change in the tenure system. Thus while the majority of agricultural land in Jasper continued to be owned, leased, and managed by individuals (and by the Hutterites, who own their land) a sizable proportion of land used by farmers had passed into cooperative use and management.

We made a detailed survey of agricultural land tenure in Local Improvement District No. II (see Fig. 2.10), which contained the most diversified array of agricultural enterprises of any statistics-collecting political unit in the region. We found that the ranchers, who constituted 35 per cent of all the enterprise operators, controlled 76 per cent of all the grazing land leased from the government, and that the farmers, who were 64 per cent of the enterprisers, had 18 per cent. Ranchers held 39 per cent of the owned or "deeded" land; farmers, 46 per cent. Hutterian colonies had another 14 per cent of the deeded land and no leased land. Grazing cooperatives held a small 5 per cent of leased grazing land. We also found that over 70 per cent of all ranch land was leased, 29 per cent deeded, while 67 per cent of the land in farms was deeded, 33 per cent leased. This 33 per cent of leased land represented an increase of about 20 percentage points in as many years, showing the movement of farmers into the leasing system as their cattle herds expanded. Much, but not all of this increase in leased land was obtained by persuading the government bureau to transfer small leased tracts from ranches to farms—a competitive situation we will discuss elsewhere.

The precise status of leased grazing land is ambiguous; although the government retains the title and monitors all transfers of lease to new holders, the lease-holder actually has a kind of use-tenure or moral right to the land, since he can will it to his kinfolk, and can "sell" it in the sense that he can put a price on the "improvements," in accordance with current market values. This price must not exceed 20 per cent of the government's assessed value of the entire spread, but the rule has not prevented a considerable inflation of ranch prices—a topic we have discussed elsewhere.

In a preceding paragraph we mentioned a number of cooperative institutions of land use. These may be described briefly here (more detailed analysis is found in Chap. 9. See Fig. 2.2 for locations.) The *community pastures* consist of large tracts of dry and poor land that were taken over by the provincial or federal governments and managed for the use of farmer cattle herds. The largest pastures were federal and managed by the Prairie Farm Rehabilitation Act (PFRA). Farmers in their vicinity become "patrons" of the pastures, pay a small use fee, and participate to some extent in the management of the pasture, although its control remains in government hands. The system is really one of collective use and is not a true cooperative, but the governments hoped that eventually the local farmers could assume complete management.

The *grazing cooperatives*, on the other hand, are true co-operative ventures, with a lease of grazing land—often from an old ranch or part of a too-big ranch—awarded by the provincial government to a group of farmers who agree to manage and finance its use. These organizations have been markedly successful, whereas the community pastures have suffered from dissension and lack of cooperative participation. Cooperation on land use and ownership has worked best among Jasper farmers if they have some form of title to the land, and/or if they constitute a natural social group of neighbors or cooperators.

The *irrigation projects* are also tracts of dry or rough land, abandoned by their former owners, taken over by provincial and federal government agencies, and developed for the production of irrigated livestock forage. The largest of these were federal, also managed by the PFRA, with a local office in Jasper town. The scheme of tenure and management is basically similar to community pastures: the irrigation plot holders—farmers and small ranchers—pay low annual rentals and fees for the water, and participate to a degree in the running of the schemes, although the governments stand most of the costs. Eventually the governments hope to persuade the local plot renters to form their own water users associations and operate the schemes themselves.

These various cooperative and collective-use ventures help to compensate for the inequities imposed on agricultural producers by the grid survey system. The irrigation systems, with their reservoirs, government assistance to producers in developing their private schemes, and the rented irrigation plots bring scarce water to the agricultural operator—water which might otherwise be lost by drainage or used only by those fortunate few whose location or topography permitted irrigation. Pasture land, in short supply for farmers because of the basically small farms (although all have been greatly enlarged since home-steading days) and because of the relatively low "carrying capacity" of the grasses of this semiarid country, was provided nearby in the form of community pastures or grazing cooperatives. Essentially the objective is to develop a farm and small-ranch livestock regime by creating specialized forage-production and pasturage (as can be seen from the placement of the facilities, visible on Fig. 2.2).

The Hutterian colonies, on the other hand, did not require these special institutions, since they bought very large tracts of land to begin with—enough to supply the average colony with all the varied soil and water resources they would need for their diversified farming and livestock operations. Thus bigness —large land areas—makes up for the uneven distribution of resources. The communal management principle of Hutterian farming can be said to supplement the cooperative forms of land use among farmers, reinforcing this adaptive trend in the region.

TYPES OF ENTERPRISES

Throughout the history of the Jasper region there have been four main types of economic enterprises: livestock-raising; crop-farming; combinations of the two; and town business establishments. The proportions of these have varied considerably at different time periods. The ranching version of livestock-raising dominated in the beginning, and was followed immediately by a number of town service businesses, some of them established by early settlers near the towns who combined them with livestock and farming enterprises. Beginning in 1910 crop-farming came to dominate, due to the homesteader influx. By the 1950's crop-farming was becoming a rare type, with the majority of farmers combining livestock and cropping on diversified farms. Ranchers held their own.

More specifically, between 1910 and 1920, the heyday of homestead farming, there were about 90 straight ranches, almost all raising cattle exclusively; a few sheep ranches; and about 2,000 small, mostly grain-raising farms, but each with a few cows and domestic livestock. By the 1960's the ranches remained without substantial change in number or land area. But the farming enterprises, as we have seen, had been drastically reduced in number and had greatly increased their land area. The average farm in 1915 had between 160 and 320 acres; the average farm in the 1960's had nearly two sections, or around 1,000 acres. Most agricultural experts expect this average amount to increase to a full two sections or more, but for the time being, with the help of the special institutions described in the previous section, a farm can operate at a modest level of income with the smaller land area.

The varieties of agricultural enterprises in the 1960's can be classified technically as follows (based on agricultural census data and terminology, and revised by our own survey):

1. *Hutterian diversified farms* (colonies). There were six of these of which four had all their land in the Jasper region as we drew its boundaries. The other two had most of their land in Jasper, but portions lay in contiguous regions. These colonies were essentially large, diversified commercial farms, with ambitious enterprises in nearly every type of agricultural production: cattle-raising; cattle-feeding or finishing; forage production; cash-grain production; sheep; poultry; eggs; dairy and numerous activities producing food for domestic consumption. With the exception of a few of the largest ranches, the colonies were the largest (by land area and income) enterprises in the region.

2. *Small diversified farms*. These were enterprises with varying emphases on livestock or grain production, but always with more of the latter than in the case of the cattle farms. Thus in most cases the majority or a substantial amount of income was provided by grain sales. A few had sheep, and more than half raised a few swine. All raised some grain to feed to livestock— a "barley-to-meat" regime. About 550 farms fell into this category, and most were located in areas where soils and topography permitted some grain cropping.

3. *Livestock farms and ranches*. These were, in the majority, farming enterprises specializing in raising beef cattle or in cattle feeding or finishing (buying calves and getting them ready for market). A few raised purebred cattle for breeding stock, and about five were sheep ranches. About 350 farms and 90 ranches in the region fell into this category. Nearly all of the farms raised some grain and forage for their stock, some of which was sold. Most of their land was unsuitable for cash grain production.

4. *Straight grain farms*. These were farms making their entire living from grains: wheat, barley, or rye. There were not more than 30 or 40 in the region (in 1920, this was the largest

category of all farms). Nearly all of these farms were located in the areas with the best soil, from the standpoint of grain production (heavy, clayey textures that will hold moisture).

5. *Dairy and poultry farms.* There were only eight in the entire region. All were located near towns and transportation arteries.

This classification shows that (1) there is a trend toward specialization—adjusting production to resources; and (2) that the majority of farms in the region still obtained a major or significant share of their income from grain production. However, the viability of agriculture in the region is made possible by livestock, and by the special facilities developed by the government to further its development. The major adaptive movement in Jasper agricultural development therefore has been to intensify livestock (especially cattle) production—a reversion to the earlier rancher use of the natural resources. Since a majority of the Indians who populated the region before the white man came relied extensively on the bison for food and raw materials, the present reliance on another hoofed, pasturing species represents a qualified reversion to a still older use of the specialized environment.

The size and productivity of the enterprises varied as follows: (1) As noted, the Hutterian colonies and four or five very large ranches were the largest enterprises in terms of land area and income. (2) Ranches, as a group, were divided between very large and very small, with about 50 per cent of all enterprises in the intermediate class of around seven sections (4480 acres) in size. Income varied greatly: from $3,000 to $100,000 annual gross, but the average was around $15,000. (3) Farms were more homogeneous than ranches in size and income: about 65 per cent of all farms had around 1,000 acres and grossed around $8,000 (not considering the great annual fluctuations typical of the region). Various factors had influenced these distributions: ranch leases were controlled by the government, and the bureau was engaged in a long-term process to reduce the number of small, substandard and also very large leases. The homogeneity of the farming enterprises was due mainly to the uniform homestead start, and also to the government's resources-development projects that tended to encourage the persistence of farms of a certain size, and enlargement of smaller farms to this size.

Technical classification of the ranching and farming occupations aside, Jasper people had their own ways of grouping enterprises. Their "folk" classification was, from the technical point of view, confused, since they often mixed economic and cultural criteria. The term "ranch" was applied by Jasperites either to an enterprise that acquired 100 per cent of its income from cattle, *or* to an enterprise the members of which lived in the ranching cultural style—regardless of the fraction of income derived from cattle. The former of these is similar to our technical term "ranch"; but many if not most of the latter were technically some type of "farm," with income shared between crops and cattle. The confusion was more apparent than real, since when a diversified farmer began to alter his cultural style of life toward the ranching mode (the wearing of Western clothing and practicing horsemanship hobbies), he was almost always beginning to emphasize cattle over crops in his production regime. Thus often the aggressively cowboyish-appearing young man walking the streets in Jasper town was actually a mixed farmer deriving 50 per cent or more of his livelihood from wheat and barley, but who was also seeking additional pasture to reduce his crop acreage and increase his livestock production—for both financial advantage and cultural prestige.

In 1960, the farms, ranches, and colonies of Jasper had 132,124 cattle. They had 201,135 acres planted in wheat, which produced on the average, about 11 bushels to the acre, and 154,929 acres planted in rye, barley, and other coarse grains and forage crops. The number of cattle was almost double the number in 1936; the wheat acreage was about 10,000 acres below the 1930's figure; and the land acreage used for other —mainly forage—crops was about 5,000 acres higher.

Jasper agriculturalists were on a "cash economy," meaning by this that they purchased most of their commodities for dollars at regional stores and dealers. However, there were some significant qualifications. In the first place, every Jasper farm and ranch had a substantial garden in which were raised vegetables and a little fruit for home consumption. Gardens are difficult things in the northern Plains, but with hard work and plenty of watering considerable produce could be raised. Most farms and ranches also provided most of their own eggs and chickens, and the ranches, their own beef. These home-raised products furnished a surprisingly large quantity of food: for one farm we computed a cash retail value, at local super-market prices, of $1,000, or about one-third of the annual food bill.

Secondly, an important exception to reliance on cash purchase was found in the case of the Hutterian colonies. These people raise nearly all of their food in their own gardens, poultry yards, and cattle feed lots. In addition, they manufacture a number of agricultural implements and nearly all common-use domestic articles. Needless to say, the savings effected by using their own labor, and buying surplus raw materials at bargain prices and collecting discarded metal and wood, make a very large contribution to their income. For one colony we found that their cash expenditures would have been doubled without this home production of food and articles.

GOVERNMENT INPUTS

The viability of the enterprise economy was aided by the government not only in the form of the resources-development projects already described, but by a host of other supports. To determine the magnitude of these, we made a study of all money coming into the region from government sources in one typical year in the early 1960's. We found, first, that nearly $800,000 was provided in the form of annual direct cash benefits (no interest, no need to repay). This category included about $350,000 in the form of payments by the federal government's Prairie Farm Assistance Act (PFAA) program of cash benefits to grain growers. If a farmer's crop yield was below a certain minimum, as figured on the basis of the resources in his district, he could obtain a cash bonus—not to exceed $800 per farmer. This seems small, but this amount in cases of marginal farmers could mean the difference between quitting farming or staying in business. Many agricultural experts criticized this system because it tended

Table 4.3. Financial Contributions by Government Agencies to Jasper Region for One Year in Early 1960's

	Federal		Provincial		Federal & Provincial		Totals
	Prairie Farm Assistance Payments	Social Welfare	Indian Family Allowances	Roads and Other Facilities	Wages Paid by Gov. Agencies	Shared-cost Benefits to Agric.	
Direct Cash Benefits: No Repayment	$350,000	$62,000	$30,000	$450,000	$800,000	$400,000	$2,092,000
Repayable Loans	Farm Credit Corp. Loans to Agriculturalists $3,000,000	—	—	—	—	—	$3,000,000
							$5,092,000

to encourage a number of small, marginal operators to remain
in farming and produce at low efficiency.

While there is truth in these criticisms, the great majority
of PFAA payments were made to the regular farmers and
ranchers, since truly marginal operators had become few. One
example of the survival effect can, however, be presented. In
the district called Greenfields, in the Cypress Hills in the
eastern half of the Jasper region (see Fig. 2.2), a community of
homestead farmers survived from about 1912 until just after
World War II, when the last several families departed. The
area had been surveyed and opened for homesteading because
of the lush green grass on the plateau. The growing season
was far too short for reliable crops, however. PFAA payments
were given to the families in Greenfields for a period of 22 years
prior to the final dissolution of the community. A total of
$248,000 was paid out. An average of 15 families lived in the
area during this period, making a total of about $15,000 per
family, or around $600 per year. This annual amount, small
as it was, made the difference between survival and departure
for many years for these marginal operators. After their final
departure, the land was sold to ranchers who now use it for
pasture and hay production.

One Jasper rancher described the yield deficiency payment
system this way (although he took his share on forage crop
payments):

Them deficiency payments ought to be called inefficiency payments. Two hundred dollars isn't going to do anybody much
good—it just helps keep these marginal fellers going when they
should get out. As the old Injun said, this is good country but
much of it is now the wrong side up.

(There is, in any case, a tug of war in North American farming between those who want to save the "family farm," whether
or not it is efficient, and those who want to get rid of the small
operators and let the bigger, business-minded producers take
over.)

Another part of the $800,000 in nonrepayable cash benefits
consisted of welfare payments. The "poor" of the region were
few in number, and consisted mainly of elderly people and

other indigents, mostly living in Jasper town and the villages. These people received about $62,000 annually. Each of the 100 or so Indians on the local reserve received about $20 per month.

The figure of $800,000 is only part of the story, however. An additional $1,200,000 was received by Jasperites in the form of wages for legitimate work performed for government agencies, or in the form of various types of repayable or shared-cost benefits. Grazing cooperatives and individual farmers could apply for shared financial assistance from the PFRA and other agencies on their various development projects; the big irrigation projects were repaired and rehabilitated at intervals by the government; road-building received considerable government financial support; agricultural supplies were sold at bargain prices through local government channels; the recreational facilities and stores in the Hills Provincial Park were subsidized by the government.

The bulk of all cash loans for agricultural activities was provided by two sources: the local private banks, all branches of eastern Canadian banks, and the Farm Credit Corporation (FCC), a federal government body. The former source of funds was almost exclusively devoted to short-term financing of annual farm and ranch operating expenses; the latter source, consisting of mainly medium-term loans, was directed toward young farmers and ranchers starting out in business. In a period of 25 years preceding our study, the FCC provided $2½ million to Jasper operators for these purposes. In the typical year used for the financial input study, the local banks loaned about $3 million dollars for operating expenses. The bank loans made a regional per capita indebtedness of $450; in a comparable area south of the border in Montana, the per capita bank indebtedness was $1,000.

Not counting the FCC and the bank loans, in a typical year Jasper people would receive about $2 million dollars from government sources. While the total figure of $2 million, or even the cash nonrepayable item of $800,000, for a population of about 7,000 seems large, actually this was small in comparison to comparable regions in the United States. (We obtained comparable figures for a county in Montana just south of the Jasper region with a nearly identical geographical milieu and economic pattern. An area equivalent to the Jasper region, with only a little more population, received almost twice as much money in all forms of payments as Jasper.) Moreover, it must be remembered that Jasperites pay income taxes, and thus they are entitled to receive some of their tax money in return. Finally, the enormous costs of developing the marginal and refractory resources of the region make either of the two figures—$2 million or $800,000—relatively small in terms of what the money could do. One reason Jasper agriculture was relatively undeveloped, and management techniques conservative, is that capital in the form of cash, credit, or services has been relatively limited during the entire history of the region.

Large or small, there is no question that the government financial inputs helped keep Jasper agriculture moving, and reduced the rate of out-migration—great though it has been. Most of the $2 million was used as working capital for the agricultural enterprises of the region, or for items, such as roads, needed to facilitate agrarian business. But it is also true, as we noted earlier, that various government financial supports prolonged settlement in districts where the climatic difficulties or the small size of the enterprises made viable agriculture impossible in terms of survival or at desired levels of income.

FARM CREDIT

We have observed that Jasper agriculture—particularly farming —has had less capital than comparable regions in both Canada and the United States. A chronic shortage of credit for development of the enterprises has been a major factor in the establishment of a conservative approach to farm and ranch management. Basically the scarcity of loan capital was due to the special difficulties attending farming in this specialized region —this, and the unwillingness or inability of Canadian bankers and the federal government to provide a more generous supply.

The credit situation had eased somewhat by the 1950's, as we noted earlier in describing the contributions of the banks and the FCC, but the available programs were inadequate for one particular need: funds to permit young men to start in ranching or farming who lacked a family to back them. In general, young men whose fathers were willing to help them get started had a better opportunity—although even here there were difficulties, as we have described. The FCC provided medium-term loans of up to $40,000, although most loans actually granted were less. The smaller the loan, the shorter the repayment period, and such loans involved relatively little security and differed from short-term bank loans for operating expenses only in the lower rate of interest. The larger, medium-term loans, ostensibly devised to help young farmers or ranchers get started, simply did not work. The regulation required that a young man had to have five years of farming experience, and had to put up the entire enterprise as security. Therefore he could not obtain any other form of credit so long as his FCC loan was outstanding. Thus the need for additional short-term sums of money to buy a purebred bull or finance a particular short-term development that might actually put the enterprise over the top, so to speak, usually could not be provided by the FCC.

A young man whose father was willing to see him through had an advantage because the father could get the loan for him —the five years of experience would be the father's not the sons's and the security offered was the *father's* enterprise. The regulations thus favored the "farm family," and encouraged the normal father-son succession cycle but militated against the young man starting fresh—and these were often the most ambitious and dedicated farmers and ranchers. Clearly the legislation had been written with the idealistic need to save the farm family—a characteristic pattern of agricultural planning and legislation in both Canada and the U.S. We have shown, however, how the entire economic picture of farming and ranching in Jasper is working against the traditional farm family—or at least the traditional type of family enterprise. Many Jasper people felt that more effort should be made to encourage the young men as individuals, and that saving the family enterprise should be forgotten.

CONSUMPTION

The consumption level of Jasper farm and ranch families was modest. Electricity entered the region during the 1950's, and nearly all farms and ranches had the basic appliances: refrigerator, radio, TV, freezer. The typical family had one passenger automobile, usually a four- or five-year–old car kept in good condition. Homes were usually the old homestead or ranch headquarters buildings, kept in repair, and modestly furnished with a mixture of old and new pieces. Often the ranchers, relatively affluent by Jasper standards, had the most modest outlays: in ranching culture, and in the region generally, there was considerable pressure to save money and not to display it in consumption. The family that decided to build a modern ranch-style or suburban house, or to invest in expensive furniture and appliances, was considered to be displaying bad taste and was suspected of "throwing money around," although the custom was increasing among the third generation. But Jasperites were still close to the frontier and its frugal values. One important definition of a "good man" was one who spent little and wisely, and who did not seek to set himself off from the majority by conspicuous consumption.

In only one sector of consumption could some Jasperites be accused of "throwing money around." This was the horse hobby: the raising of horses for riding and show, their expensive equipment, and other expenditures related to the activity. Only a minority of Jasperites engaged in this—perhaps half of the ranchers and a small minority of farmers—but the expenses were considerable. Horses eat more grass than cattle do, and require special feeding in the winter; good or pedigreed horses are expensive purchases. Reactions to these activities on the part of Jasperites were governed by the community's perception of the ability of the family to sustain them: small operators were criticized because it was obvious that money needed for family consumption or production was being drained off by them. At best, however, the feelings were ambivalent, since everyone acknowledged the important symbolic value of the horse hobby in Jasper culture: it represented the authentic heritage of the frontier and the Old West.

We commented earlier on one of the "paradoxes" of Great Plains ecology, noting that as population declines, per capita income tends to increase, owing to the increase in acreage. However, as population declines, tax revenues fall, which creates another round of relative deprivation in the sense of poorer services—schooling, roads, recreation, professional services, and the like. Sociologists and economists have referred to this latter effect as the "social cost of space." The Great Plains populations may aspire to urban middle-income levels of consumption and services, but they cannot obtain these services unless the government steps in to help pay the bills. Thus a characteristic pattern is for a farm family to experience an income rise as they acquire more land, but then to realize that even these gains do not give them the consumption level they desire—at which point they are likely to sell the farm and leave. (In other words, their labor and farm resources have acquired intolerably high opportunity costs.) Those people who do decide to stay finance their farming existence out of their willingness to take less in the way of goods and services.

In the next chapter we shall describe the social roles and economy of the Jasper Indians, noting that these people lack the wherewithal to accumulate enough cash at any one time to finance a more stable adaptation to the local economy and society. It is useful to distinguish this pattern from that described above. In both cases—the Indians and the farmers—one finds a degree of deprivation, but there are two important differences: (1) In the first place, the farmers more frequently have a surplus, however small, available for investment—it is the difference between a net income that hovers around $2,500 a year for the former, and a gross income of about $1,000 for an Indian family. (2) Secondly, the farmers have a cultural style that already includes the habits and strategies needed to make the investment—the objectives of "maximization," or at least of accumulation. The Indians, we will find, lack this style. These differences mean that the farmers are "deprived" more in the sense of status than of finances, even though many of them accommodated to this disparity between their monetary rewards and the middle-class status they identify with. The Indians, of course, have neither status nor money, and lack access to the many government benefits enjoyed by the farmers.

Historically, of course, Jasper farmers, and some ranchers, did pass through an era of economic marginality: the drought-and-depression decade of the late 1920's and '30's. During this period most Jasper farms did not provide even a minimal living, and many farmers had to depend on government handouts of food, in order to survive. It was this difficult experience that bred the strategies of caution and limited investment we describe in the next section of the chapter. The effects of this experience on the farmers were to push them toward political action—that is, they felt the deprivation of status and aspiration as keenly as the economic deprivation. The Indians have rarely or never formulated a policy of action, and it is a rare Indian who has seriously entertained aspirations toward a middle-class way of life and security.

FARM MANAGEMENT

Economists and social scientists interested in the agrarian development of the new nations of Africa, Asia, and Latin America use the term "backwardness" to describe the conservative peasant or former tribal peoples who may constitute the majority of the populations of these countries. To be "backward" means to practice self-subsistent agriculture, to be conservative in investments, wary of innovations designed to improve productivity, to avoid extensive relationships with landlords, creditors, and government agencies, and to live in a traditional manner, avoiding manufactured gadgets and luxury items. If this is a description of backwardness, then to a degree Jasper ranchers and farmers are "backward." However, it is confusing to call them this, since they are thoroughly committed to entrepreneurial farming, and like other businessman farmers, they want to make money and are aware of the economic devices needed to do so. Certainly Jasper agriculture was not self-subsistent agriculture—all of its products (excepting the home-consumed produce) were sold on the market.

However, many traits associated with economic backwardness in the emerging nations were found to be present in Jasper farm management. These 'traits' took the form of practical procedures concerned with the actual operation of the enterprise, and also a series of particular cultural values and social attitudes. The latter will be described in greater detail in other chapters. For the time being we can say that the general economic deprivation suffered by Jasper *farmers,* and the financial stability of the *ranchers,* had, with the help of the pioneer traditions, been converted into a cultural style that upheld such conservative patterns as desirable. This mechanism is not dissimilar from that considered to characterize peasants.

However, there is a difference. While Jasper operators had a culturally reinforced conservatism, and therefore to some extent resembled peasants, this reinforcement was relatively weak when compared with typical peasant societies. As heirs to the Anglo-American entrepreneurial tradition, there is a built-in responsiveness to economic opportunity that makes a population of farm operators of this type more inclined to change, when opportunity presents itself, than the usual peasant population. In fact Jasper operators, particularly the younger ones, *were* changing, although the change seemed slow, and in some districts was not sufficient to stem the tide of ambitious, secular-minded outsiders on a hunt for land. How hard do old ways die? How long will it take to outlive the conservative managerial traditions, backed up by values and status prestige? Probably not more than one human generation.

As we see it, farm management is always—even in entrepreneurial agriculture—a complex texture of response to quantity of available resources, economic knowledge, cultural styles, reactions to risk and opportunity costs, and choosing between alternatives. The needs of the family are taken into account as well as the needs of the enterprise, an important matter which will be discussed in detail in Chapters 6 and 7. Security can be even more important than wealth. In our interview questionnaires we asked farmers how they would handle various amounts of money under various circumstances. The tone of these answers was conservative: a majority always chose uses for the money which were not productive in the classical sense of affording new opportunities to make additional income. Cash savings, investment in securities, retirement, or an occasional new house or car, were the favored uses. The respondents explained that they were leery of going into debt, since they had had bad experiences with debt during droughts and depressions, and that they had learned that money invested in resources often did not pay off, due to these same factors. Their actual financial behavior corresponded to these attitudes.

Moreover, ranchers and farmers showed considerable skepticism over new ideas and techniques advocated by agricultural extension services. They pointed out, with justification, that these techniques did not always work in their own, specialized environment, and that their costs were often higher than the experts claimed. The majority of farmers and ranchers felt that they were better off taking modest gains by tried and true methods: raising the same crops in carefully calculated quantities year after year; never plowing up all the summer-fallow on the hunch of an unusually wet year, or sinking all available cash into feeder cattle on the assumption of high prices; and staying out of debt as much as possible. The per capita figure of indebtedness to the local banks is a modest one as compared to other agricultural regions in the Plains.

This approach to the management of ranch and farm enterprises is essentially one of avoiding risks because of the uncertainty of all factors affecting production and marketing. Uncertainty is the degree of inability to predict what will happen —in the weather or markets—and risk is the subjective assessment of just how serious the consequences of uncertainty may be. Such assessments can accumulate and form attitudes or traditions which then influence management decisions. These attitudes may be more or less subject to change when conditions alter—individuals differ in their flexibility.

A number of other factors influence this perception of risk. When the enterprises are small relative to the available resources, they are more vulnerable to resource deficiencies and economic hazards. Economists speak of an "economy of scale," which means that when resources and facilities are relatively abundant, risks can be absorbed, capital can be used to finance productive routines even though they may not always pay off as expected, and returns are large relative to costs. Jasper enterprises, with the exception of a majority of ranches, a very few farms, and of course Hutterian colonies, were small relative to the available resources. Their operators had to be cautious because the farms were not large enough to permit the accumulation of large amounts of capital, machinery, and other facilities which could handle large crops or herds and thereby easily cover costs and fluctuations. Smallness begets smallness, so to speak; the operator of a relatively small enterprise in a high-risk or high-uncertainty situation will, if he does not receive outside help from government or private sources, tend to keep his investments and needs low and his returns modest—which in turn increases his opportunity costs of innovation and development. If these attitudes become culturally sanctioned as the "right" way to run a farm or ranch, there will be relatively less flexibility in responding to change even when better opportunities and subsidies appear. Characteristically the lag will be less among North American or European farmers than in our peasants, but the problem of traditional conservatism will still be present.

How small is small? We noted that most Jasper farms were around 1,000 acres—a "large" amount of land in the humid Midwest, but a "small" amount when compared to an average cattle-grain farm in western North Dakota of about 3,000 acres. Hutterian colonies had from 6,000 to 17,000 acres. The biggest ranch had two whole townships; a few were undersized; the majority averaged about nine sections (nine square miles). While these figures sound large, the productivity of the land and water resources was proportionately small. Yet with additional development, some of these farms and ranches were increasing their productivity. Government aids were beginning to make a difference during the period of our study, and some farmers and ranchers were starting innovative experiments. Their deep-rooted caution was beginning to change with changing resources (remembering that "resources" always includes financial and social as well as natural facilities).

Some observers—and many farm and ranch operators themselves—call Great Plains agriculturalists "gamblers," implying that they take risks like card players. This is not entirely wrong, but it is too simple a label. A gambler in the strict sense is a man who goes for broke, who takes risks freely, hoping that if he does this often enough, he will eventually make a lucky hit or a "killing." Some wheat farmers in the Great Plains have followed this particular strategy, but it is no longer a common form of behavior. In Jasper it was nonexistent. "Gambling" in the Jasper sense meant that the operators followed conservative, bet-hedging strategies, as do cautious poker players who never stay in the game on a long shot but who only bet on a sure thing and collect a series of small winnings. As a matter of fact, we found that the "get-rich-quick" gambler left in the first generation of farm settlement in Jasper because he discovered that the country was just too risky to count on long shots. Thus the development of conservative strategies in Jasper farm management was not only a matter of learning, but to some degree, involved the elimination of certain types of personalities who favored more daring approaches. (See Chapter 7 for a more detailed discussion.)

We also found differences in the sources of these conservative strategies between ranchers and farmers. The ranchers, as we have pointed out, were better endowed with natural resources and followed a mode of production which was better adapted to the northern Plains resource pattern. Their conservatism was really a matter of what the local people often called "sitting" or "coasting"; that is, they were doing so well (according to their modest consumption standards) that they felt no need to expand their holdings or to intensify their resources. On the other hand, most farmers could not coast—they had to work hard for what they got, and the costs of doing anything different were felt to be so great that they followed conservative strategies. There is also some evidence that they were influenced by the ranchers' conservative attitudes, as well. Ranching culture was a tradition in the region, and constituted a standard of behavior for others to emulate.

Basically what Jasper agriculturalists were doing was to follow an "averaging game." By this we mean that they were trying to stay in business by striking a reasonable though modest average income, avoiding the consequences of fluctuation as much as possible. They were not always able to do this, of course, since the fluctuation in markets and weather was so marked. Due to inadequate capitalization and credit, however, their cautious strategies were adaptive, providing they were willing to accept less in the way of financial returns and a level of living. This kind of strategy had become a cultural definition of the ideal kind of farmer or rancher: cautious, steady, cheerful in the face of adversity. The concept also coincided with persisting frontier values, which held that a man was good if he saved money, provided reasonably well for his family, and did not "push too hard for the dollar." We shall see in later chapters how these attitudes were also reinforced by the social system.

Since the whole question of management strategies lay at the heart of our economic studies, we made an effort to classify the styles of farm and ranch operation. After considerable study of the management procedures of a large number of ranchers and farmers, we found that these reduced to two major types, with a third sometimes emerging clearly enough to be considered separately. The men manifesting the two principal styles of management we called "Conservatives" and "Developers." These patterns of management follow the patterns already suggested: the Conservatives were those who played the cautious, saving, averaging game, refraining from excessive investments and innovations, preferring to live simply and accept modest returns. The Developers were those who simply showed more financial daring, an interest in income, and a willingness to invest in resources development to increase productivity. The third type we called the "Expanders"—the local people called them "land grabbers"—and this term adequately describes their activities. They were really a special form of Developer who concentrated on land accumulation. We have not distinguished them from Developers because they followed the same basic philosophy of management.

We wanted to know two things: (1) how these management styles were divided between ranchers and farmers; and (2) how they were divided among the generations of the ranch and farm operators. By "generation" we meant the position in the family cycle occupied by the present operator: if he was the man who founded the enterprise, he was "first generation"; his son, or a purchaser, would be "second generation," and so on. Generally speaking, since the settlement of the Jasper region was fairly uniform as to time and type of enterprise, no ranches were first-generation; most were second, a plurality, third; and a very few, fourth. A number of farms were still in the first-generation stage; the great majority were second, and a minority, third.

Table 4.4 presents the classification of management strategies by ranch and farm operators. (The sample used was our Regional Schedule sample stratified by size and type of enterprise and augmented to some extent by specialized studies of other farms and ranches.) The first thing to note is that the proportion of ranchers in the Conservative category is considerably higher than farmers—a finding in conformity with all other observations plus those of agricultural experts on the region. There are also more Developers among farmers: 33 per cent of the farmers as against 24 per cent of the ranchers. These figures also conform to all other data and observations.

Table 4.5 shows the data reclassified by generation of operator. In both ranch and farm categories, the majority of Conservatives are found in the second generation, and among the total number of second-generation operators, Conservatives far outnumber Developers. It is otherwise with the third-generation operators: there are twice as many Developers as Conservatives. This suggests that among the younger operators, one out of two is likely to be expansionistic, innovative, and desirous of higher income.

A classification of management styles is one thing; the effect of these on the regional economy is another. One must be careful here, since even a very few innovative people in a mass of conservatives can have a considerable effect on the statistics

Table 4.4 Classification of Jasper Farmers and Ranchers by Management Strategies

	Farmers (63)	Ranchers (40)
Conservatives	42 or 66%	30 or 76%
Developers	21 or 33%	10 or 24%

Table 4.5. *Jasper Management Strategies
by Generation of Operator*
FARMERS (63)

	1st gen. Total: 5	2nd Gen. Total: 43	3rd Gen. Total: 15
Conservatives	5	33	5
Developers	0	10	10

RANCHERS (40)

	1st gen. Total: 3	2nd Gen. Total: 32	3rd Gen. Total: 5
Conservatives	3	26	1
Developers	0	6	4

of agricultural productivity of a region. Our study did not penetrate quite this far: we have no quantitative evidence to show how effective the Developers were becoming in terms of increased regional income. One thing was clear, however— more and more operators were finding it necessary to begin intensive development of their enterprises if they were to stay in business. This meant that they had to overcome some of the cultural reinforcements of conservative management behavior— something not always easy to do, and certainly not in the 1962– 64 period being done by a large majority of even the younger operators.

There were other factors involved in the differing styles of management behavior, and particularly with reference to the tendency for the younger operators to be more innovative. We studied the history of a number of enterprises over their entire two- or three-generation span, and the behavior of their several owners. This study showed us that the operator of an enterprise was most likely to invest in or otherwise develop his enterprise when a "crunch" appeared as a result of the coincidence of needs for increased consumption in the family and needs for investment in the enterprise. An example of this would be when a young man took over an enterprise from his father (or buying one), found that the resources were not sufficiently developed to give his wife the income she desired or needed for two young children. If, on the other hand, the young man had been able to buy the enterprise before his marriage, or before the children were born, there would have been less pressure to develop it. There were several other points in the *family cycle* where coincidence with investment needs in the *enterprise cycle* resulted in development activity: for example, when aged parents were ready to retire and in need of cash, or when additional households had to be supported by the enterprise (as in the case of a young married man and his wife still "working off the place" from the young man's father and living in the old homestead). We also found that when children became of sufficient age to add their labor to their father's, development behavior was likely to appear, since this lowered the cost of the activities. (See Chap. 7 for further analysis.)

If external pressures also coincided with family or enterprise needs, additional pressure mounted on the operator. If strong needs for money emerged at a time when farm prices were unusually low, or drought conditions had lowered yields, many families would sell out or simply migrate, since they simply were unable to respond to the development challenge even if they wanted to, lacking even the smallest surplus to get a "start." Thus we were able to show that the same factors that encourage enterprise development will also, under extreme circumstances, impede or suppress it.

In any case, if we look at the pattern of management styles as a cultural-historical phenomenon, we can generalize as follows: The first generation consisted of rugged, courageous men who did what they had to do to establish semi-subsistence enterprises on the frontier; they were hard workers and given the limited knowledge and resources of the period, were willing to try anything. Their basic economic outlook was conservative however, insofar as they emphasized savings over investments, stability over expansion and development. Their sons learned this general philosophy from their fathers and, in addition, came into control of the farms during the worst period of drought and depression. The combination of these influences bred the cautious strategies we have described. The third generation of operators were coming into ownership of the ranches, and just beginning on the farms, during our period of research. Improved economic conditions were encouraging some of them to consume more and to practice a more innovative approach to agriculture. But since most of them had learned the conservative habits of management from their fathers, their numbers were not large. Change was beginning, but it would take another generation, and also continued prosperity, to bring a larger number of operators into the Developer-Expander category. (As a matter of fact, there were actually more Expanders than included in the category, but we deliberately excluded a number of outsiders who had moved into the region in the 1960's to take advantage of available land.)

Thus the shift toward a more innovative disposition in the later generations was associated with the increasing investment value of the enterprises. For two generations Jasper ranchers and farmers valued their enterprises in terms of their fluctuating productivity; land, though it was felt to be a good thing to accumulate, was considered to be worth no more than the average low income it produced. This attitude, and the fact that the Jasper region was a kind of backwater, kept land values —and agricultural values generally—low. In the 1950's and '60's, better farm prices, the competition for land triggered by the entry of the Hutterian colonies, and the growing interest in farmland by outsiders, pushed farmland values from about $15 an acre in 1949, to $50 or more by 1963. A medium-sized ranch (that is, its "improvements") of around 5,000 acres sold for $50,000 in the 1940's; by the mid-1960's it could command over $100,000.

These changes were accompanied by changes in the conception of agricultural values by Jasper operators. Enterprises and land were coming to be valued in terms of opportunity costs, or their potential productivity—what they could produce with improved methods of management and farming or pasture management, or what the labor of the operator was worth in terms of other types of jobs, or a rising level of living. In other words, many Jasper operators were beginning to conceive of agricultural properties as investments, and not merely as a means to a stable and modest way of life.

One result of this change was the emergence of the economic ritual known locally as the "land deal." Competition for land (which we discuss in greater detail in Chap. 9) had reached the point where sales of land, especially whole ranch or farm properties, had become surrounded by considerable tension and secrecy. The number of potential buyers, and the fact that if the land was leased ranching pasture the government had ultimate control over the sale, meant that intense competition would develop between potential buyers to attract the favorable attention of both the seller and the government bureau concerned with monitoring the disposition of the lease. Offers for land were secretly conveyed to the sellers and secret negotiations would proceed to the point where agreement or the lack of it was reached—while other buyers, aware of activity through the grapevine, would be impatiently hanging around the neighborhood, waiting for a chance to get in and make their offer.

This change in the conception of agriculture also had its inconvenient effects in the form of increasing difficulties for local young men to succeed to their fathers' enterprises. The enhanced market value of the enterprises meant that fathers were often unwilling to simply give the farm or ranch to a son or other relative, but required him to pay for it, since they felt it was time they extracted some financial benefit. The increasing push toward productivity also required sons to refinance farms on takeover in order to produce enough to meet these new standards, to afford retiring parents a decent income, or to satisfy their young wives' consumption needs. The difficulties of succession made it easier for outsiders to buy farms and ranches, and thus many of the "places" that had been in the hands of a single family for two or three generations were beginning to fall into alien hands. These events had their impact on family relationships, and we shall discuss this in greater detail in Chapters 6 and 7.

EDUCATION AND OCCUPATIONAL OPPORTUNITY

The difficulties of succession and the diminishing number of agricultural enterprises meant that Jasper young people were required to find jobs in fields other than agriculture. But since such jobs were scarce, out-migration of young people was a necessity. At the same time, the occupational situation affecting young people was inextricably bound up with the nature of education, since the out-migrating young people require training for jobs on the outside. We conclude this chapter on the Jasper economy with a discussion of the linkage between opportunity, migration, and education.

Whether a Jasper boy took over his father's enterprise, bought a new one, or left home for a town job, or whether he completed high school or went on to college were all decisions bound up with the nature of schooling in Jasper, the distance one had to travel to attend school, and the attitudes of one's parents toward education. A young woman had fewer decisions to make; she was barred by local custom from inheriting a farm or ranch, and her parents expected her to complete high school and leave for further training or jobs, or perhaps to marry a local boy.

Until the early 1950's, Jasper country young people went to country schools, the traditional one-room schoolhouses serving the old school districts, established in the frontier period. The lucky ones, located near small towns, went to the town high schools. The cost of maintaining country schools, and the difficulties of getting teachers, led to the school consolidation movement, and by the 1960's, only one or two of the country schools were left in operation. The great majority of country children were bussed—often many miles—into consolidated schools located in the towns. Most of them were in Jasper town, although one of the southern towns (Eldora—see Fig. 2.10) had schools serving the districts south of the Hills. The long bus rides were hard on many children and in the severe winters buses often did not make the trip. Difficult schooling conditions were a major factor in inducing many farm parents to sell their remote properties and move elsewhere.

Education in Saskatchewan is organized on a provincial basis. While the local municipalities control their own schools, the teachers are prepared by the Province and made available to the local schools at their choice. The curricula are consequently generalized, and emphasize the subject matter of urban middle-class intellectual culture. In rural areas like Jasper, vocational subjects are not taught intensively: there was no way for Jasper youth to be adequately trained in shop, business, clerical work, or agriculture, for that matter. Teachers may come from anywhere: other rural areas, cities, the British Isles. This arrangement certainly provides a cosmopolitan atmosphere which has its desirable features, but in regions with their own distinctive history and institutions, or with vocational training needs, like Jasper, school children often find the curriculum unrewarding, and remote from local traditions. The Jasper region has had a number of interesting books written about it, including works by Wallace Stegner, the distinguished American novelist. None of these books, though sometimes read by parents, were used in the school curriculum during the period of our study.

In addition to problems of curriculum relevance, the school system in Jasper had to compete with the practical need for ranch and farm boys to spend much time on the enterprise if they were to learn the routines. This need to be on hand so as to permit on-the-spot training by the father was coupled with ambivalent attitudes toward education, especially high school and college, on the part of parents—particularly fathers. This ambivalence was more pronounced among ranchers than farmers, and this is reasonable insofar as the opportunities for succession were greater on ranches than farms. The need for farm sons to migrate was correspondingly greater, and hence farm parents tended to be more encouraging on the subject of education.

Education for girls was a different story. The girl was expected to leave the region, since she did not inherit farms and ranches. Thus both ranch and farm parents insisted that she complete high school and then look for a town job or a local husband. Many girls went to distant cities to enter secretarial schools, nursing, medical technology, and other fields receptive to women. If the girl married a local rancher or farmer, she would probably have more education than her husband, and her additional training often served the enterprise in good stead, especially in areas requiring superior literacy or mathematics, such as bookkeeping and income tax preparation.

The actual amount of education enjoyed by Jasperites, as measured by number of grades completed, is not easy to generalize about, since it varied by age group, neighborhood, and occupation. We studied educational accomplishments in several ways: local school records, questions on education in our Regional Schedule sample, and a special augmented sample of families studied in the social organizational project. We found that in general (1) farmers had completed more grades than ranchers, although the group of farmers who had experienced the drought-and-depression era, mostly men in their 40's and 50's, had less education than the comparable group of ranchers. This was a result of the greater stability of the ranching population during the crisis years. Many of the farmers had had to leave the region for a time, interrupting their schooling. (2) All older ranchers and farmers—men over 50—had uniformly low educational levels; most had left school—or had simply never had any schools available—before the 8th grade. (3) Among the young farm men who had recently succeeded to their fathers' enterprises, more had completed 10th and 12th grade than the comparable group of ranchers. This held true for the young boys still in school: more of the farm boys were staying in school than the ranch boys. But we also found that (4) among both ranch and farm boys who had recently migrated away from the region, the great majority—around 75 per cent —had a 10th-grade or better education, and about half had training or college in addition to high school. This shows that departure from the region is associated with higher educational accomplishment. (5) Among wives of ranchers and farmers, all age groups, there were no significant differences: the majority of each had had a 10th-grade education or better.

We can conclude from these and other figures that farmers generally have somewhat more schooling than ranchers; that the educational levels of all men were relatively low; that the educational levels of all women were relatively high. The actual numbers of people with high school diplomas and college educations in Jasper were very small: among the young successor ranchers in our sample, about 10 per cent of the total; among farm men, 6.6 per cent of the total. However, the field staff concluded that there was much more encouragement of college training in the farm families, and proportionately more farm boys were in college.

The precise value of a grade- and high-school education for ranchers and farmers is difficult to measure. We have already noted that practical training on the enterprise is needed in any case, and that school often interferes with this. Moreover, the more school, the greater the desire of the boy to leave and enter urban occupations. As agriculture becomes more of a business, however, the need for training in mathematics and business management procedures becomes more acute, and many ranchers and farmers were beginning to realize this during the period of research. Those ranchers and farmers with longer educational exposure also had a larger proportion of higher-income enterprises than the operators with less schooling, although for the ranchers this was a result of the inheritance of a prosperous enterprise—and the prosperity also accounted for the education. It was evidenced also by the very great concern of all parents for the long distances traveled to school, and the quality of the educational experience. There was evidence to show that Jasper people were beginning to realize the value of education, but at the same time the curriculum did not really serve their needs either for local purposes, or for training in fields other than agriculture.

A study of the records of the Jasper consolidated town high school (and confirmed by our sample survey) revealed that girls did much better in school than boys. The records also showed that boys with the best academic records—and always this meant a high-school diploma—were also the most likely to leave the region in search of higher education, skill training, or urban jobs. Town boys were also more likely to do better in school, and to migrate, than were country boys. While proportionately more farm sons than ranch boys were completing high school during the 1960's, the farm boys with high-school diplomas were just as prone to migrate as any others. Thus the practical skills of ranching and farming were not easily compatible with formal education beyond the 8th or 9th grade—a selective process was in operation, favoring the retention of the less academically inclined boys. Since many or most of these latter boys were candidates for succession, this also meant that they were often the more passive siblings, prone to accept their father's controls and probably less inclined toward innovation and enterprise development. Thus the conservative management style, so typical of Jasper enterprises, received a certain amount of reinforcement from the educational process.

Although a large number of young men (and women) left (and had to leave) country occupations, we have noted that the occupational opportunities in the region itself, and in this part of Canada generally, were very limited. Thus, a young man or woman with college training and a professional career in mind, would be required to go to distant cities—in the U.S. or British Columbia, or Saskatoon, Calgary, Winnipeg, or in eastern Canada. In the Jasper region a young man without special training, and with, say, a 9th-grade education, could expect to make no more than $6 a day in farm labor, manual labor, or menial service jobs. With a high-school diploma he would be qualified to operate one of the large road machines and receive about $350 per month. If he was a skilled mechanic, preferably with a certificate of special training, he might make around $300 a month. These jobs were few in number, however; there were only about 20 of the road machine jobs; 25 mechanic's jobs; 50 or so reasonably remunerative ranch-farm labor jobs; perhaps 30 manual labor jobs in various government agencies and on the roads; and about 25 service jobs, like clerks in stores. Banks hired a few local girls as secretaries and clerks, but teller and junior executive positions almost always went to trained outsiders brought in for the purpose. The same was true for many of the managerial jobs, although a few local men could expect to get some of the bulk farm commodities and fuel station management positions. In the two small cities located 60 and 80 miles from Jasper, similar jobs were available, and in much larger number, but the better-trained town boys usually had a far better opportunity for acquiring them. Jasper youth—especially the boys—were caught in a difficult situation: they were being forced to migrate in ever-larger numbers but were inadequately prepared to cope with the occupational situation in larger communities. It is no wonder that many boys, especially sons of the prestigeful ranchers, did everything possible to find a ranch or to work as ranch hands; their limited education exposure provided them with training for little other than menial positions in towns and cities. It is also no surprise to find that the more academically competent boys were the most likely to migrate; their intellectual skills would permit them to more easily compensate for their deficiencies in special training and on-the-job learning. Girls, of course, were in a better position: their superior application to scholarship, and the structure of training programs for female occupations, made it easier for them to find jobs on the outside.

There is in this situation one of the paradoxes of the North American rural economy: the limited economic opportunities are handled in a way which benefits the remaining people— but not the young, not those who most need encouragement and support to stay in the locality. Security for the remaining population is achieved at the cost of preventing the great majority of the young people from remaining in the region, or from obtaining nonagricultural jobs. Only the Jasper Hutterites completely escaped this paradox: their communal society and economy provided enough savings to finance the retirement of the aged and also gave every young person a satisfactory position in the colony; there was no need for individual migration, and their labor in the colony was highly remunerative for the group as a whole. When the colony became too large, it divided in two, and one-half would buy land elsewhere to establish a new colony.

BIBLIOGRAPHIC NOTES

The historical events surrounding the settlement of the Jasper region and adjoining parts of Canada and the United States are related in Paul S. Sharp, *Whoop-Up Country: A History of the Canadian-American West,* University of Minnesota Press, 1955. A more literary account, but particularly good on the early history of the Cypress Hills and Jasper country, is found in Wallace Stegner, *Wolf Willow,* Viking Press, 1962.

For accounts of the homesteading process and homesteader culture in Canada and the United States, see A. S. Morton and C. Martin, *A History of Prairie Settlement:* Vol. II, *Canadian Frontiers of Settlement,* Macmillan (Toronto), 1938; Paul F. Sharp, "The American Farmer and the Last Best West," *Agricultural History,* 21 (1947), pp. 65–74; Everett Dick, *The Sod House Frontier,* Johnson Publ. Co., Lincoln, Nebraska, 1954; Louis B. Wright, *Culture on the Moving Frontier,* Harper Torchbooks, 1961.

For histories of agriculture in Saskatchewan and the Prairie Provinces, see H. G. L. Strange, *A Short History of Prairie Agrictulture,* Searle Grain Co. (Winnipeg), 1956; Vernon C. Fowke, *The National Policy and the Wheat Economy,* University of Toronto Press, 1957. The fluctuations in the agricultural economy caused by changes in price and moisture levels are analyzed in C. Schwartz, *The Search for Stability: Contemporary Saskatchewan,* McClelland & Stewart, 1959. A study of one of the several optimistic movements that swept the Western plains shortly after the homesteading period, relating to the possibilities of an abundant agriculture, is Mary W. H. Hargreaves, "Dry Farming alias Scientific Farming," *Agricultural History,* Vol. 22 (1948), pp. 39–55.

Histories of Populist and agrarian cooperative movements in North America are found in Paul S. Sharp, *The Agrarian Revolt in Western Canada,* University of Minnesota Press, 1948; John D. Hicks, *The Populist Revolt,* University of Minnesota Press, 1931; A. A. Bruce, *The Non-Partisan League,* Macmillan, 1921; Harold S. Patton, *Grain Growers Cooperation in Western Canada,* Harvard University Press, 1928. Some additional studies of the cooperative movement in Canada are Jim Wright, *Prairie Progress: Consumer Cooperation in Saskatchewan,* Modern Press, 1956; Henry Cooperstock, "Cooperative Farming as a Variant Social Pattern," in B. Blishen and others, *Canadian Society,* Free Press, 1961. (See also Chap. 9 and notes.)

The definitive study of the CCF party and its rise and fall is Seymour M. Lipset, *Agrarian Socialism,* Doubleday Anchor ed., 1968. A critical study is Leo Zakuta, *A Protest Movement Becalmed,* University of Toronto Press, 1964.

The problem of the "family farm" in North American agriculture has attracted a wide critical literature. One recent study dealing in part with the problem is Harold F. Breimyer, *Individual Fseedom and the Economic Organization of Agriculture,* University of Illinois Press, 1965, Chap. 6. A more technical study is found in Joseph Ackerman and M. Harris, *Family Farm Policy,* University of Chicago Press, 1947.

The concept of "social space" and its higher costs of living is dealt with in a basic and classic article, A. H. Anderson, "Space as a Social Cost," *Journal of Farm Economics,* Vol. 32, No. 3 (1950). An extended discussion of the sociological implications is found in Carl Kraenzel, "Sutland and Yonland Setting for Community Organization in the Great Plains," *Rural Sociology,* Vol. 18 (1953), pp. 344–58. The term "sutland" refers to the nucleated service center towns in the Great Plains that, despite small permanent populations, supply many services to the hinterland, or "yonland."

Economic and occupational opportunities generally are more

limited in Canada than in the U.S. This is the result of fewer resources and a later start at development, and also of some rigidities in
the Canadian social structure. The latter are expertly portrayed by
John Porter in his *The Vertical Mosaic: An Analysis of Social Class
and Power in Canada,* University of Toronto Press, 1965, Chaps. 2, 5,
and 6.

Agricultural economists have attempted to measure the value of
education by showing the relationship of the number of years a person
spent in school to his income, thus giving a cash value to a given
number of years. In a study of Nebraska farmers, (*Land and People in
the Northern Plains Transition Area,* University of Nebraska Press,
1966, p. 195) by Howard W. Ottoson and associates, it was found that
each year in school was worth about $47 in accumulated capital per
year. In other words, the longer one went to school, the greater the
share of accumulated capital—acknowledging plenty of exceptions, of
course. We performed similar computations, and found that (1) there
was no reliable relationship between years in school and income for
the ranchers, which in turn is consistent with the indifference to education, especially college, shown by Jasper ranchers. (2) For farmers, we
found that the relationship is much closer, and each year in school was
worth about $30. Such computations should not be given too much
weight, since many other factors enter the picture. For a summary of
the relationship between education and management skills in farming
in the underdeveloped nations, see Richard Bradfield, "The Role of
Educated People in Agricultural Development," in A. H. Moseman,
ed., *Agricultural Sciences for the Developing Nations,* American Association for the Advancement of Science, Publ. No. 76 (1964). A study
of North American farm youth migrants to the city is found in A. O.
Haller, "The Occupational Achievement Process of Farm-Reared Youth
in Urban Industrial Society," *Rural Sociology,* Vol. 25 (1960), pp.
321–33.

For a study of reactions to drought and economic fluctuation in a
community of New Mexico bean farmers, see Evon Z. Vogt, *Modern
Homesteaders,* Harvard University Press, 1955. An account of the
economy and ecology of the "five cultures" of the New Mexico region
studied in Vogt's project can be found in E. Z. Vogt and Ethel Albert,
People of Rimrock: A Study of Values in Five Cultures, Harvard University Press, 1966, Chap. 6. A study of an Alberta farming community
suffering from drought is Jean Burnet, *Next Year Country,* University
of Toronto Press, 1951. This latter study was made during the era of
pessimism and despair in the northern Plains, and accordingly can be
taken to represent what Jasper was like in the same period. Actually
the two areas represented are only about 150 miles apart.

Standard treatments of agricultural innovation are found in Everett Rogers, *The Diffusion of Innovations,* Free Press, 1962, and N. F. Lionberger, *Adoption of New Ideas and Practices,* Iowa State University Press, 1960. An analysis of innovation in the context of risk and social status is given by Frank Cancian, "Stratification and Risk-taking: A Theory Tested on Agricultural Innovation," *American Sociological Review,* Vol. 32 (1967), pp. 912–27. A study of rational economic behavior in the context of irrigation, among Texas farmers, is: Jack P. Gibbs, "Human Ecology and Rational Economic Behavior: Agricultural Practices as a Case in Point," *Rural Sociology,* Vol. 29; 138–141, 1964. A study of the effects of technology on farm labor and society is found in Harland Padfield and William E. Martin, *Farmers, Workers and Machines: Technological Social Change in Farm Industries of Arizona,* University of Arizona Press, 1965. For analyses of reaction to change among peasants, see George M. Foster, *Traditional Cultures and the Impact of Technological Change,* Harper, 1962, and Charles J. Erasmus, *Man Takes Control: Cultural Development and American Aid,* University of Minnesota Press, 1961. (See also notes for Chap. 10 of this volume.)

FIVE

The Indians

In the next four chapters we shall describe the adaptations made by each of the major groups of the contemporary Jasper population. We begin with the Plains Cree Indians, [1] the first inhabitants of Jasper, displaced by the Euro-Americans, as the Amerinds were everywhere on the continent, driven ever westward and eventually into enclaves called reserves in Canada and reservations in the United States. Whether reserve or reservation, the condition of the Indians within these enclaves has been rarely prosperous or even physically healthy. The Jasper reserve was one of the more disturbing cases: a group of from 100 to 120 Indians—the number fluctuated—inhabited a tract of about 3,000 acres in the aspen bush forest near the crest of the Cypress Hills—land that lacked sufficient pasture for cattle and with a growing season too short and with too little open land for crop production. Perhaps one small family of parents and children could have made a modest living by ranching the area at contemporary levels of cost and income, without substantial development and intensification of its resources.

Jasper Indians lived, at intervals, in old shacks, plywood one-room houses, or tents on the reserve, in a camp on the Jasper town dump or in shacks on the edge of town, or simply in their jalopies—they were not required to stay on the reserve if they did not wish to. They supported themselves with odd jobs of labor, by an occasional swindle of a gullible or sympathetic white, and on their monthly relief allowances of about $100

1. This chapter was written in collaboration with Niels Braroe, who did the basic historical research and field work on the Indian population.

per household from the government. Essentially still a migratory or at least ambulatory people, retaining much of the pre-reserve outlook, these Indians had found no permanent position in the Jasper economy.

Our study of the Indian inhabitants of Jasper will begin with a review of the history of the northern Plains tribes and the Jasper enclave, and will proceed to a description of key features of Indian life and culture before contemporary adaptation to the Jasper region.

HISTORY AND CULTURE

The northern Great Plains portion of Canada was a transition zone for Indian tribes inhabiting the northern forest and the Plains proper. By the middle of the eighteenth century, the Gros Ventre and Assiniboine lived in the eastern portion and the Blackfoot and affiliated tribes in the west. To the north were bands of people speaking an Algonquian language—collectively called *Cree*. The former tribes were, by the seventeenth century, bison-hunting, horse-riding Plains nomads, while the Cree were still forest hunters, only occasionally moving out onto the Plains. The first written accounts of the Cree in the seventeenth century (by Jesuit missionaries) describe them as hunting and gathering peoples centered mainly on the west coast of Hudson Bay, where the modern Woodland Cree Indians still live. During the early nineteenth century portions of the Cree people moved south into the lake country and out on the Plains. By the end of the first quarter of this century, the Cree were a Plains group.

This movement was caused mainly by the fur trade. As the Hudson's Bay Company expanded its activities, all of the tribes were affected since most of the furs were obtained through them. The vigorous Plains tribes were less influenced by this business, however, since they could always retreat into their organized bison-hunting life. But the Cree, with ties to the forests where the fur-bearing animals were found, were drawn into the traders' orbit, and by the end of the eighteenth century had become greatly dependent upon European tools, weapons, and consumption items of all kinds, including food. As the eastern forests and streams were denuded of beaver, the Cree moved west in search of furs, and some of the bands became horse-bison Plains Indians in the process, largely severing their contacts with their forest-hunting relatives, though a few continued to move back and forth. For a time, the Cree were middlemen in the trade between whites and tribes further west. As this happened, a kind of no-man's land developed between the Plains Cree and the other tribes to the east and south; the Cypress Hills and the Jasper region were in the heart of this zone. The Blackfoot eventually dominated the area, maintaining garrisons in or near the Hills in order to keep other Indians from permanent habitation. The presence of grizzly bears in the Hills also discouraged Indian occupance. The Hudson's Bay Company more or less collaborated in this policy, since they were anxious to maintain the bison herds, to ensure the supply of bison meat (in the form of pemmican) for the posts, and to make profitable sales of guns and other articles to the Indians who did the hunting and trading.

By the early part of the nineteenth century the situation had developed into a stable military frontier, with the Cree and their occasional allies, the Assiniboine, raiding the Blackfoot but generally fleeing before the implacable Blackfoot could retaliate in force. But the no-man's–land policy held, and the long delay of white settlement of the region was due to Blackfoot hostility and the collaborative desire of the Company to keep whites out.

The culture of the Plains Cree Indians by the mid-nineteenth century was thus already a product of a century and more of culture change: the ecological move from forest to Plains and the involvement with the fur trade and the Hudson's Bay Company. This was not an "aboriginal" culture, but one already adapted to a Euro-American frontier society. Moreover, the population of the "Cree" bands was actually quite diverse: individual Indians and whole families could move freely between bands; members and families of other tribes might find a home in a Cree band, and people with French or English names— *Métis* (half-breeds)—could live in the bands, as Indians, hunt bison for cash payments, or join white society as employees of the Company; or, after about 1880, serve as scouts for the Royal Northwest Mounted Police.

The bands are described as loosely organized aggregates, varying in size and geographical range over short periods of time. Each band claimed an imprecisely defined territory, usually along a river valley. All of the bands in the vicinity of Jasper were more or less adapted to bison-hunting, but occasional hunting and gathering forays into the Cypress Hills, and dealings with the fur traders to the east, preserved the flexible, relatively unspecialized nature of their adaptation. Life was migratory, with the bands moving on the Plains in search of bison and deer, or in and out of the forested islands and brushy coulees and river bottoms as their food quest, fur trapping, or fear of the Blackfoot dictated. There were, however, certain rhythms: about late June one or several bands would come together to hold the annual Sun Dance—one of the great Plains ceremonials the Cree adopted along with the other features of the culture. Bison drives were usually associated with the Sun Dance. Late in the summer the coulees and hills were searched for edible vegetable foods, and in fall, deer and elk were hunted in the valleys and the hills. If fur trapping was contemplated, bands would head for the northern forests at the onset of winter and would camp near the Company posts and bring the pelts to the factor, receiving European articles and food in return.

Thus the Cree adaptation to the Plains was partial in the sense that the bison and the horse were not the sole determinants of migratory movements. The Cree retained a measure of their older forest-hunting habits and collaborated with the fur traders in the hunting and trapping of the beaver and other animals. This was in contrast to the more southerly Plains tribes who had converted entirely to true pastoral life based on the raising of horses and the hunting of bison. Symmes C. Oliver has worked out the extent to which the various Plains tribes based their band size and migrations on the habits of the bison: he found that most bison scattered in the summer into small groups to forage on the open Plains, and congregated during the fall for breeding purposes, when they formed large herds. Likewise,

the true Plains tribes lived in small scattered hunting groups
during the spring and summer and gathered for organized
bison drives of the large herds during the fall. The winter encampments of the tribes were a logical conclusion of their
fall nucleation. The pattern was reflected in their social and
ceremonial life as well: like the bison, the fall and winter
assemblages were opportunities for courtship and mating; the
organized fall drives required police organizations and structures and also afforded an opportunity for Sun Dances and
other tribal ceremonies. Since the Cree, even the "Plains Cree"
groups, were less attached to bison hunting, they did not
display so marked a development of the seasonal Plains patterns
and social forms.

The nomadic adaptation to the Plains, followed in some
degree by all tribes living within their borders, was based
on the seasonal distribution of resources and the dominance
of grasses within the resource supply. Indians who adopted
Plains culture, or a version of it, found it necessary to carry
out the various activities in their social round in different locations: hunting bison on the open plains; slaughtering and preparing meat and hides in wooded and watered coulees; ceremonials in great riverbottom or plateau campgrounds; winter
camps in the forest fringe; trapping or game hunting in the
forests.

It is useful to note that the early open-range cattleman in
Jasper and elsewhere in the Plains lived a rather similar life.
While they had a cabin in a coulee, along a stream, as headquarters, much of their time was spent on horseback herding
cattle on the round-ups, brandings, and annual drives of the
animals to market. Like the Plains Indians, the early cattlemen had their "winter encampment" at the home ranch, herded
cattle in the fall and spring, drove them to market in summer,
and caroused in the hotels and bars of the market town with
their fellows—the "Sun Dance" of the cattlemen! There is a
genuine ecological parallel to the Plains Indians, based on the
same circumstances: the specialized resources encourage dependence on a hoofed, grazing species, which in turn requires an
ambulatory existence.

Indians who took to the Plains to hunt bison generally

preserved some features of their original, pre-Plains social organization. Tribes like the Crow, who had been corn-growing village-dwellers, kept their formally organized political system with its recognized chiefs and politico-ceremonial groups after their entry into the Plains. The Plains Cree had been forest hunters with an exceedingly simple social system based on kinship and loose bands, with informal chieftainship—features which persisted after the adoption of Plains culture. There were no formally recognized procedures for selecting chiefs, no fixed membership number per band, no formally organized constituency. A man was recognized as a leader if he had demonstrated ability in hunting and war. He was expected to be generous, providing for relatives and financing ceremonials like the Sun Dance for the whole group. Decision-making among the Cree was implemented by holding gatherings of the responsible men of the band whenever the occasion arose—legal processes and formal authority were flexible and informal.

A feature of Cree social organization derived from Plains culture was the warrior society or lodge—one for each band. Those ambitious young men who showed promise were given recognition of special status and eventually were invited by the older men to sit in the Warrior Lodge—a kind of men's club, police force, and planning council for hunts and raids. The Warrior Lodge was headed by the War Chief, who exercised authority during the spring and summer when large encampments were built, and during the hunts and bison drives; that is, only in connection with Warrior Society activities.

The big hunts or drives were always collective operations, and individuals were not permitted to hunt alone while the official hunting camp was in existence. This rule applied to the hunting of bison and deer primarily, and was not observed when the Cree hunted smaller and more isolated game in the forests or elsewhere. An effort was made to equalize the hunting operation so that the men with the fastest horses would not have the advantage. Animals hunted collectively were divided evenly between all participants in the hunt to ensure a food supply for all family units. Formal punishment was meted out by the Warrior Society to anyone who violated these rules. Punishment usually took the form of destruction of the culprit's property, but if he mended his ways, restitution was made after a few days. The purpose of the sanction was to restore an individual as a functioning member of the group; it was not vindictive.

This sketch of Plains Cree social organization focuses on those features which were critical in forging attitudes toward the individual and the group, since these are key factors in understanding the socio-economic adaptation of the reserve Indians to modern Jasper environment and culture. As a way of life, the bison-driving and slaughtering episode lasted only about two human generations after the Cree had emerged on the Plains, after which it was modified by a number of events which we shall summarize briefly:

The most important of these was the extinction of the bison. We noted the practice of the Hudson's Bay Company in encouraging bison slaughter for the purpose of supplying meat to the posts and the Indian allies of the Company. By the mid-1870's this practice, plus the regular tribal hunts, and the new practice of slaughtering bison for hides, contributed to the diminution of the herds in the Canadian section of the Plains (the last bison were seen in the Cypress Hills area about 1877). Isaac Cowie, a Company agent who in 1913 published a memoir of his work during the 1860's and '70's, described the scene in the Jasper region north of the Hills about 1868, as follows:

Next morning, the four lines of cart and travois tracks were fresher, and on every side the bones of the buffalo, off which the hides and flesh had been stripped by the hunters, were scattered over the undulating plain. Mixed with these were the bloated and blown-out carcasses of hundreds of the noble animals wantonly slain in the sheer love of slaughter, and left untouched by the young bucks to provide a festering feast for the flocks of villainous vultures, which, slimy with filthy gore, hovered over the field and disputed with the ravening wolves for the disgusting prey. For miles, the air stank with the foul odors of this wilful waste, so soon to be followed by woeful want involving the innocent with the guilty. Neither warning nor entreaty of their elders could restrain the young men from the senseless massacre of the innocent herds of the universal purveyor of the prairie Indian. (p. 297)

Cowie describes here the consequences of the Company involvement in the bison economy: the economic value of the animals encouraged the tribes to increase their slaughtering, tipping the balance against survival of the species. The Indians had never known conservation: their relatively small population, and purely domestic use of the bison provided a built-in limit on the numbers of animals killed, but throughout the history of the bison economy in the Great Plains the evidence suggests that more animals were killed than the Indians could actually use. Even in prehistoric bison kill sites, the depth and character of the bone deposits indicates that sometimes no more than half of the animals slaughtered were utilized, although the vast numbers of the animals prevented serious decimation. However, with the breakdown of the restriction of the animals for domestic use, the balanced ecology of the system was destroyed, and the Indians went on a rampage. The Indians were encouraged by their belief that their connections with the fur and commercial bison trade would provide them with support for an indefinite period.

With the bison disappearing in Canada—before they did in the United States—the Company built new posts in the west, closer to the Jasper region, and began sending out regular trading parties to the Indians in the area, thus increasing contact. The Métis people, always employed to some extent as cart drivers to pick up furs and bison products, came into their own during this period ('60's and '70's), since large numbers of them were hired by the Company as hunters, trader middlemen, interpreters, and in other liaison capacities. Since Cree-derived Métis and tribal Cree were now in much closer contact, the distinction between the two began to blur. By the time the Royal Northwest Mounted Police established their pioneer post in the Cypress Hills, the Jasper Cree were a mixed group of true Plains Cree, with a few French and English Métis and odds and ends of the "allied tribes"—particularly Assiniboine.

Another factor which hastened the breakdown of the Plains culture and the integrity of the tribal groups were the great smallpox epidemics of the late eighteenth and late nineteenth centuries—caused by the increased contacts of whites with the tribes and by the large concentrations of Indians brought together by the stepped-up bison hunting operations. Historians of the epidemic have pointed out that the debilitating effects

had by 1873 virtually eliminated warfare among the old con-
tenders in the northern Plains, the year of the last battle between
Blackfoot and Cree. The Cree were never again able to muster
a coherent front for tribal warfare. These epidemics depleted
the ranks of the tribes, reduced their vitality and determination
to control their involvements with whites, and discouraged their
resistance to contact and settlement. It was not until after the
1869–70 epidemic that American whiskey and fur-traders were
able to open a post in Blackfoot country in southern Alberta,
not far from Jasper, and to use the area as a channel for
hide shipments south into the United States.

Thus as the bison vanished and smallpox sapped the vitality of the tribes, the whites moved in, and after 1871 the
whiskey trade became a major factor in the northern Plains.
The Cree and Assiniboine became dependent on the Indian
agency of the Canadian Northwest Territories, after 1871 the
successor of the Hudson's Bay Company in the area, and a few
bands began to move north into the reserves allotted to them.
The whiskey traders moving into the vacuum created by the
withdrawal of the Company from whiskey trading, instigated a
series of disorderly episodes, one of the most famous of which
was the Cypress Hills Massacre; a slaughter of thirty-odd Assiniboine by a dozen wolf-hunters from Montana, in a coulee in the
Hills in the heart of the Jasper region. In 1883, the Canadian
government decided to organize a frontier constabulary, and in
1874, Colonel McCleod's 300 pioneer Royal Northwest Mounted
Police rode and marched all the way west to establish a fort
in the Cypress Hills and one in southern Alberta. This stopped
the whiskey trade.

But it did not solve the Indian problem. The tribes, now
augmented by refugees from the Indian wars in the United
States, congregated around the forts by the thousands, rioting,
drinking, begging, demanding support, and refusing to head
north to the new reserves. The Mounties dealt with the problem
in their inimitable way, enforcing order by stern but fair
rule, exerting a moral authority as well as a punitive stance.
White settlers—mainly the pioneer ranchers, began filtering
into the area, and the Mounted Police succeeded in preventing

Indian attacks on these people. Thus the Canadian Plains Indian did not become the setting for major and destructive Indian wars for a combination of reasons: the smallpox, the destruction of the bison herds, and the peculiar good timing and consistent law-enforcement of the Mounties.

In 1885 occurred the second and major Riel Rebellion. Louis Riel was a sometime schoolteacher, reformer, politician, and agitator who had aroused the Métis in 1869, was defeated (or rather, his force evaporated at the appearance of a small punitive expedition) and exiled, and then returned in the 1880's to rally the Métis and their Indian allies against the land survey and settlement policies of the new Dominion. These policies, developed by Eastern politicians out of touch with the history of the old West, were working out so as to deprive the Métis of their control over lands along the Saskatchewan River system. The Métis were a "non-people": they had signed no treaties with the government and had no access to food or free distribution of agricultural equipment. Riel invited the Indians to participate in the Rebellion in the hope of securing better terms with the government, and Poundmaker, a Cree leader, accepted. After a series of small battles, which generally ended in favor of the Cree or Métis, the latter were defeated decisively in a major engagement by General Middleton and a mixed force of militia and Mounties, and the Rebellion was over. Louis Riel, an eccentric with genuine heroic qualities, was hanged— an act Canadians continue to regret.

The end of the Rebellion marked the end of the relatively free Indian occupancy of the Plains. The policy of forcible removal delayed for want of adequate preparation in the northern reserves, now had to be carried out to clear the way for settlement. For a few years after 1879 there had been an Indian agricultural training farm near Jasper, on the north slope of the Hills, but this was abandoned in order to remove all Indians comfortably north of the CPR tracks. Small groups of Indians returned to the hills, however, saying that they had been promised a reserve there. A small reserve was eventually established for them about 1915—although to this day the Jasper Band is listed as "non-treaty." The population was, and remains, a microcosm of the ethnic composition of the Plains Cree in the last days of the 1870's and '80's: many French family names; mostly Cree-speaking; with at least one Assiniboine family.

Associated with them, but not legally considered "Indians," and not members of the official Band List of the reserve, were about ten families of Métis, who occupied small, substandard ranch properties or retirement shacks in various portions of the Hills. Most of these were descendants of Métis who had worked for the Mounties as scouts. Several families had intermarried with the official Indians of the reserve: in their physical appearance, their economic adaptations to the Jasper region, and their integration into the social life of the Band itself, they were practically indistinguishable from Band Indians.

There are no reliable eye-witness accounts of the life of the Jasper Indians before and during the early reservation period in the Cypress Hills, but during the nineteenth and early twentieth century the Northwest Mounted Police published annual reports which sometimes mentioned the Indians and the dealings the Police had with them. One of the most colorful of these accounts is found in the annual report of the Commissioner for a year in the early 1880's. Here is a passage from it that also gives other details that help define the atmosphere of the old Jasper frontier:

The Office of the Commissioner
North-West Mounted Police
Regina, N.W.T., 1st January, 188—

Sir,——— I have the honour to submit herewith my Annual Report for the year ending 31st December, 188—.

In January last I acknowledged the receipt of your letter of the 28th December, 188—, with which you enclosed, for my information and guidance, copies of correspondence from Washington, U.S., relating to the notice given by the United States Government of possible collision between their troops and bands of Indians in the Milk River country. Such collision was feared from the fact of representations having been made to the United States Government to the effect that the portion of the country above alluded to was overrun by half-breeds, Crees, hostile Sioux and armed Yanktons, as well as the presence of white hunters in their midst. Had the intervention of the United States troops been considered necessary, it was then assumed that such collision might take place in the vicinity of the Canadian frontier. You therefore directed me to notify the officer commanding our post at Wood Mountain, in order to place him on his guard in case of such contingency arising.

I therefore promptly gave instructions to the officers commanding our posts at Wood Mountain and Fort Smith, forwarding them copies of the correspondence from Washington, and directing that, should there be any foundation for the reports which had reached the United States Government, I was to be advised thereof.

Happily, the fears entertained by that Government were not realized. On the 27th of January last I forwarded you a report on the subject from Inspector Macdonell, the officer commanding our post at Wood Mountain, which report it is needless here to recapitulate, further than to add he was not of opinion that any of our halfbreeds and Indians were at that time south of the International Boundary Line, nor did he consider it probable that any collision would take place, notwithstanding the fact that he was aware of the evil influences created among the American Indians by the presence, in the American reservation, of a large number of white hunters, described as being a lawless set, principally composed of professional horse-thieves and outlaws. The statements and surmises, as set forth in Inspector Macdonel's report, eventually proved themselves to be sound ones.

During the past winter everything was quiet in and about the headquarter district. The Indians on the various reserves east of Regina gave no trouble. During these winter months, the principal duty that devolved upon that portion of the Division stationed at headquarters was the suppression of liquor traffic; men being stationed at suitable points along the railway, eastward and westward of Regina with a view of accomplishing this object. This, in itself, sufficiently taxed our resources, as the strength of the Division at headquarters was not great, owing to the lack of barrack and stable accommodations that then existed, a large portion of the division wintering in our old post at Fort Qu'Appelle. This detachment was withdrawn at headquarters on further buildings being erected, which supplied the necessary accommodation.

A large number of Indians spent last winter in the vicinity of the Cypress Hills; their conduct, on the whole, was fairly good, though requiring constant police surveillance from the division then stationed at Fort Smith.

Track-laying on the Canadian Pacific Railroad ceased in the month of January, at a point some 12 or 13 miles eastward of the station now known as Jasper. Several parties of workmen employed by the railway company wintered in the Cypress Hills, cutting and getting out timber. These men, ignorant of Indian habits, were on different occasions needlessly alarmed by rumours that reached them of the hostile intentions of the Indians in the vicinity. On one occasion, a timid attempt was made by a few Indians to stop their work; such attempt at intimidation was prompted on the part of the Indians by a desire to procure presents of food from the contractors. On representation being made to the officer commanding at Fort Smith, prompt and effectual steps were taken to secure quietude and prevent any similar occurrence. On this subject Superintendent Shurtliffe reports to me as follows:——

"On the 7th inst. Mr. La France, a railway contractor, who was cutting ties in the neighbourhood of Jasper, came to me and complained that a body of Indians, under 'Front-man,' had visited his camp and forbidden them to cut any more timber, saying that it was the property of the Indians, and that they had also demanded provisions from them.

"Mr. La France and his men being thoroughly frightened, at once left the bush and repaired to the police outpost at Jasper and claimed protection.

"On hearing Mr. La France's complaint, I sent for 'Front-man,' and explained that it was a very serious matter to interfere with any men working in connection with the railway, and convinced him that it would not be well for him or any other Indian to do anything having a tendency to obstruct the progress of the road.

"On being assured that he would have no further trouble, Mr. La France resumed work. . . ."

During the month of April, work was resumed on the Canadian Pacific Railway, and large numbers of men and horses were pushed forward to the end of the track by that Company. With this began what may be termed the commencement of our season's work. Order had to be maintained among the railway navvies, and every effort used for the prevention of whiskey smuggling. As the track-laying proceeded westward towards Medicine Hat, I found it necessary to place a strong detachment at the point. This detachment rendered excellent service. Owing to the heavy nature of the engineering work, through the Seven Persons Coulee to Medicine Hat, this latter place was for a considerable time considered as a terminus, where large bodies of men were collected, and where a settlement at once grew up. This being the case the services of our detachment were in constant demand in the suppression of liquor traffic, the prevention of horse stealing, quelling small strikes, and generally maintaining order. . . .

As an evidence of the exertion we put forward, with a view of preventing any horses stolen from American territory remaining in this country, I may quote the following extract from a report made me, by the officer commanding our post at Jasper, which bears on horse stealing during the past summer. "Three men came in from I.C. Baker & Co.'s ranch, in Montana, and stated that a war party of Cree Indians had stolen thirty-four head of their best horses. On discovering their loss, they at once followed up the Indian trail; they arrived at Fort Smith a little in advance of the Indians. The raiders, on reaching the Cypress Hills, had divided into three parties, each of whom followed a separate trail to their camp, which was about 30 miles from Fort Smith. Within half an hour after the arrival of these men, I had a detachment of ten men, under Sergeant Paterson, on their way to intercept the raiders. When 10 miles out they overtook seven Indians with seventeen head of horses.

"Sergeant Paterson at once arrested them, and sent horses and Indians to Fort Smith, in charge of four men. On arriving within 6 miles of the camp, he saw another party of Indians with more of the stolen horses. These were also sent to the Fort.

"On reaching the camp, Sergeant Paterson found the balance of the horses stolen, with the exception of three, which the Indians afterward stated they left on the way. J. G. Baker's men were on their way to Montana with the recovered horses within twelve hours after their bringing in the tidings of the theft. The eleven arrested Indians of the party were afterwards sentenced to two years in the Manitoba Penitentiary. So far as our Indians were concerned, this summary justice had the effect of putting an end to their raiding expeditions. . . ."

JASPER INDIANS TODAY

The 1960's population of the Jasper reserve had few connections with the original group under "Front-man" that remained in the Hills after the removal. Only two families could be considered to be descendants of the original band; the remainder were Indians or transitional Indian-Métis who had joined the Jasper group in subsequent decades. In fact, during the period of our research, at least three Jasper Indians departed and as many joined, or "drifted in" as the whites have it, from northern reserves or Montana. (There is a comparable reservation of half-Cree half-Cherokee people south of the Jasper region, across the line in the United States.) All of these people migrate relatively freely when the spirit moves them or when the promise of a job invites from enclave to enclave in the northern Plains. Without a permanent footing in the economy—no cash surplus to provide roots—there is nothing to stop them from doing so.

The Jasper reserve was considered by the Indian Affairs Branch as a marginal and very difficult case. It was too small to attract massive support, and its society was too disorganized to absorb the limited help that slender budgets could give it; the bureau felt that the reserve would be better disbanded and its members distributed to the northern Cree reserves. This plan was offered to the Jasper Indians in the early 1950's, but they rejected it on the basis of the poverty and immorality of the northern reserves, and probably out of general mistrust of white authority. By the 1960's, the condition of the Jasper Indians, and their role in the regional society, had deteriorated considerably.

The official residence of the Jasper Indians was their reserve in the Cypress Hills, about 20 miles southeast of Jasper town. The altitude is 3,700 feet; much of the land is covered with a dense aspen forest consisting mainly of very old and very young trees: the middle-size specimens have nearly all been cut by the Indians to sell as fenceposts. The area has a number of springs and running brooks, and does not want for water, although the Indians have permitted some of these sources to become polluted. The forest is alive with colorful wildflowers from June through October, and a variety of edible berries abound, some of which are picked and eaten by the Indians, or sold to the ranchers nearby. (However, wild foods do not form a significant part of Indian diet or income.) At the edge of the forest, great vistas of the Plains can be seen, and to the north, the town of Jasper can be picked out far below by the flashes of light reflected from its aluminum-painted grain elevator along the CPR tracks.

The few neighbors of the Indians consist of the ranchers with pasture land on the "Bench," a local name used for this part of the Hills. These people were considered to be the "rougher type of rancher" by other Jasper residents; their "spreads" had small pasture areas, they used casual methods of management and had a reputation for cheerful violence and horseplay, much of it carried out with the Indians. To the southeast of the reserve was a Hutterian colony, but at the time of our research the Indians and Hutterites had no dealings with each other; Hutterites regarded Indians as pagan savages, beyond the pale, though they also pitied them.

At the time of the study, there were about 100 Indians on the reserve, but most previous census reports indicated that this was a low point: the average population appears to have been relatively stable since 1885, with the number about 125. In 1963 there were 25 Indian children under five years of age; 46 from six to 25 years; 24 persons from 26 to 55; and four who were 56 or older. The somewhat disproportionately large number of children reflects an increased birth rate and, since Indian women now have their children in the Jasper town hospital, decreasing infant mortality. The sex ratio favored men over women: about seven more males. The population was divided into 12 fluid household units of which about six were parent-child groups, the remainder mixtures of different relatives: mothers alone with children and an older person; grandmothers and grandfathers with or without assorted grandchildren from broken marriages. Residence had a marked ambulatory pattern: individuals and groups would move from household to household after quarrels or after protracted drunken sprees in town. Or relatives from other reserves might "visit" for periods lasting up to five years. Children ate or slept in whatever house they happened to be visiting or playing in at the time. Many people lived in tents during the summer, others would remain for days at a time in a tent/jalopy camp on the town dump or in one or two shacks at the edge of town owned by Métis families or those few whites who associated with Indians. The population was divided into six surname groups, most related to one another by marriage. While the entire group had an official existence as a Band, with each person's name entered on an official document, there was at the time of study no band chief, and no implementation of the corporate existence of the group. (Indeed, the "Band Fund" administered by the Indian Affairs Branch contained less than $10!) There was an amorphous sense of group identity defined largely in terms of the discrimination and segregation patterns practiced by whites against the Indians, and implemented by common language and culture and mechanisms of free sharing and transfer of possessions.

The looseness of the social structure was reflected in the constant going and coming of Indians. The whole population was rarely on the reserve at any one time: individuals and families would be traveling in their old cars to pow-wows, Sun Dances, or festivities at other reserves; to temporary laboring jobs; cutting trees in the woods on or off the reserve ("off" was illegal, but constantly done); or simply cruising around. Their mobility was historically a part of the old Cree migratory culture, but functionally a response to the lack of roots and a sustaining economy of the contemporary reserve culture. It was, in another sense, a part of the "jalopy culture" of contemporary Indian reservation life everywhere in North America: the automobile confers mobility on people without definite ties to the larger community. The car is not only a means of transportation, but a means for amusement, a way to kill time and, on occasion, a place to live and sleep. Indians could be seen living in these old cars on the town dump, on the reserve, or occasionally in the yard of a Bench ranch while the Indian car owner was working for the rancher. Jalopies could be seen on every day coming off the reserve for a spree in town, and returning the next day or so, full of sleeping, laughing, quarreling Indians. "Beer bottle Indians" was a local term applied by some whites to the Indian practice of throwing the empties out of the car windows at night, and then returning the next day to pick them up to sell them to the hotel beer parlors.

None of the Indians were Christianized, although one or two had been married in a town church, not out of religious attachment but to legalize the union for financial gain (to obtain the government family allowance). The majority believed in fragments of Cree and Assiniboine folklore, magic, spells, and various conceptions of spiritual beings. Little rituals accompanied many daily events; often before drinking a bottle of beer, Indians would pour a little on the ground as an offering to the generations of dead Cree. Songs and chants were sung in both Cree and Assiniboine; drum beating and singing was a regular part of the "pow-wow" demonstration the Indians invariably put on (for a fee) for Jasper town festivals. Rain dances were held nearly every year on the reserve; the tattered old lodges were one of the interesting sights of the district. The words and music for the Rain or Sun Dance ceremonials were known by all of the older men and one or two of the younger.

The educational situation on the reserve had been a source of anxiety for the Indian agents and white friends of the Indians for years. There had been really no education at all until the Indian Affairs Branch built a school on the reserve in 1958. Attendance by children at the school was intermittent and casual, and very little had ever been learned according to the white teacher in 1963. In 1965, the school was finally closed in admission of defeat and the children were bussed into the consolidated schools in Jasper town. By 1966 it was evident that the practice was having an effect: one or two Indian children took part in school functions and scholarly competitions, and the dress and behavior of most of the children had begun to change toward the white model. There were, however, no children of high-school age in school. It was believed and hoped by some Jasperites that the change in educational procedure was devised in part as a means of gradually liquidating the reserve.

The following excerpts from a brief oral autobiography of a 44-year-old Indian man provide a typical life trajectory:

I can't remember much before I was seven years old. Things have changed a lot in the last twenty years—the Indian's life, I mean.

We used to haul wood into town—that time was use wood in town. I was about ten years old, I guess about '28 or '29. We used to use horses; it would take six hours to take a team to town. We used to camp for the night, then in the morning we'd cut up the wood for burning. We did this year 'round. We used to charge one dollar a wagon box load. We went sometime with my dad, sometime with my mother's dad, sometime my mother, or Charlie or Joe [brothers]. We buy some stuff in the store—everything, sugar, butter, flour. Everything was cheap that time. That time father was live this place. Lived in a tent. We had log house that time like this too, but we used tent when we went to town. Stay sometimes two nights when we finish selling wood.

My father he was cuttin' posts, tryin' livin' that time. That time there was no help at all [government relief]. I think my old grandfather was workin' over here—we call 'im that Gus Anders, but he died. He worked for 'im twenty years, eighteen anyway. Haul hay, help plowin', everything; feed cattle winter and summer. He [Anders] live there eighteen years, had three [Indian] girls live with him, and some boys. My dad was one of 'em.

There was no school then. Old Indian fellas didn't want us to go school in town. Old folks was afraid we would go to war then. That time was war—1919. I guess lotta Indians went that war—lotta Indians kill 'em up East. Young fellas they learn to read they go into Army, that's what the old fellas afraid.

There was lotsa Indians that time, more than now. All pull out around '28 or '29, '30 I think. They can't live very much— this place no good, no work, long ways to town, that'sa reason. Round 1919 there was a big flu here, too, and in town. Lotsa Indians, they die then. Lotsa white mans die too.

We was pull out from here. Left 1936 with my old dad and mother. We went Moose Mountain. At that time die my old grandmother. My mother's mother died in the States when we were at Rain Dance, same spring died that old fella. Lived there about two years. After that two years we come back from Moose mountain. That time was 1940. We don't like that place, water no good, lotsa sickness. No good place.

In '42 died my old mother. So we scattered all over. We tried workin' here, workin' all over the place. My father got married again in '41. That's his own sister-in-law. No more kids with that lady. He met her Moose Mountain, she Jimmy's wife. He went back there again that year and married her. I went then too.

About '39 I start ride horses in stampede. I rode all over. Last time was '57 up here in Greenfields [the Jasper amateur rodeo in the Hills]. Then I quit. I made maybe $140 the whole time. I rode bareback and saddle bronc, and wild horse race. That's all I ride.

I was start bronc riding that time—'39—when I met wife that time over Moose Mountain. Live with that girl there. I was stay with that father-in-law. Had a kid about one year later. Wife catch cold and die pneumonia in that winter—that was about 1940. Then I come back here. The baby stayed with that grandfather. Indian agent ask me sign paper so that baby stay with old folks. He was supposed to stay there and come here when he twenty-one, but he din't do it. I think he married now, but I don't know when. See him five years ago, we went down Moose Mountain for Sun Dance, in 1958.

So I come back here by myself. I stay with Dave [a friend] and we cut posts, we live that way. Was huntin' a little bit—deers and coyotes. I live with that Dave until 1942. He die 1953. For while I work for old George Marshall, nice guy, he treat us pretty good. His wife nice woman too. We start at seven o'clock and quit about five o'clock evening—right time to work and right time to quit. They didn't work us too hard.

But then I was bronc ridin', so I went East maybe two-three weeks. We work out winters, maybe sometime spring, summer.

Then we go ridin'. Lotsa work then, but not no more. I guess the ranchers got lotsa machinery now, they don't need no man now. . . .

Several patterns are typical and important: the confusion over dates and the imprecision of relating movements and experiences; the lack of roots in any one place and the willingness to roam, making a living where one can; the casual ties between relatives; the sense of a deteriorating role for the Indian in Jasper.

ECONOMIC ADAPTATIONS

Jasper Indians seem to have made a low but steady income down to about World War II. While their economic behavior was casual and intermittent, there were a number of income-producing activities which were always available. At different times, they concentrated on farm and ranch labor, manual labor in town, cutters and salesmen of firewood and fenceposts, trappers, hide-tanners, and craftsmen who made beadwork moccasins, and polished bison horns for local sale and for travelers on the CPR trains stopping at Jasper, or for tourists at the park in the Hills. With a more assured income, and with memories of the old frontier still fresh, they also appear to have been treated by whites with greater respect than at present. Many of the old pioneer ranchers and farmers had firm friends among the Indians; more than one claimed to have been in the habit of inviting Indians to dinner, and of providing gifts at Christmas or at the birth of a new baby—customs unbelievable in the deteriorated situation of the 1960's. Indians were always invited into town to appear at festivals (they still were in the '60's, but it was now a matter of a perfunctory performance for a fee), and to receive honors along with whites. The Indians were an important symbol of the old frontier and the pride the pioneers took in its development. The Jasper Indians were "our Indians" as more than one old timer put it, invariably concluding his story by deploring the contemporary sad state of affairs.

For the Indian by the 1950's and '60's had lost whatever meager socioeconomic status he might have had in Jasper society, although he retained a little of his symbolic or ceremonial significance as "our Indians." But many merchants in town discouraged Indians from coming into their stores; restaurant proprietors, by tacit agreement, confined the Indians to one cafe, and of the two hotel beer parlors, only one received Indians regularly. Their low incomes forced the Indians to be very selective in their business dealings: only one garageman in town would repair their cars, usually knowing he would rarely receive full payment; only one grocery store manager would give them money on credit, letting them use relief chits as collateral (an illegal practice)—and so on. Indians "hung out" in vacant lots, in the laundromat, behind the beer halls or garages, in one old empty building, or in a shack or two on the outskirts of town.

In the period of the study, the Jasper Indians received a small cash income from the following sources:

1. A monthly relief allowance from the government. For a household of two adults and four children this would provide about $85 per month. In the case of families with husbands and young men who worked occasionally, this relief allowance formed one-half or more of the annual income. For aged people living alone, it was the whole income, although gifts of food and clothing from other Indians would make up what was lacking.

2. The sale of fenceposts, which was intermittent, but accounted for between one-half to three-fourths of the income of some families.

3. Manual labor, on an intermittent basis, from ranchers, the highway department, and similar employers. This means of getting income, while once very important, had diminished almost to the vanishing point by 1963.

4. Fees from white ranchers who rented pasture land from the Indians, paid grazing fees for an occasional cow or two, or bought hay from Indian land by baling it and giving the Indians a share. Indians could either use the hay for their own cattle or sell the hay in town for 50¢ a bale (the latter the more common custom).

5. The sale of cows given to the Indians by Indian Affairs. This was strictly illegal; these cattle were inalienable, and were designed to give the Indians a start at ranching. In 1958 the Indians had received 57 head; by 1962 there were only about half this amount on the reserve. Some, of course, had been eaten.

6. Borrowing and begging money; minor swindling of whites for gasoline or beer money; getting advances on wages or fence-posts and then not following through—and similar illegal or extralegal devices designed to provide pocket money or emergency sums.

7. Occasional trapping of small fur animals and sale of the pelts. Relatively inconsequential.

Actually, it is extremely difficult to estimate income for any given Indian family, and nearly impossible to do so for the reserve as a whole. For one thing, Indians were reluctant to report earned wages, since this would jeopardize their receiving full relief payments. For another, since many sources of income were illegal—such as the selling of hay, etc.—they tended to conceal these. Finally, it is doubtful if Indians themselves knew with any accuracy what their incomes were. They kept records neither of income or expenditures. The latter are of course difficult to estimate in light of Indian tendencies to act "impulsively" and "extravagantly" with respect to money, at least from the white man's point of view.

The annual income produced from various means for an Indian family of two adults and about five children, ranged from roughly $1,000 to $1,500, but fluctuated considerably, depending upon the opportunities in category 3. Income in this category also varied depending upon the desire of the Indian to undertake a job which might require his steady and faithful presence each day for a month or more. By the 1960's, the Indian habit of looking for cash rather than steady jobs whenever a specific objective was in view had become dysfunctional because the jobs were too few in number, and those that turned up required relatively conscientious work, not casual labor. When a growing shortage of casual laboring jobs developed due largely to haying mechanization on Jasper ranches, the Indian Affairs Branch inaugurated the monthly relief check. For Indians, whose culture did not value work as a calling, or in general did not accept the philosophy of a consistent "job" to support a family, this relief check simply became a means of avoiding what jobs there might have been. The Indians referred to the day relief checks arrived as "pay-day." Jasper whites who had considerable sympathy for or anxiety about the Indian situation universally condemned the relief allowance as the one measure which had worsened the lot of the Indian—although they were not so articulate about the unwillingness of Jasper employers to take a chance on Indian labor. Their argument was that relief robbed the Indian of initiative and the will to be self-supporting.

In the past many Indian families had resided in shacks on the property of ranchers, working as a family for the enterprise. By the 1960's, this practice had almost entirely ceased. Between 1963 and 1965, it was attempted on only two ranches, and in both cases it ended in disaster: the Indian became increasingly unreliable, going into town and drinking up his wages, being prevailed upon by his relatives and friends to share his wind-fall, and encouraged to steal from the rancher. Ranchers declared that their relations with the Indians had reached an impossible state of affairs, and that they could no longer make these residential arrangements.

The Indian habit of "conning" or swindling whites out of small sums of money was a consistent feature of the interaction pattern, and while it did not provide a significant part of the annual income, it was a matter of considerable sociological interest. We found that in numerous cases, the white knew perfectly well he was being swindled: an Indian truck or jalopy would cough to a stop before the ranch or farm gate, and an Indian would walk in, explaining to the rancher that he wanted to borrow some gasoline, or $2 to buy some in town, saying he would pay the man back next week. The rancher would invariably provide the favor, knowing full well he would never be repaid, and knowing also that the Indians were capable of simply camping in the car in front of his house, saying that there was not enough gas to get further. In a typical but spectacular instance, a rancher agreed to buy a windmill and water pump from the Indians. This sale was illegal, since a permit would have had to be obtained from the Indian agent, whose office was over 200 miles from Jasper. The rancher took the apparatus apart and hauled it home. That same night, a group of Indians crept into the yard, stole several pieces of the equipment, and took them into town and resold them to a junk dealer. None of these instances, petty or imposing, were ever reported by ranchers to the Mounted Police.

The ranchers and townspeople involved in these curious dealings invariably explained them either by expressing sympathy for the Indians, who needed things and had no security or money to get them, or in a comic, anecdotal bluster, regarded the stories as evidence of the rough old frontier way that has such symbolic power in Jasper. In either case, however, the whites regarded the Indian behavior as proof of childlike qualities: the behavior was used as evidence that the Indians were incurably childish and irresponsible. "They're not really adult people, you know—just like children, and you have to accept that." This attitude confirmed the white image of the Indians, and thus indirectly sanctions discrimination and segregation.

But it does more: it conceals and rationalizes the exploitation of the Indians by ranchers whose property surrounded the reserve and with whom the Indians had the most frequent interactions. These men bought and sold Indian property illegally; made deals with the Indians for pasturing and hay-cutting which were to the Indians' disadvantage and often as outright a swindle as those practiced by the Indians themselves. Indians sometimes retaliated with violence: fights between the Indians and ranchers, both in the Hills and in town behind the beer parlors, occasionally occurred. These battles also were not reported to the Mounties, who of course knew full well what was going on. The Mounted Police routinely arrested Indians for drunkenness or traffic violations, or for major crimes, like a rare shooting, but this was the limit of their concern. The Mounties, too, saw the Indians as irresponsible kids, or as "savages," as one sergeant remarked in an unguarded moment. Actually the Mounted Police attitude toward the Indians was identical to that held by them in the early days of the frontier, when they curbed violence but followed a policy of ignoring petty infractions and Indian internal disputes.

People everywhere in this kind of marginal, impecunious position tend to have loose social organization with few organized groups and structures. In their place one finds "personal networks" of influence and manipulation. Most Jasper Indian men had several whites with whom they had a variety of friendly, swindling, and hostile relationships—people on whom they might count for help from time to time, or people whom they could use to some advantage in their struggle to exist and to enjoy life. Indians had these same network-like relationships among themselves: instead of a tightly organized society on the reserve, there was a loose band of people with a variety of relationships of mutual aid and mild exploitation. An Indian family which abandoned their house for a month or so would almost always find a group of Indians living in it upon return; an Indian who wanted money to buy beer would borrow it from another (or a white), and eventually pay it back in the form of a lift to town when his car was running; and so on.

Thus in order to survive, Jasper Indians had to develop ingenious strategies of manipulation of the socioeconomic environment. They were neither more nor less skilled in these strategies than other marginal populations, and to some degree they were manipulated and exploited, in turn, by the ranchers and other whites. Actually the Bench ranchers were, in the larger Jasper context, another kind of marginal group: the least affluent members of the ranching community, and with the least assured prestige and recognition in that generally elite group. Many of them were known as "characters," and in a sense were considered by other and higher-status ranchers and farmers as somewhat irresponsible people.

The ranchers however, were in a very different position from that of the Indians. The ranchers could play the rules of the game of two groups: the ranching community as a whole, and the Indian-Bench rancher community in the Hills. The ranchers, while "characters," still had respect as entrepreneurs, and by demonstrating skill could increase their social credit (a term for a special kind of status, defined in Chaps. 6 and 7). One Bench rancher, raised on an old Hills ranch adjacent to the reserve and accustomed from childhood to play the swindle-and-mayhem game with the Indians had bought a ranch "on the flat" (at the base of the north slope, not far from town), and was managing it with increasing evidence of financial acumen and an interest in developing his pasture land for greater productivity. This man was accepted as a member of the middle-status rank of ranchers, but at times continued to have his battles with the Indians. "Old Dan Hunt—he can deal with the best of 'em now—but he still has his fist fights with the Indians back of the old Jasper Hotel." This dual role-playing by the Bench ranchers was one of the key factors in their unique status: relatively low in the ranching hierarchy, but also the object of prideful anecdotes because of their symbolization of the good old days.

Through the years since the establishment of the reserve the Jasper Indians did not develop a "Protestant ethic" of conscientious work and a sustaining economic enterprise. The slender budgets of the Indian Affairs Branch, and its unwillingness to do very much for this undersized and isolated reserve, prevented it from supplying the kind of equipment, funds, or vocational training which would have been necessary for the Indians to make the shift from a migratory, live-from-day-to-day way of life, to a sedentary income-and-capital-oriented economy. It was argued by Jasper whites that if the Indians had enjoyed leadership which could have helped them to mobilize and use their own labor and determination as "social capital," they might have done more with their slender resources (developed more pasture, or bred cattle instead of selling them one by one). The surviving Cree social organization, however, with its lack of clear cut authority and leadership patterns, its emphasis on headstrong "warrior" male behavior, its emphasis on sharing and disposing of possessions to people with need for them, lacked the impetus for this kind of organization. Added to this, of course, is the fact that the Indians' resources were hopelessly inadequate. When jobs had been frequent, and wood for fenceposts was abundant, and people in town still needed fuel for their wood stoves, these deficiencies in Cree economic behavior were not so critical. And then, too, there was less visible difference between whites and Indians in material possessions. But with the drying up of these sources of income, the Indians were forced back into manipulative strategies in order to get what they wanted and needed, aside from the relief income. It is clear that the reserve could not support its members by agricultural means alone. And, even the old reliable means of income had become corrupted by the situation: fenceposts were supposed to be dipped in blue vitriol to protect against rot, but since the cost and time investment of this operation was considerable, Indians often bought cheap laundry blueing for the task, thus swindling the unwary buyer (although some buyers knew full well they were not getting what they paid for—and found ways of not paying the Indians the full price).

The marginal role of the Indian was illustrated clearly in his participation in rodeos and other local sports and festivals. Jasper people often mildly boasted about the participation of the Indians in the old Greenfields Stampede in the Hills, but in fact the Indian role was confined to bucking horses and steer-riding, the two "rough" sports of the rodeo that do not necessarily require the specialized ranch training, like calf roping and steer decorating, or the elaborate barrel racing and other "show" events. Indian spectators sat over at one side of the arena where no one else would sit because of the prevailing wind and the dust from the grounds, and it was understood that Indians were not to invade the better spots.

At the same time, some of the values of the Indian male were shared with those of the rancher. Masculinity, taciturness, individualism—these are all values which find an echo in the old Plains Cree social organization. The Indians were aware of their similarity, and so found it possible to identify with the ranching-and-riding culture; their participation in the rodeo was a symbol of this identification. By successfully swindling a white man, particularly a rancher, the Indians manifested their equality in their own eyes, and thereby avoided destructive loss of identity. The white, in turn, found his conception of the Indian as an irresponsible child fully validated.

The Indian population of Jasper is an example of a society which has minimal adaptability to natural resources insofar as development of these resources is concerned. It was also a society lacking a sufficient cash surplus to acquire a "stake" in the local economy. But the Indians succeeded fairly well in manipulating the social resources of the white community to obtain a degree of satisfaction and a survival income.

BIBLIOGRAPHIC NOTES

The Indians of the Great Plains were the first to be studied intensively by the first generation of professionally trained ethnologists, since the latter completed their training only shortly after the Indians had been placed on reservations in the West. Some of the more illuminating works from the standpoint of the ecological approach are Clark Wissler, "Influence of the Horse in the Development of Plains Culture," *American Anthropologist*, 16: 1 (1914); George E. Hyde, *Indians of the High Plains*, University of Oklahoma Press, 1959; Symmes C. Oliver, *Ecology and Cultural Continuity as Contributing Factors in the Social Organization of the Plains Indians, University of California Publications in American Archeology and Ethnology*, Vol. 48, No. 1 (1962); W. W. Newcome, "A Re-examination of the Causes of Plains Warfare," *American Anthropologist*, 52 (1950), pp. 317–330; Waldo R. Wedel, "Some Aspects of Human Ecology in the Central Plains," *American Anthropologist*, 55 (1953), pp. 499–514.

The definitive study of the role of the bison in Indian and white culture, and a history of the exploitation of these useful animals, is found in Frank G. Roe, *The North American Buffalo*, University of Toronto Press, 1951. See also H. Clyde Wilson, "An Inquiry into the Nature of Plains Indian Cultural Development," *American Anthropologist;* 65 (1963), pp. 355–69. For prehistoric aspects of Indian-bison relationships, see Helen M. Wormington and Richard G. Forbes, "An Introduction to the Archeology of Alberta, Canada," *Proceedings,* Denver museum of Natural History, Vol. II, Denver, Colorado (1965).

The Cree Indians of Canada were a humble woodland and hunting group and even the bands that entered the Plains and took up bison hunting were unspectacular as compared with the more famous and flamboyant Plains tribes to the south. The standard monograph on the people is David Mandelbaum, *The Plains Cree*, Anthropological Papers, American Museum of Natural History, Vol. 37, Pt. 2 (1940). Another and more recent specialized study is Verne Duesenberry, *The Montana Cree: A Study in Religious Persistence*, Almquist & Wikesell, 1962. A general description of the Cree and their neighbors is found in Douglas Leechman, *Native Tribes of Canada*, Gage, 1956. Material on the Cree migrations described in the chapter can be found in Frank R. Secoy, *Changing Military Patterns on the Great Plains,* Monographs of the American Ethnological Society, No. 21 (1953).

A novelized version of the life of a group of Indians like those of Jasper on a reservation in Montana is provided in Dan Cushman, *Stay Away Joe,* Viking Press, 1953. Some of these people are relatives of the Jasper Indians. A motion picture based on the novel, and starring, of all people, Elvis Presley as "Joe," the Indian who becomes a rodeo star, was released in 1968. A description of the Piapot and Front-man bands and their culture is found in Abel Watetch, *Payepot and His People,* Saskatoon, Modern Press, 1959.

The term *Métis* is French patois for "half-breed," and is applied to a variety of populations representing intermarriage between various Indian groups and Scotch, English, and French settlers. Most of these marriages took place during the period when western Canada was under the control of the Hudson's Bay Company. These people are one of the true "forgotten" populations of North America, and have become objects of interest to social scientists only in the past several years. A good general description is found in Wallace Stegner, *Wolf Willow,* Chap. 4. An available technical study is B. Y. Card and G. K. Hirabayashi, *The Metis in Alberta Society,* University of Alberta Committee for Social Research, 1963. The two rebellions of Métis and Indians led by Louis Riel are described in George F. G. Stanley, *The Birth of Western Canada,* University of Toronto Press, 1960—which also has much information on the Métis people. Louis Riel is biographized in William McCartney Davison, *Louis Riel: 1844–1885,* Albertan Publishing Co., 1955.

There are many books on the fur trade and the Hudson's Bay Co. The eyewitness account by Cowie, quoted in the text, is taken from Isaac Cowie, *The Company of Adventurers,* Wm. Briggs, 1913. A standard history is H. A. Innis, *The Fur Trade in Canada,* Yale University Press, 1930.

The role of the Royal Northwest Mounted Police (now called Royal Canadian Mounted Police) and their unique qualities are described by Wallace Stegner in Chap. 8 of *Wolf Willow;* and two other books, Phillips Allen, *The Living Legend,* Little Brown, 1954, and Joseph K. Howard, *Strange Empire,* Morrow, 1955. Actually most of the literature on the Mounted Police is adulatory to an extreme; there is little objective assessment. The student who seeks the correct flavor of the period can find a good deal in the published volumes of RNWMP reports for the late nineteenth and early twentieth centuries. These include a series from Jasper as well although the reader must be warned that our name for the town is fictitious. The official reports give a picture of a youthful frontier constabulary with its share of deserters, drunks, and failures to "get their man."

The Cypress Hills Massacre mentioned in the text was the subject of a 1959 Hollywood film. The film company used several Jasper ranches as locales, and Jasper ranchers and Indians were used in bit parts. Metropolitan Opera singer Teresa Stratas played the role of an Indian in the usual fictitious white-man-Indian-girl love story. The film, which was not even a hit in Jasper when it got to town, was entitled *The Canadians*. Perhaps its most enduring contribution to civilization was the improvement of a useful back road out of the Hills Park.

The mutual swindling and hostile interaction between Jasper Indians and whites described in the chapter is treated in greater detail in Niels W. Braroe, "Reciprocal Exploitation in an Indian-White Community," *Southwestern Journal of Anthropology,* Vol. 21 (1965), pp. 166–178. The type of adaptive behavior displayed by the Indians has been found to be typical of economically marginal people the world over. Descriptions for two New World Negro groups are found in Norman Whitten, "Strategies of Adaptive Mobility in the Columbian-Ecuadorian Littoral," *American Anthropologist,* Vol. 71 (1969), pp. 238–242, and "Network Analysis and Processes of Adaptation among Ecuadorian and Nova Scotian Negroes," in M. Freilich, ed., *Marginal Natives: Anthropologists at Work,* Harper & Row, 1959.

SIX

The Ranchers

In the next two chapters we shall describe the adaptations made to the Jasper region by the Euro-American settlers, classified here in terms of the two major agrarian adaptations worked out over the three generations of settlement. From a cultural standpoint, however, this is a study of Westerners in Canada, and there is little difference between these people and their neighbors across the unfenced and undefended border. Like their American cousins, the Canadian settlers found a land of enormous skies and refractory but stimulating climates; of vigorous and mobile aborigines, of antelope and bison, railroads and wagons, hope and hard work. The North American West was one of the world's last frontiers, and one of such color and energy that it has shaped an entire literature and dominates sections of the mass media in the Great Society of North America, and even of Europe.

The symbolic importance of the West is very great, since relatively few civilizations have drawn so heavily upon their pioneer past for a sense of value and direction. Perhaps this is merely a matter of chronology; there has never been a civilization that developed as rapidly as the North American, benefiting, as it did, from the urban and industrial progress of Europe. But whether this is a matter of time or a matter of cultural style, the North Americans, and especially the people of its Western plains, have built upon the virtues of self-sufficiency and the lone individual who does everything by himself. Logically, if not ecologically, this is a paradoxical conception: to stress the self-sufficient individual is to violate every notion of organized society and the mutuality which has made possible the vast sweep of human achievement. Still, it happened: the ranch, the farm, begun as a shack on the creek or the windy plain, grazed, broken, husbanded, built up section by section, the soil improved or the water impounded, until in the second or third generation, the proprietor has a *place*.

While this experience was a real one, repeated countless times on the Western frontier, it also became an ideal. Conditions differ today: the individual can rarely do it on his own but must cope with and use a world of government organization, management and supply, the market, of cooperating groups and tax computations. While the values continue to emphasize the individual and his accomplishments, in fact interlocking relationships between individuals, and between them and the institutions of the larger society, have become the order of the day. The Westerner must cope with a much more complex world, and often he resents it. In Jasper, this attitude, as we shall see, is most characteristic of the ranchers, since farmers, out of necessity, established a more intimate relationship to bureaucratic society.

THE SETTLEMENT

And so we begin with the ranchers—the first agrarian settlers of the Jasper region. We have already described how the Mounted Police came west to control the traffic in whiskey, horses, and men which flowed freely back and forth across the wilderness frontier between the United States and Canada— that border which for many years was little more than a fictional line. The Mounted Police and United States Cavalry officers freely exchanged visits; the cattlemen ran livestock on both sides; the Indians commuted freely (and still do); a farmer might have land across the line without even a fence dividing the fields. This was the "Whoop-up Country" of Alberta, Montana, and Saskatchewan, named for the old local term for a horse or cattle round-up. The Mounties established a fort: a colony of log cabins in a great ravine in the hills, and there, before their removal, the Indians camped and bartered, fought and caroused.

The Cypress Hills, long a terra incognito full of grizzlies and guarded by the somber Blackfoot Indians, now became a place of frontier commerce and settlement.

The first cattle and horse raisers settled near the Mounted Police fort for safety and also to take advantage of the wagon trail from the East which terminated there. In a few years—in 1882—the railroad reached a point north of the Cypress Hills, and the town of Jasper was born. Now the cattlemen came in larger numbers, filtering into the hills or out onto the plains, to take out their tiny patch of homestead land as a base, to build their log huts and corrals. They were a mixed breed: railroad workers who decided to settle down; remittance men from the British Isles, black sheep of good families; young men from the cities of Eastern Canada and the United States; and, in increasing numbers, cowhands from the overstocked American ranges on the prowl for good grazing land and with an itch to have their own "outfit."

This passage from an old Jasper rancher's pioneer reminiscences typifies the breed:

At a place called Mapleton, I got a job off a farmer, stooking and helping the thresh. That was the dirtiest house I ever seen. It was full of kids and flies. He had a hard time getting his stooks threshed, as each crew would quit after eating only one meal at his house. In the spring, I hit out for greener pastures, and wound up in Billings, Montana. About 70 miles out of Billings I got a job off an old Scotsman, herding his sheep. He finally canned me because I couldn't get it through my head to let the sheep spread out to eat. I drifted on aways and got a job in a shearing shed. When that was finished, I went on a few miles and wound up as cook's helper on a big sheep ranch. My wages at that place were $20 a month. I next went to Dixon, N.D., and spent a month haying. When I left Dixon, I caught a cattle train at night and sat on top of a car loaded with big steers. A big thunderstorm forced me to take cover in the cattle car. The steers were crowded in as tight as they could stand, so I had to sit on the back of one. I thought the steer would tear the side of the car out, but he quieted down after awhile, and as soon as the storm quit I got out of there. Whoever owned the cattle, whether they knew it or not, had one steer broke to ride.

A majority of the earliest ranchers were bachelors, but as time passed, an increasing number brought or found wives, often in pioneer homestead farm families, then raised big, brawling families of their own. In one ranching district, 26 of the 38 rancher pioneers were single, and only 12 were married—and most of the latter were the later comers.

Here is a typical story from one of the mimeographed district "history books":

Ed Scofield got into the Eldora and Massacre Creek district about 1897. He come up from Chinook, Montana, where he was working cattle for a big outfit, but he got to thinking he wanted to start out for himself. The range was getting pretty crowded down there so he went up to Canada to look things over. He found some ranchers along Massacre Creek near Fort Smith, where he camped, the McKenzie's, the Wallfield's, the Rammel's and one or two others along there. He found a good spot and built a cabin, but the next few years he worked for some of the ranchers to get a little stake. I think one winter he worked in Jasper in the old Wallace Harness Shop there, but he wasn't one much for the indoors. He started raising cows in 1899, and then his brother George from Indiana come out and joined him. Ed and George they set up quite a place there in the creek bottom. There wasn't any land subdivided then, they just ran the cows out together and every spring they and the neighbors would round 'em all up. That was the Massacre Creek Roundup, it was called.

Ed's settlement was just a case of squatting on wilderness land, but by the time George came, they would have taken out a homestead around their shack in the creek bottom, and this 160 acres of land was all they had to call a "ranch." Their cows and horses, however, wandered over thousands of free acres. By 1908 or '09 they would have had to accept a government lease on several sections of land in the vicinity, since the land was surveyed and the homesteaders were coming in. The amount of land in their grazing lease would have been determined by the number of animals they were accustomed to pasture, and the amount of persuasion they could bring to bear on the government land bureau.

Ed and George didn't like the homesteaders, and called them "land grabbers," "sod busters," "mossbacks," and other uncomplimentary terms. But there was little serious trouble between cattlemen and homesteaders—the presence of the Mounted Police discouraged the open wars that were so frequent in

the United States West. Many ranchers helped the impecunious
and tender homesteaders with food and shelter—not entirely on
altruistic grounds, since the homesteaders also furnished a
labor force and some good female cooks! From the viewpoint
of the farmers, the ranchers were rough, untutored landgrab-
bers—but of course they were willing to accept help and work
for them in time of need—which was often. There was only an
occasional disappearance of a range steer or cow, the mysterious
destruction of a hundred yards of fencing, or an invasion of a
farmstead by a troupe of tough old range cattle to scare the
farm wife out of her wits. Guns worn openly were taboo,
also; the Canadian West was not so wild as the American, but
it was just as raw. An old Jasper rancher actually wrote this
in his will:

This is a codicil to my last will and testament, bearing date the
28th day of September 1919, and which I direct to be taken as
part thereof. I give, devise, and bequeath to George Winser my
Navajo saddle blanket; to William Vincent Smith my rope; to
Pete LaPlante my rifle; in recognition of the fact that they are
respectively the best rider, the best foot-roper, and the best shot
in the Hills. Finally I leave to each and every Mossback my
perpetual curse, as some reward to them for their labors in de-
stroying the Open Range, by means of that most pernicious of
all implements, the plow. As witness my hand this 9th day of
May 1922.

The early cattle and horse ranchers came to Jasper to find
land, to have adventures, to do as they pleased. A rough and
mobile lot, they were not interested in civilization and required
only minimal services. An annual visit to Jasper town, with a
horse and wagon, gave them all the supplies they needed
and the touch of "city life" they wanted. In the 1960's there
were still one or two ranching families in the Hills who got
to town only once or twice a year, but the breed was passing,
and the old liking for isolation and the wilderness was, for most
ranchers, mainly a nostalgic attitude. Yet this attitude was not
entirely symbolic: ranchers still valued the long distances between their places, and though their wives usually said they
disagreed, the women seemed actually proud of their ability
to cope with isolation and other disabilities of a rancher's

wife. A few families renounced telephones or proudly described the troubles they might have in the winter, when the roads were blocked and the lines were down. Still, human contacts were never rejected: the ranching tradition held much stock in the friendly gesture: "There was always a meal waitin' for you; you put your horse in the barn first and then walked into the house!" The traditions of hospitality and friendliness are universal in pastoral, dispersed societies the world over: among the Arabs, in Central Asia, and of course among the Plains Indians. It is a functional custom in a world where exposure and isolation can be real dangers and where necessity lays a foundation for reciprocity.

Ranchers, like other people who develop very close contacts with nature, have a streak of romanticism and poetry. One old Jasper cowhand, writing his memoirs in the 1950's, lapsed into nostalgia:

One time of the year things get a little rough for me and that is the Spring. When the south Wind blows soft, carrying the smell of green grass, I get a longing in my old heart for the wide open spaces. As I lean back in my chair, many of the scenes out of the past come vividly back to life. Strange as it may seem, many of these are horses I have ridden and trained. They are truly the cowboy's best friend. I recall the blizzard when my horse brought me home from a cold lurking death. Through the past I seem to live again the breath taking moments when my strong swimming horse carried me safely to the shore of the flood swollen river. (I never did learn how to swim.) Nights of thunder and lightning, out with the herd where a man was thoroughly at the mercy of God and his horse. The balls of fire which glowed on the tips of the cattle's horns. These ghostly lights, mingling with the smell of sulfur in the air, gave a cowboy a feeling of being in another world.

It was also a society that extolled conventions of chivalry. To help a man in need was as important as accomplishing things on your own: helpfulness was the mark of the honorable man just as individual success was the mark of the competent one. Women were there to honor and cherish—the ranch housewife was a provider of necessities, a hard worker when the occasion required, and a companion in loneliness. Open gossip was avoided, but a man could expect to be coolly appraised by his peers and judged for his worth. It was also a masculine culture, with great emphasis on strength, fortitude, and ability to take punishment and privation without complaint. Its masculinity, as in other pastoral societies, was based ultimately on its technological relationship to an animal species: the physical strength associated with the tasks of cattle raising and horse-breaking.

There was a fascination for anecdotes. Story telling or ballad-singing accompanied every poker game or round-up or branding: the day old Pete Smith got mad at his Ford and tried to rope and throw it; the winter night Abe Grant bought the little prairie hotel because they refused him a room; the time Jack Randall went over to his thievin' neighbor and said "next time you take one of my calves I'll see to it you get throwed and branded like the maverick you are"; the big Winter of 1906-07 when a thousand head of stock from the old Diamond-X drifted against the railroad fence and froze standing up; the day and night Eddie James drove that mail buggy through the Hills in a blizzard to deliver one letter. These anecdotes were not just folktales, colorful and apocryphal though they might be, but were cautionary stories told to make points: the rugged, loyal, honorable breed of men and women, the people who could experience adversity and come back smiling and friendly. There was no room on the ranching frontier for the griper and the timid, or the man who stuck to himself. The ideal was not always followed, but the pressures were strong and the total environment of the frontier enforced the rules.

The necessary reliance upon one's own abilities and strength encouraged the growth of an individualistic value system. These values continue to be extolled and form an inner core of ranching culture, as they do everywhere in the West. At the same time, the differential access to resources meant that some Jasper ranchers have become wealthier than others, and have correspondingly greater influence in the community. Still, the emphasis on individualistic and egalitarian values has meant that the less fortunate or competent are entitled to assistance from the wealthier, since it is believed publicly that their position is not their "fault," but due to "bad luck." This mechanism has tended to create a series of paternalistic relations between the larger and smaller ranching families, in which the lesser provide labor and other services in exchange for loans, assistance in establishing herds, and the like. These paternalistic relationships are viewed with ambivalence, since they can seem to deny the validity of "doing it on your own"—at the same time they grow out of the need to believe in these values. A small rancher in this kind of relationship to a big man will often seek to disguise the relationship by treating the latter with deliberate casualness, or emphasizing the use of the given name, to symbolize an equality that is, in fact, denied economically.

There was a strong relationship between the ranching culture and its forms of land tenure and use of resources. The individualism and isolationism, and of course, the hospitality, were adjustments to the dispersed settlement pattern. The ranch houses were never closer than three miles, and the average was closer to nine: strung out along the creeks and coulees leading down the slopes of the Hills. The riders—today, the men in their pickup trucks—would head for town or a distant neighbor with the assurance that along the way a friend in need could be found if necessary. Out on the range, or on the large fenced tracts, a man could find peace and isolation, but in the knowledge that his neighbor would be riding his own fences or moving his herd only a few miles away. The distances did not completely isolate men—for people who valued privacy or isolation, distances permitted them to control the amount of contact they had with others. On the whole, the pioneers who came out West to ranch either valued isolation or were not particularly frightened by it. Of course, a number found themselves getting into pioneer range ranching even though the relative isolation and distances were unpleasant. In such cases, they simply had to make an adjustment. Moreover, early ranching was by no means devoid of group assemblies: there were the usual district dances and picnics, and once or twice a year everyone in a given district would come together and round up all the horses and cows for branding or sale, or go from ranch to ranch, on a reciprocal basis, and have a fine

old time doing it—just as the roaming Plains Indians gathered
for an annual Sun Dance which brought all the bands together
for business, socializing, and religious observances.

SOCIAL ECOLOGY

The history of the ranching economic and social adaptations
to the Jasper region and its surround may be summarized by
beginning with the basic fact that the natural resources of the
region are ideally suited to livestock raising; or that livestock
production can be carried on profitably with minimal special
facilities or enhancement of the resources. The early arrival
of the cattlemen and the absence of a need to invest large
amounts of money in land permitted an easy experimentation
with the environment, and the establishment, by the time
fencing began, of viable enterprise units. While the fixed-tenure
leasing system did introduce an element of insecurity, since
the rancher could not be sure he would retain title, the use-
lessness of much of the available land for farming confirmed
ranchers' use-tenure, and from time to time their own political
action also helped. In any case, the relative profitability of livestock (prices have fluctuated, but less so than for grain) plus
the low grazing fees charged by the government on its leases,
and the generally low overhead cost of ranching—has further
contributed to the economic security of their operations.

Such relative economic security also made ranchers good
credit risks, and they were sustained during the period of the
drought and Depression by local bankers and financiers, whereas
many farmers were foreclosed or simply went broke and
departed.

Economically secure enterprises also led to social stability.
Over half of the Jasper ranchers in the 1960's represented
families who had come there in the 1890's and the first decade
of the twentieth century. Most ranches had undergone orderly
succession by sons from their fathers for two or three generations,
although a few ranches had passed through prolonged periods
of family disputes, particularly battles between sons, and between
fathers and sons. The majority of ranch families—particularly

the old "core" groups of Town and Hills ranchers (see Chap. 3) were interconnected by marriage.

Stability and success in a traditional way of operating the enterprise also led to conservative methods of management, although this was beginning to change in the 1960's. Ranching as a specific way of using resources contains fewer opportunities for important innovation than in the case of crop farming, where new plant varieties and ways of treating and using the soil appear constantly. The straight ranching methods of raising beef cattle mostly on native pasture have continued to pay well; cross breeding has helped, but conversion to a crossbred herd takes several years, and there are difficulties: purebred cattle strains are often not as rugged as the standard breeds. Pasture can be improved with sown tame grasses, but this is often a difficult and ambiguously successful venture. The irrigation ditches and fields can be improved also. It is hard to increase productivity on many ranch units, however, and once a reasonably profitable regime has developed, the rancher is unwilling to change. Consequently Jasper ranchers on the whole continued to operate their enterprises in tried and true ways, saving much of their proceeds and investing relatively little. The most intensive experiments with resources enhancement or breed improvement were occurring on the medium-sized ranches, in the hands of ambitious families who were beginning to feel a need for larger incomes. Jasper ranchers probably could have increased their incomes by developing certain non-ranching activities, such as cattle finishing, but with one or two exceptions of ranchers who went into the sideline business of cattle trucking they rejected this kind of supplementation on the grounds that Jasper's distance from larger centers made such businesses risky—although this situation was beginning to change in the 1960's.

Stability led also to continued individualistic operation, and a rejection of cooperative and collective organization. The exception to the latter was, of course, the traditional voluntary combinations of ranchers for branding purposes. A few ranchers also were influential in organizing the community for the promotion of irrigation. But on the whole the ranchers vigorously condemned the combinations of farmers who espoused the collectivist philosophy of the CCF party and government in their effort to obtain more resources and more government emergency aids during depressions and severe droughts.

Finally, economic and demographic stability also led to the confirmation of the old cultural traditions and their continued utilization. To some extent adherence to these beliefs was encouraged by the need to defend them against culture change, as previously noted, but there is also no doubt that the traditions were strong because the economy had been successful and could operate with an individualistic stance.

As we have noted, Jasper ranching began with horses and ended with cattle. But there were also sheep, and in 1918, the peak of the sheep industry, Jasper shipped more wool than any other region in western Canada. Sheep raising declined rapidly, however, due to assorted causes, with cultural factors perhaps dominant. A man can actually make more money with sheep on a given land area than with cattle, but the pasture has to be top-grade and the management of a flock requires constant attendance. There was no tradition of sheepherding in Jasper ranching or farming culture, and once the casual frontier characters and eccentrics willing to become lonely sheepherders diminished in number, there was no one to take their place. Sheep herding moreover always had low prestige in the West: it was degrading and unromantic, unassociated with the legendry of the cattle kingdom and the masculine rancher stereotype. For these and other reasons sheep production declined in Jasper nearly to the vanishing point in the 1960's— only the Hutterian colonies practised it on a fairly large scale.

JASPER RANCHERS TODAY

Jasper has a regional cultural style and a regional social system, although the patterns are loose and variable. Ranchers were the earliest Euro-American settlers, but after the home-steading period, they constituted—and still constitute—a distinct minority in the population. There were about 90 true ranches in the region, over against about 1,000 farms—although about 350 of these farms were really small ranches in terms of their economic production, if not culture. Since ranchers retired into Jasper town more consistently than farmers, many of whom preferred more salubrious climates, they constituted a disproportionate slice of the town's population.

Despite their small numbers, the culture of the ranching community of Jasper had high prestige in the region, and most of the big ranchers constituted a social elite. As guardians of the old Western frontier tradition, ranching pastimes and values formed an important stylistic component of Jasper regional culture, and Jasper farmers were more inclined to wear Western costumes than farmers in other parts of Saskatchewan. The high prestige of ranch culture, and economic power of some ranchers, was manifested principally by the respect accorded them by Jasper people of all occupations, and by people outside the region. When Jasper was represented in national media, it was always the ranching culture that was featured.

The power of some ranchers was manifested by their influence on town affairs, rather than on agrarian politics, where the farmers were dominant. Jasper town (and its organizations) was usually run by a group of town businessmen and retired ranchers, and the latter were usually much more affluent than retired farmers. Some businessmen had investments in ranches, and some ranchers in town businesses. This was a major factor in the conservative cast of Jasper town culture. a culture not very encouraging toward prospective outsiders who wanted to establish business, and protective of the old buildings and other souvenirs of the old frontier days. The local museum was operated by retired ranchers who carefully preserved the memorabilia of the early ranches and the wilderness: the grizzly bear skulls from the Hills; the mess table from the old Diamond X; photos of the roundups on the open range, and minerals or fossils found on ranch property.

While some ranchers had considerable power in the region the ranching community itself was divided into several subcutural groups (described in Chap. 3) with differing prestige positions. The highest-prestige groups (and earliest-comers) were the Town and Hills Ranchers—really the regional country elite; the lowest group was the rough-and-ready Bench Ranchers; and the Sandhill and Shortgrass ranchers having varying prestige depending on income and reputation. The latter two groups were not as closely tied to Jasper traditions and the kinship network.

These prestige differences among Jasper ranchers were related, but not identical, to the "social credit" mechanisms of status that we describe in detail in the next chapter. Briefly, "social credit" is something that an individual achieves on the basis of certain personal qualities and abilities—especially his efficiency and skill in operating his enterprise, or her effectiveness as a mother and hostess, in the case of a woman. Jasper ranchers were differentiated on a social credit basis as were farmers; but in addition, the various district and economic groupings of ranchers had cultural prestige rating within the ranching community (the community often denied any such thing, however), and in the region generally. Comparable group distinctions in prestige or status were much less visible among farmers. Thus a Bench rancher might be called "good for a Bencher," but this type of qualified dual status label was very rare for farmers.

Ranchers also had their own organizations, as well as occasionally participating in organizations open to membership by farmers and townsmen. Specific ranching voluntary organizations were the roping and riding clubs, usually one for each ranching district. These organizations provided recreation for the ranching society and were also agencies for the socialization of young men and women in the traditions of horsemanship and the skills of ranching horse culture. A regional organization of considerable prestige, the Jasper Light Horse Association, headquartered in Jasper town, was open to all comers, and included a number of farm families interested in horsemanship. The ranching fraternity dominated its policies, however, and ranching people usually monopolized the prizes given at the club's annual field day at the Jasper Agricultural Arena. A few Jasper ranchers also were influential in town civic clubs and lodges, but their relatively small numbers meant that in this sphere they were usually subordinate to the farmers or townsmen. The Jasper Old Timer's Association, another town-based group, tended to be dominated by ranchers since its membership was chosen on the basis of the date of entry into the region of the family unit or ancestor. The cutoff date was 1905. Since most farmers entered after 1905, the membership was heavily ranching in character.

The seasonal round of ranching everywhere is governed by the needs of the livestock population. It is a full year of activities since, cattle, unlike crops, do not have a dormant season. In Jasper the basic cycle had several variants, depending upon the regime of the particular rancher. The winter season was similar for all: a period of constant inspection and feeding in which the rancher had to tour his pasture areas delivering bales of hay and keeping the water sources open and running. In unusually inclement weather, he would need to move his herd into more sheltered areas. If the winter was very cold, he might run short of hay, and have to seek out supplies he could buy. Spring is the time of calving, and summer the period of weaning and branding and the constant manipulation of the herds to ensure adequate natural pasture. Fall, for the Jasper "cow-calf" rancher, was the time of selloff of spring calves and culled cows, but some ranchers wintered their calves to get higher prices for the heavier animals in spring. Some ranchers mixed the two regimes. In any case, the animals need care the year 'round, and only rarely does a rancher have the time to take a vacation. This enforced presence on the range helps to cement the rancher's identification with the locality. His pride in his stability and localism is the valuational aspect of his economic adaptation.

This localism is reflected in his commercial style. Most ranchers sold their animals to private buyers who came to the ranch to inspect them and make an offer. In describing this system ranchers manifested a noticeable satisfaction in their ability to keep their transactions private. The various other methods of cattle selling—auctions, rail grading, direct to packers, through the Wheat Pool—involved exposure of the price paid for the animals, or the acceptance of standardized prices without the opportunity to bargain. Ranchers preferred to feel they were romantic, isolated entrepreneurs with an indispensable product— the world must come to them.

At the same time, as ranching has experienced some of the

cost-price squeezes affecting all agriculture, and as their own levels of living have slowly risen, needs for intensification of ranch resources have developed. Rancher anxiety over the security of ranch lease tenure increased as farmers schemed to obtain sections of lease for their grazing cooperatives and community pastures. Consequently some ranchers—particularly the Town, Hills and Shortgrass people—stepped up their participation in the various provincial and national cattlemen's associations, and have engaged in politicking with government officials involved in land and water management. This has made ranchers more commercially and politically minded, and has brought them into closer contact with the outside. As this has happened, their reverence for the romantic isolation and the old frontier traditions has become quixotic. "Hypocritical" would be far too strong a term, although some of the Jasper farmers used it. All peoples tend to intensify their basic traditions when they appear threatened by culture change, especially when the traditions are still relatively fresh. In the case of the Jasper ranchers, the major threats were economic and ideological, although the mass media and proximity to the town have had their effects.

The Family and the Enterprise

Ranching society is a special case of the North American institution of the "farm family": a kinship group of parents, children, and occasionally other relatives who own and operate a business. This means that the roles people play in the kin group and their economic roles in the enterprise are closely related and can be functionally identical. The situation differs from the norms and actuality of urban society, where family businesses are uncommon and where the vast majority of people earn their living in occupations separate from the kinship group.

The "developmental cycle" of the nuclear family of parents and children and its associated enterprise involves the prospect of a takeover of the ranch by the son from the father, and the eventual retirement of the parents. The successor then begins to prepare his own son for a similar succession. Although ranches did occasionally come up for sale, their very high prices, plus the fact that lease regulations forbade division of the property, meant that the great majority of ranches were obtainable only by the process of succession—or in kinship terminology, the transition from a "family of orientation" to a "family of procreation." In spite of the scarcity of available ranches, the high prestige of ranching as an occupation in the region and the diffuse elite status of ranchers in regional society meant that kin ties were powerful factors tending to keep the ranch men in the region and community. Emigration out of the region and into urban occupations was looked down upon by the ranching population, in particular by the men, and for good reasons, since the only jobs open to these usually under-educated young men were poorly paid in contrast to what they could make as ranchers. A boy would rather work as a cowboy, however ill-paid he might be, than become a garage mechanic in a local town or distant city, and in many if not most cases he would lack the qualifications to become a mechanic. The roping and riding clubs of the ranching districts in Jasper were local versions of the professional rodeo circuits, and every ranch boy (and some farmers' sons) who participated in the local club events had a secret dream of becoming a famous rodeo rider. About one ranch out of 15 could boast of a son who had spent a year or two in the professional circuits, although none had become star performers. The glamor and symbolism of a little rodeo experience was sufficient; both ranching fathers and mothers quietly opposed the rodeo as a permanent career, since they were well acquainted with its precarious income and brutalized existence.

Young men therefore did everything possible to stay in ranching, since this was the only real career suitable for them. Coincident with the fact that ranching culture did not value education for the men (although this was changing) there was considerable evidence that most of the skills needed to run a ranch were best learned in practice, although training in economics and business could undoubtedly benefit the young rancher. But any education beyond local schools, or even attending the Jasper high school, required time away from the ranch, and this removed the boy from exposure to practical experience at the time he could gain most from participation. This would work to the advantage of the one who succeeded, but to the disadvantage of those who might have to find other occupations. One local rancher, known as a bit of a cynic, defined ranching as "the best paid manual labor in the world."

The situation was different for the ranch daughter. The cultural traditions did not include recognition of the woman's role in running a ranch—in the entire region, there were only two cases of this, both atypical and unusual. The typical woman had two possible roles: she could marry a rancher, or she could migrate to the city and be trained in a woman's occupation: nursing and teaching had the highest prestige. While the girl's effective ties with her family were strong, entrance into adult status and occupation did not depend on her position in the enterprise, as it did for the son. Her relatives in the city might help her get established, but she severed her ties with the family enterprise (though not the family itself) once she migrated. Therefore education was more highly valued for women. The role disparity between men and women also led to the common phenomenon of a marriage in which the rancher was a relatively rough, uneducated person, while his wife was a high-school or secretarial graduate, urban middle-class in outlook and appearance, often much more highly skilled in bookkeeping and related sedentary skills than her husband. Such women could be effective partners in the operation of the ranch enterprise, but the role had to be played down and their services concealed or simply not discussed openly. Women thus could be a quiet but important force for social and economic change on Jasper ranches.

The process of succession was rarely abrupt. In the usual case the son began to take responsibility in his late 'teens, with the father continuing to dominate management until the son was in his late '20's. It was not unusual for a father to continue to intervene up to the time of his death. In a few cases the elderly parents retired into a small house on the ranch property, instead of to a town house, creating a three-generation ranch household unit. Residence was usually patrilocal: there were very few cases of a ranch son moving into his wife's family and enterprise. However, when the opportunity of acquiring a ranch required matrilocal residence, the son-in-law was quite willing to undergo it. The patrilocality was thus largely a situational affair, and was a de facto consequence of the custom of ranch daughters migrating. In some cases the pattern was similar to the classic Japanese farm family: the young married son and his family inhabited a small house while the still-active parents lived in the old ranchhouse. When the son took over effective control, the two families switched residence.

The prolonged activity of the fathers in the ranch enterprise meant that the majority of sons had to accept what we have called a "bound-dependent" role well into life. Their subordination to their fathers, as a de facto pattern, clashed with the strong values the ranching and regional culture placed on independence, individualism, and masculine competence. In some cases the dependent role of the son and the continued dominance of the father was linked to the increasing market value of the ranches. As pointed out in Chapter 4, ranches had virtually doubled in sale value from the late 1940's to the 1960's. Many fathers (probably unconsciously) felt some reluctance to simply turn over the ranch to their sons without extracting some of the enhanced value. "Sale agreements" in which a father sold the ranch to his son for labor wages, or on a contract requiring the son to turn over a percentage of the profits after retirement of the parents, were increasingly common. On the other hand, and in contrast to the farms, succession to a ranch by a son did not require proportionately high refinancing charges for developing the productivity of the ranch. These costs had risen, of course, but the relatively high income of the ranches—due to the fact that the majority were "economic units"—meant that ranch sons often had to do less than farm sons to increase their productivity in order to pay off retiring parents or to satisfy their wives' consumption demands. But the effects of the rising costs of staying in agriculture were being felt by ranches, too, and probably would be to an increasing extent.

The incompatibility of these various patterns was responsible for considerable open conflict and hostility between father and son, and between brothers—a theme often exploited in popular and serious literature on the West. The more sons, the more violent the conflict. A typical case would find a father unwilling to decide among his quarrelsome offspring as to who should succeed to the ranch. Attempts would be made to permit them all to collaborate on the operation of the ranch, but fights would soon drive some of the boys away, leaving the scene to the most compliant brother. Sometimes he might also decide to leave, in which case another would return to take over—who in turn might throw it all up when he discovered the magnitude of his financial obligations to his parents. Eventually some or most of the boys would drift back to Jasper or neighboring regions after "failing" at urban occupations, and would acquire ranches through various kinship and friendship connections. These variable patterns of succession were encouraged by flexible inheritance patterns, competition for land in the community, and other features of North American society which prevent the development of predictable patterns of succession, like primogeniture. The land bureau of the provincial government also encouraged flexibility by insisting on skill and competence as a basic requirement for the transfer of leases from one owner-operator to another (e.g., from father to son). Even direct testamentary succession did not always ensure retention of the ranch by the heir if he was markedly incompetent, since the bureau could intervene in favor of other relatives in extreme cases. The regulations which required that a ranch lease had to be operated by a single owner, and not a group of brothers or relatives, forced the issue of decision among the possible heirs or successors, encouraging the period of quarrelsome elimination. The bureau's regulations had the effect of strengthening the nuclear family control of the ranch enterprise, and discouraging the tendency toward operation by an extended kin group.

Thus the solution to one problem—continuity of the family enterprise—creates new problems: divisiveness in the family and violation of the norms of masculine independence. The new family of procreation is aided in its establishment by the parents of the husband, who provide the only important means of livelihood in an economy with few occupational alternatives. But the "price" the young couple pays for this help is considerable in light of the culture's emphasis on independence. A man must accept dependence and financial burdens for long years in order to be able to run a ranch and enjoy the elite status of rancher in the regional society.

Grandparents had an important role in ranching society. Slightly under one-third of the women married to ranchers came from outside the Jasper region, though usually from neighboring regions. Where the wife was from the outside, her parents were much less involved in the life of her family of procreation than the parents of her husband, who lived in the region (and often on the ranch itself). Children whose parents were from the immediate region generally had two sets of grandparents available for affection and help. The most important role played by grandparents who lived in town was to provide a temporary home for the child during the winter school season in town. The cold and the icy roads made school bussing difficult and extremely time-consuming, and if parents had one set of their own parents living in town (about one-third did), the child would be boarded there for indefinite periods. This pattern was looked at askance by many of the ranch fathers who disliked town life and believed their sons would be "spoiled" for ranch life. There was good evidence that they were right. Residence in town did contribute to father-son friction and tended to encourage a "wild" period among boys. Most ranch sons passed through this period, often marked by abrupt departure from the ranch for a few weeks, months, or even years, and there was evidence that increased town contacts, caused by the consolidated school system, was intensifying it.

Growing up on a ranch involves hard work and much physical exposure to a hard climate, and the ranch child is unquestionably a more rugged type than his urban counterpart, and perhaps even more so than the sons of farmers. The need to feed and care for the cattle in the long, sub-zero winters, the exhausting haying operations, and the handling of cattle and horses are all tasks requiring considerable physical stamina and entailing risk of injury. Some tasks, like haying, were slowly being mechanized in Jasper (which has lagged behind many other Western regions in its acceptance of advanced machinery), but the other burdens remain heavy.

But growing up on a ranch also contains some of the most

enjoyable experience a child can have in North American
society. One learns to ride horses in early childhood and can
compete in the numerous horse shows and amateur rodeos by
the time he is nine or ten. Girls are as active in these sports
as boys—the Jasper taboo against women operating ranches
does not extend to their participation in Western equestrian
sports. Boys were encouraged to operate the tractors and hay
balers as soon as possible, since they were indispensable helpers
in an age of scarce and expensive labor. There was plenty of
wandering and riding over the range and in the wooded
coulees, with hunting and fishing, trapping, and an occasional
"trail ride" for all the ranchers and their sons through the
Hills.

The life of the ranch is something city relatives envy and
admire, and the summers were for many ranches a period
of continual house guests as the kinship network doubles back
on itself. These guests tire the ranch wife, but provide un-
skilled but helpful labor during the summer haying season
and the June branding. Summer is also a time of opportunity
for practical jokes and sprees. The tenderfeet from the towns
and cities have the opportunity to fall off horses into the mud
(carefully arranged by their teen-age hosts), to participate in
fraudulent "snipe hunts," to hang around in town on Saturday
night with the ranch sons and the hired hands, or to attend
the community dances in the lodge in the Hills Park. The
visiting girls learn to bake bread and cakes, prepare the picnics
held on the creek banks or in the Park, and fall in love with
one of the ranch boys. Although this visiting can be a nuisance,
and is always a burden on the ranch wife, the custom does maintain and reinforce reciprocity between kinsmen, which could be
important later, especially for the ranch girls.

THE AGROECOLOGY OF RANCHING

Ranching began in the Jasper region with an approximately
equal emphasis on horses and cattle. The last decade of the
nineteenth century and the first decade of the twentieth were
still within the "horsepower" era, but by 1910 the horse rapidly

began to recede as the automobile and powered machinery began taking over urban industry and transportation. Consequently horse raising rapidly diminished in Jasper as elsewhere, and cattle became the mainstay. For a period in the teens, sheep were also an important livestock crop in Jasper, but after 1920 they rapidly diminished in importance, and in the 1960's, aside from the Hutterites, a mere handful of sheep ranchers were left.

The big change in ranching came with the fencing of the range and the establishment of fixed pasture areas that had to be managed as specific units of resources. We have noted how this was associated with the coming of the railroads and the land survey of the West. Behind it also were some ecological difficulties with the old frontier manner of raising cattle on the open range; while its use of resources was not maladaptive —insofar as grasslands are ideally suited to the pasturing of a hoofed species—it was remarkably inefficient in some of its manifestations. The cattle, of mixed breeds of longhorns and British types, were not well suited to the long, cold winters and were also vulnerable to the recurrent droughts and heat. Lack of control of the herds on the range meant that portions were severely grazed and other areas largely unused. During exceptionally severe winters, like that of 1906–07, Jasper cattle died by the thousands, and in some districts as much as 75 per cent of the total herd died. Many of the cattlemen themselves were willing to take these losses, since their wants were few and their expenses low, but the government and the private interests, concerned with obtaining larger returns from the land, felt that farming or limited ranching might provide the answer.

The fundamental ecological strategy of modern fenced ranching is to maintain a herd of cattle (plus a few horses) of a size sufficient to make maximum use of the finite grass and water resources without seriously depleting these resources. When the range was fenced, creating "ranches," the cattleman was forced to calculate his resources with considerable precision—on a trial-and-error basis. At the time fencing began, there was no precise information available which would permit him to calculate the "carrying capacity" of his pasture with abstract formulae, although such information exists at the present. Most contemporary Jasper ranchers, however, prefer to trust their own accumulated experience and their ability to experiment, on a trial-and-error basis, with new procedures.

In order to make maximum use of resources without injuring them, the rancher must control the grazing behavior of his livestock. Cattle, if permitted to wander at will, inevitably concentrate near sources of water, which results in over-use of the grass in that location. Consequently a rancher is required to develop means to force the animals to move over the entire grazing area in some kind of routine pattern. Since each ranch has a unique topography, and ranches differ in the lushness of their grass and water resources, grazing patterns will differ for each. This means that a rancher must have an intimate knowledge of the natural microenvironment of his ranch; the successful rancher is the one who has developed this knowledge over years of experimentation. But there is always room for a change, and slight adjustments in grazing patterns may serve to increase the number of cattle any ranch is capable of supporting; the efficient or aspiring rancher is one who constantly experiments with such alterations in routine.

In controlling his cattle, the rancher takes note of the following: (1) cattle should graze those portions of the pasture lands which have an optimal protein content at particular times. The higher the altitude, the higher the protein content in the warmer months, but the shorter the grazing season because of frost;—hence the high fields should contain the cattle during the summer. (2) Cattle are attracted by water, and by blocks of salt placed in the field for their use. If salt is placed near a water source, the cattle will intensively over-graze the immediate area; hence salt should be placed away from the water source. (3) Cattle tend to move naturally down slopes, not up; hence if grazing is required at higher altitudes, fences must be built to keep the cattle there. (4) A maximal but conservationist use of grass can be achieved by two systems: (a) by permitting the cattle to graze one area intensively, and then permitting this to recover during the entire following year; or (b) by permitting the animals to graze all the fields to some extent in rotation, thus not over-using any field at any time. In addition, irrigation of meadows will provide hay and alfalfa for winter feeding, relieving pressure on pasture. (5) Cows with calves need more grass than dry cows and steers; hence they should be given first grazing in any pasture area. (6) Cows need shelter during the calving season and all cattle need occasional shelter during the winter.

In order to follow every one of these principles, a ranch would have to have an ideal habitat: high fields and low, more than one water source (strategically separated), and low areas overgrown with brush and trees. Naturally not all ranches will have this kind of environment, and therefore compromises and trial-and-error experiments must be made with the available resources. To maximize the size of the herd, new water sources may have to be developed by building dams, or by building new or better irrigation systems for hay fields, or by digging wells; pastures with thin grass cover may have to be sown with grass seed suited to the soil; compromises with grazing may have to be made, and risks of over-use taken. A general conservationist philosophy is necessary to maintain a ranch in optimal condition, but this may have to be strained or violated at intervals in order to produce the amount of cattle needed to supply the desired income.

The contemporary rancher who wishes to maximize his production must know his resources with an intimacy not required in the old days, when ranchers had few wants and their cattle were not confined to limited pasturage. The farmer without livestock, or who feeds and finishes cattle in a fenced lot, is usually not required to know his terrain with this degree of intimacy. His fields are generally flat and featureless; his cropping patterns can be established and followed with little change. The emphasis in farming is not so much on constant manipulation of topography and water, but on routine treatment of the soil with cultivating implements, occasional replenishment of its fertility with fertilizer, or experiments with new crop varieties. *Timing* is extremely important in farming and in farming experiments, whereas it is much less so in ranching, except, of course, when the rancher is a crop farmer: i.e., his irrigated forage plots and hay fields.

Generally speaking, the larger the ranch, the more likely it is that it will have the varied resources and topography needed to raise cattle with maximum efficiency. This rule applied to the Hills and Slope areas of the Jasper region, but was not always relevant to the ranches in the Sandhill and Shortgrass areas, where topography and resources were uniform over large areas. For this very reason, these latter ranches were less productive than the ranches with smaller areas—but more varied topography and more abundant water—in the Hills districts. These facts meant that the larger ranches in the Hills-Slope zone of the Jasper region tended to be the most conservatively operated, since their owners found it relatively easy to raise a large herd without substantial modification of the resources. While they could have increased the number of their animals by introducing new water sources, tame grasses, better irrigation, and the like, they usually did not do so since their income needs were being met by the existing conservative regime.

On the other hand, the most innovative ranchers were those with medium to small pasture areas but with families that had high consumption desires. These ranch families were also the most cosmopolitan in outlook and interests, and usually the ones most favorable to education and most involved in town affairs and status-seeking. Here we have an interesting relationship between aspirations, felt resource deficiency, and economic innovation: a classic cultural-ecological process. Thus while ranching is a localized rural occupation and culture, a rancher can be drawn into town life and consumption patterns if his present resources are inadequate for the needs for stimulation and consumption developing in his family. As one rancher remarked, "When a fella starts building dams and dugouts all over the place, find out what kind of a wife he has!"

The larger ranchers were also subject to less damage by a number of difficulties and disasters which can plague the smaller operator. Disease in his herd, losses in the winter due to cold and exposure, variable calving rates, and other problems can be compensated for by the relatively large income he derives from the large size of his herd. Smaller ranchers must operate on closer margins; an annual loss rate of 1 or 2 per cent in his herd can make the difference between profits or breakeven, whereas a big rancher can take a regular loss rate of 3 per cent and still profit. While ranching in the Jasper region as a whole

was a profitable undertaking due to the low grazing fees on
the leases, and the relatively high productivity of most ranches,
there were the usual differences between ranches based on the
principle of "economy of scale."

This system of raising livestock is, of course, based on fixed
pasturage and on the production of the animals for sale on
the market. It can be contrasted with subsistence herding as
practiced by many African peoples, where the cattle are raised
on open range or pasture lands, followed around by the people,
and used directly for food, as well as for objects of social
and economic exchange within the society (e.g., as a "bride
price"). Tribal people raising cattle for subsistence purposes
must take into account many of the same factors noted here
for commercial ranchers, but the rhythms and causes of particular practices will differ. Basically, subsistence herding does not
bring food and water to the animals, but lets them seek it, or
takes them to the sources. In ranching on limited tracts of
land, water is provided by dugouts and other devices; grass
is husbanded and enhanced by sowing cultivated species; alfalfa
is raised on irrigated tracts and fed to the animals in the winter.
These are considerable differences, but there is also no doubt
that the modern rancher, as indicated above, has to consider
many of the same factors noted for subsistence herding: variability of rainfall, and the need to move the animals to exploit
pasture areas. That is, the need for the modern commercial
rancher to consider the "ecosystem" of his range and its cattle
is an evident as it is for the African herder—perhaps even
more so.

Ranching as a cultural style has intimate contacts with natural
phenomena: grass, topography, water, and animals. The nostalgic
attitudes held by ranchers toward the old wilderness and the
wild species are in part simply the persistence of traditions
based on the frontier experience, but they are also meaningful
symbolizations of the intimate ecology of the ranching operation. Ranchers view cattle as economic objects, but they also
have a mystique about these animals and their own ability to
manipulate them. "He really knows cow, that feller. He can
tell what she's going to do every time before she does it," remarked a rancher about his neighbor. Horses are still functional

in ranching everywhere in the West, since the horse is the best means to control cattle when moving them from field to field, or in the branding and roundup procedures. A horse is not an economic object to the rancher, but a friend and associate. The rancher's pastimes—the riding, calfthrowing, and roping events of the rodeo, the events of the horse show like the barrel race which requires a horse to change course instantaneously, and many others—are all based on the functional activities of ranching. The whole Western style of horsemanship is a projection of the ranching occupation itself, as are the distinctive costumes.

All of these things have been virtually done to death by the mass media, which appear to have an inexhaustible fascination for the ranching way of life. The symbols and activities have become so familiar that the average TV viewer or novel reader is inclined to take them as legend, not realizing that the way of life is a genuine one, and the cultural ecology one of considerable intricacy. The ranching culture developed along with the mass media in North American life: the life had become a legend in its very first decade during the nineteenth century, and this means that it has become a kind of legend for many of its practitioners as well. Ranchers, and especially their sons and daughters, are conscious of television images of their own way of life; at least one ranch in Jasper has called itself "Ponderosa" after the ranch in the TV program. The pull of the ranching occupation in Jasper is thus not only the result of the solidarity and profitability of ranching, but also of the glamorizing influence of the international mass media. Jasper itself appears frequently in Canadian TV broadcasts and in advertisements in national magazines: invariably it is the ranching industry which is featured. The much more numerous farmers are given less attention.

The future of Jasper ranching is not entirely clear. There is probably no doubt that some form of straight livestock production will continue indefinitely in the Hills, since this area is too rough and too cold for the raising of cash grain crops. But it could easily become a domain of community pastures for farmer and small ranch cattle. The same can be said of the Sandhill area. The Shortgrass areas, and parts of the ranching leases on the Slopes, probably will even more definitely pass out of control of the ranchers and be taken over by farmers for community pasture and grazing cooperatives. Farmers, with smaller pasture areas and herds, are required to intensify their use and supply of resources; often they can raise more cattle per land area than ranchers because they are required to, having less land. Farmers covet ranch land, and they have been successful in acquiring a few leases for their own grazing cooperatives—waiting until a ranch lease is up for transfer, or when a ranching family has produced no suitable heir, and then mounting a campaign against the land bureau in charge of lease assignments. Such activity on the part of the farmers can be expected to continue.

Another problem of modern ranching, in Jasper and elsewhere, arises from the changing opportunity cost structure of the industry. During the 1960's the situation was transitional and complex. Opportunity costs of staying in ranching or using the invested capital in some other way could be computed as either high or low, depending upon one's perspective. If one defined costs as high, he would be attentive to the fact that ranch properties had achieved a very high market value, for various reasons: the operator's discovery of their sale value, noted before; the local competition for lease land; urban hobbyists desiring ranch properties as tax shelters; and others. A Jasper rancher making a net income of around $6,000 a year might be making it on a medium-sized ranch worth $200,000 on a cash sale—which means that if he were able to realize this on a sale, and invest the money in certain types of urban business, he might eventually be making $10,000 net.

However, if one takes into account other factors, the opportunity costs of ranching were relatively low. For one thing, the average rancher, as we have shown, was deficient in the training, skills, and incentives for entering other businesses—and these factors must be considered in figuring opportunity costs. Secondly, the capital appreciation of Jasper ranches made them exceedingly sound long-term investments, even though their rate of return was not as high as a different type of business might provide. Yet their returns were higher, and also much more stable and secure, than the returns of farming.

Moreover, even though most of their land was leased, and

not subject to direct sale, the rancher was allowed to sell the "improvements," which in effect meant selling the land at the going price, or near to it.

Jasper ranchers were aware of the complex nature of their economic position. They might experience an inner struggle over their strong cultural identification with ranching as a way of life and their desire to realize greater returns on their investment and conclude that "all us ranchers are hobbyists," since they finance the ranch enterprise, in part, out of their own labor and desire to stay in the country. The prestige of being a rancher thus has a definite price tag. On the other hand, most ranchers resolved the issue in favor of ranching, and displayed pride in their hard work and dedication. Still, the situation was sufficiently fluid to encourage the breakup of an increasing number of old ranch families and the sale of the ranch properties to outsiders, or to farmers. Ranching will probably continue in Jasper, but the era of the old family ranches, with succession and kinship traditions, may be drawing to a close.

BIBLIOGRAPHIC NOTES

The symbolic significance of the west in North American culture is treated in Henry Nash Smith, *Virgin Land,* Harvard University Press, 1950. A serious analysis of the problem of individualism in modern society is provided in John W. Gardner, *Self-Renewal,* Harper & Row, 1964, especially Chap. 5.

The resemblance between the societies of the Plains Indians and the early range cattlemen has been noted by a number of writers, including Walter Webb, in Chap. 6 of his classic book, *The Great Plains*. Additional discussions are found in Joe B. Frantz and J. E. Choate, *The American Cowboy,* University of Oklahoma Press, 1955, pp. 40, 54, 110, 111. See also Gail N. Egan and G. A. Agogino, "Man's Use of Bison and Cattle on the High Plains," *Great Plains Journal,* 5 (1965), pp. 34–43. For some studies of ranching and pastoralism elsewhere, see Lawrence Krader, "Culture and Environment in Interior Asia," *Studies in Human Ecology,* Social Science Monograph III, Pan American Union (1960); Frederic Barth, "Ecologic Relationships of

Ethnic Groups in Swat, Northern Pakistan," *American Anthropologist:* 58 (1956), pp. 1079–89; Rada and Neville Dyson-Hudson, "Subsistence Herding in Uganda," *Scientific American,* Vol. 22 (1969), pp. 76–89. Arnold Strickon, "Class and Kinship in Argentina," *Ethnology,* 1 (1962), pp. 500–15 (concerning wealthy ranching families); Strickon, "The Euro-American Ranching Complex as a Cultural Type," in Anthony Leeds, ed., *Man, Culture and Animals,* Publ. No. 78, American Association for the Advancement of Science (1965). As Strickon points out, the entire North American cattle-raising pattern is derived from the Spanish prototype in Mexico, from the basic cowboy costume to a large number of everyday terms (e.g., "chaps," "hackamore," "lariat," "ranch," etc.). A good history of the early development of the Spanish pattern is found in Richard J. Morrisey, "The Northward Expansion of Cattle Ranching in New Spain, 1550–1600," *Agricultural History,* Vol. 25 (1951), pp. 115–21.

One ecological problem associated with livestock-raising peoples is not dealt with in this chapter: the relationship of the size of the herd to the size of the human population. In studies of tribal pastoralists this relationship develops fairly stable characteristics, or at least displays regular fluctuations, returning to an average condition. Hence a complex relationship develops between factors that tend to change the size of the herd and factors that do likewise to the human population. These factors are both natural and social: e.g., a drought, or a particular form of a divorce. In nomadic or transhumant pastoralists, the human population unit is the herding family. A study of the interplay between various social and resource factors influencing cattle and human populations is provided by D. Stenning, "Household Viability among the Pastoral Fulani," in J. Goody (ed.), *The Developmental Cycle in Domestic Groups,* Cambridge University Press, 1958. In sedentary pastoral economies associated with societies at a high level of economic integration, as in the case of our ranchers, the external opportunities and financial inputs probably invalidate the workings of these various internal factors directly governing population size. However, the general principle of an ecological relationship between humans and animals would still hold, however indirect the influences. It probably applies to much larger areas and demographic groupings, and not necessarily to individual family units. Jasper ranching families were all sizes—there was no discernible tendency to hold to a particular level. Yet as we noted in Chapter 2, the population of the Jasper ranching society was small and stable, the numbers controlled by the availability of government grazing land.

For studies of past and contemporary Western ranching society and its cultural traditions, see Charles L. Sonnichsen, *Cowboys and Cattle Kings: Life on the Range Today,* University of Oklahoma Press, 1950, and Joe B. Frantz and J. E. Choate, *The American Cowboy: Myth and Reality,* University of Oklahoma Press, 1955; Lewis Atherton, *The Cattle Kings,* Indiana University Press, 1961; Edgar B. Bronson, *Reminiscences of a Ranchman,* University of Nebraska Press, 1963; Ernest S. Osgood, *The Day of the Cattleman,* University of Minnesota Press, 1929; Andy Adams, *Log of a Cowboy,* Houghton Mifflin, 1903.

For accounts of life in the early Canadian ranches, see Ike Blasingame, *Dakota Cowboy,* Putnam, 1958 (a long episode in this book deals with Blasingame's experiences on the Matador Ranch on the South Saskatchewan River not far from Jasper); John R. Craig, *Ranching with Lords and Commons,* Toronto 1903; L. V. Kelley, *The Range Men,* Argonaut Press, 1965; C. M. McInnis, *In the Shadow of the Rockies,* Rivingtons, 1930. A graphic, though somewhat romanticized, account of the life of the modern rancher, based on experiences of a young urban family on a Canadian ranch (actually owned by a relative of one of the Jasper ranchers) is Gray Campbell, *We Found Peace,* Thomas Allen, 1953.

For a survey of paternalistic practices in various cultures, see J. W. Bennett, "Paternalism," in the *International Encyclopedia of the Social Sciences,* edited by D. L. Sills, and published by Macmillan, 1968. A study of paternalistic relationships in Japanese agrarian society is found in J. W. Bennett and Iwao Ishino, *Paternalism in the Japanese Economy,* University of Minnesota Press, 1963.

In our discussion of the ranch family and the problem of succession, we made reference to the concept of "developmental cycle" in the domestic family group. This concept was developed first in a monograph edited by Jack Goody: *The Developmental Cycle in Domestic Groups,* Monographs in Social Anthropology, No. 1, Cambridge University Press (1962).

For additional data on the Jasper case of the farm and ranch family, see Seena Kohl and J. W. Bennett, "Kinship, Succession, and the Migration of Young People in a Canadian Agricultural Community," *International Journal of Comparative Sociology,* 6 (1965), pp. 95–116. Additional studies of the farm family and its problems are Harold F. Breimyer, *Individual Freedom and the Organization of Agriculture,* University of Illinois Press, 1965, many references; *The Family Farm,* Subcommittee on Family Farms, Committee on Agriculture, House of Representatives, 84th Congress, U.S. Government Printing Office, 1956; and Royal Commission on Agriculture and Rural Life,

Report No. 10, *The Home and Family in Rural Saskatchewan,* Queen's Printer, 1956.

For studies of the relation of education to the agricultural enterprise, see Howard W. Ottoson and others, *Land and People in the Northern Plains Transition Area,* University of Nebraska Press, 1966, pp. 195, 230, 245; A. O. Haller, "Research Problems on the Occupational Achievement Levels of Farm-Reared People," *Rural Sociology,* 23 (1960), pp. 321–33.

Toward the end of the chapter we discuss the role of the ranch woman, noting that in many instances she is a force for change and innovation due to her influence on the consumption habits of the family and her relatively high educational level as compared with her husband. In many tribal and peasant societies, women have consistently been forces for conservatism. See, for example, Louise Spindler, *Menomini Women and Culture Change,* Memoir 91, American Anthropological Association (1962).

SEVEN

The Farmers

After the ranchers came the farmers, on the Canadian Pacific "settlers' specials" and in wagons drawn by horses and oxen, from the British Isles, eastern Canada, the Midwest United States, and, eventually, from all over Europe. Free land brought them; "the Last Best West," as Saskatchewan was called, offered the Western frontier's final opportunity to thousands of people with dreams of establishing a homestead and a family. The earlier, pre-1910 farmer pioneers were largely indistinguishable from the cattlemen: adventurous types, interested in any way of making a living, some of whom, like the ranchers near town, combined crops, horses, and cattle with small businesses. But the majority came in 1910 and after, and the great majority of these were family men from the country and small towns: farmers, tradesmen, laborers, who hoped to create a satisfying rural civilization with its neat checkerboard countryside and numerous towns and hamlets. In a typical Jasper district, 40 per cent of the pioneer farmers were married; in a typical ranching district only 25 per cent of the pioneer ranchers had wives.

All a man had to do was file a claim for a free homestead of 160 acres, and pay $3 an acre for a 160 acre "pre-emption." To prove his serious intentions he had to build a shack on the original homestead and break some of the land for crop. Many of the homesteaders were interested in nothing other than land: they hoped to establish ownership and then sell out to the highest bidder. The settlement of many of the new districts was thus a confused affair, with people filing and breaking, leaving and selling out, replacement settlers arriving, and the process continuing in most districts down to 1920, after which the decline in the number of farmers became a steady one, with no replacements. The years 1910–12 were good ones from the standpoint of rainfall, and this encouraged the influx. Few listened to the pessimistic predictions of the ranchers or the earlier farmer settlers, who warned that the country was too dry and uncertain for profitable crop farming. Here is a typical story:

We had heard about the land of milk and honey so three or four neighbors and myself set off for Canada by train in the Fall of 1910. I had thought I might go to the Kilgard District but Marty Kungsholm thought he had a better idea so we got off at Jasper. We hired a guy by the name of Jones to drive the lot of us south of the Hills. We drove all around, picked out our claims, and went back to Jasper and filed. I filed blind, on the ————, and then went back to Ontario. The next year my brother and I came out and built shacks and got some breaking done so we wouldn't get contested. In 1912 we loaded up a railroad car with settler's effects and brought our wives out. We got off in Jasper and loaded up the wagons for the trip south. . . . The neighbors were coming in fast. There was Newharts, and Winthrops, and Tuborgs, and Swensons, and the Stankos, Koslowskys, Winsleys, and many others, all around. Every little 160-acre quarter had a shack on it. Lots of neighbors. We had the first school in 1913, the teacher was Miss Johnson, and then there was also Miss Glenn, and a Miss Simpson, old Bill Simpson's daughter by then. We had good times, too, dances every Saturday night in the schoolhouse.

And so in the farming districts the hard work began: carrying off the glacial boulders, turning the tough prairie sod with clumsy oxen and crude plows. The summer heat was hard to bear, and much of the work was done in the cool of the morning and evening, or even at night by the light of the moon. Surface water was scarce, and many of the homesteaders had to carry their water several miles from a neighborhood well. Wood for the stove was nonexistent on the prairie, and long trips into the hills with a team and wagon to cut winter firewood was a routine fall activity. There were no graded roads, just rutted tracks across the prairie, and no bridges across the creeks and coulees. Prairie fires were a constant danger,

the ranchers might turn their cattle into newly planted fields
out of resentment, grasshoppers might eat the new crops, and
hail could ruin them in a matter of minutes. As the disasters
struck, the summer soldiers among the settlers packed up and
left, and the population began to thin out, finally to hit bottom
in the really serious decade of drought and depression in the
1930's.

The experiences of the homesteaders provoked a large, ram-
bling literature of poesy saturated with a mixture of affection
and gallows humor:

> Saskatchewan, Saskatchewan,
> As knee deep in the prairie snow I stand,
> I look away across the plain,
> And wonder why I ever came.
> I want to leave but cannot go,
> Because of blizzards, ice, and snow.
> The lovely vales and deep ravines,
> Of snow and hunger now are scenes;
> The rabbits chew the poplar trees,
> And have to move around or freeze.

The farmer was there to establish a civilization, and in contrast to the rancher's attitude, the wilderness was for him something to tame, not to glory in. He had to remove the brush,
plow up the ancient sod, pulverize the clods, remove the rocks,
and kill the wild animals that might disturb his crops and barnyard livestock. In later times he would modify the natural
contours of the land to facilitate drainage, fertilize the soil,
dig irrigation canals, and fight the weeds that were taking over
the fallow land. All this activity was looked upon with disdain
and irritation by the rancher, who knew that the prairie fires,
the dust storms, and gullying fields were caused by the farmer's
invasion of the land. To the rancher this was a gigantic violation
of the natural principles of conservation and the desirability
of making-do with minimal disturbance of the original flora
and fauna. Some of the rancher's attitudes were inconsistent
insofar as he tolerated wild animals only if they did not disturb
his stock or eat his herd's feed, and insofar as on occasion he
let his herd overgraze the pasture and cause erosion. Moreover,
the rancher had to engage in some of the farmer's practices

as needs emerged for irrigation and pastures of higher productivity. But on the whole, the rancher's natural conservationist attitudes were consistent with his actual practices.

The farmer's cultural objectives—to establish a settled countryside—were in harmony with his form of land tenure: the private ownership of small, surveyed plots. He conceived of the land as divided into rectilinear sections, each under the control of a different farm operator, with villages and towns evenly spaced to provide the services and the social life he needed. Schools were also spaced to give each neighborhood its educational facilities. The railroad built branch lines to the north and south of the Hills to serve the new country neighborhoods, and towns were established at about 8-mile intervals along the line, spaced in accordance with the time and distance that wagons loaded with grain would have to drive to the pickup spot.

Most farmers came to Jasper with little or no capital. Consequently the tasks of establishing a home and countryside had to be shared cooperatively. The man with a team would lend them to neighbors who had a plow; the skilled carpenter would build his neighbor's house in exchange for seed grain; the harvest, an onerous chore before machinery, was a cooperative venture of the entire district, a custom analogous to the ranching roundup and branding.

The spring of 1928 was very busy for us. We planted 2,400 trees for a shelterbelt, and I am proud to say that every one grew, thanks to my boys who helped carry water from the creek to water them. They certainly looked very lovely. Later that spring, we also decided to build a new house, and with the help of Tom Murphy, our house soon went up. When shingling time arrived, all the neighbors came and helped. I had made some beer for the occasion, but it wasn't quite done brewing, and every bottle, when opened, blew up and half went skyward, nearly drowning the men on the roof. We all had a lot of fun. We were nicely moved into the house, with only the partition up, when all of the neighbors came and surprised us with a house-warming party. Much fun and merriment was had by all. We had very nice neighbors all around us, and we helped each other when and where help was needed.

These cooperative strategies, required to establish farming in a difficult environment during a period of rising agricultural costs, prepared Saskatchewan farmers for collective action against the railroads and grain elevator companies at a later date— a movement which established the pooled grain and farmer-livestock marketing systems of the Canadian prairies and their political analogs, like the CCF party and government of the Province of Saskatchewan. The cooperative habits were reinforced also by a number of farmer leaders who had been trained in the English cooperative movement and Fabian socialist doctrines.

Life on the frontier was hazardous, and especially so since the homesteaders had no money, and the conveniences and necessities of eastern towns and countryside were nonexistent. There were no doctors, and pioneer reminiscences are full of accounts of elderly people and infants dying for lack of medical attention. At the same time, resourcefulness and self-help could go a long way:

It came the time when many of the Embassy children had to have their tonsils and adenoids out, so we the people, the Home Makers Club got together and planned to hold a clinic in Embassy. We had an ideal empty building. We could clean it up with sweeping and lots of soap and water. We tacked oilcloth down on the floor. In the back part of the store we had an oil stove for heating water, stands with wash bowls, curtained that off from the operating room. Stretchers were improvised as also an operating table by one of the boys that always came to our aid in making things. We bon ami'd the front windows so not to have the light too bright and also kept people from looking in when the Drs. were at work. In the back main part of the building were rooms used by the owners as living quarters which made ideal rooms for recovery. They were clean and with cots and beds it was complete. We had made arrangements with 2 White-mud doctors to operate. We looked it over and wondered what they would think of it. They were a wee bit late but they arrived and we guessed they sort of wondered what kind of a place they would operate in. They took one look and said, "Well we never expected a real operating room. You people are to be congratulated." We were pleased and quite satisfied with our work. Then the children were frightened but we managed to get them without much trouble. Always the thought with me was hemhorrage. One of the Drs. was supposed to stay over night but for some reason he couldn't. He left me directions and medicine to give, but we were very lucky, all got along fine. No one slept that night and we took turns staying with the children. We were pleased and all said the Home Makers are great workers.

An active social and cultural life was part of the ideal. In most of the towns and town-country districts of the Jasper region the farmer settlers built, as their initial community projects, a school, a church, and a public hall for political meetings and the Agricultural Society. These societies (by the 1960's largely moribund) were extremely important in the early years after 1910, since they symbolized the intention of building an agrarian civilization and also of doing it in close social harmony and interaction. Special financial incentives were given the establishment of such societies by the various governments that controlled the region from the 1870's through the establishment of the Province—the Agricultural Society was as much a deliberate creation as the school districts.

In any case, the farmer settlers were gregarious people, accustomed to small-town life, and they expected to reestablish this life on the frontier. Dances in the schoolhouse or town hall, frequent picnics, card games, musicals, and amateur dramatics were common. Each village and town had social clubs within a year or two after the settlers arrived, and Saskatchewan towns are still famous for their plethora of organizations. Jasper town, with only 2,500 people, had over 35 organizations in the 1960's; so many that leadership was diffused and confused. Churches were an important element in the culture; the great majority were Protestants, and within a few years after homesteading the scarcity of ministers and the general melting-pot atmosphere of the prairies led the Lutherans, Presbyterians, and Congregationalists to amalgamate into the United Church of Canada. Jasper town in the 1960's had 12 churches, and the number was growing as the town continued to receive retired farmers.

As a group, farmers were far more attentive to church affairs than ranchers, although Jasper culture in general could not be described as deeply religious. The interest of farmers in church was linked to their gregarious social activities, since church-going, with its picnics and festivities, provided one important dimension of this. Church attendance was much higher for farm women than men, and highest of all for retired farm people living in town. Retired ranchers in town also attended more frequently than the population on the ranches. There is no question that the relatively large number of churches in Jasper town and other hamlets is to be explained as a phase of the social life of the retired. Aside from this special function of religion, its continuity in the farming community had its historical base in the religious traditions of the homesteading population. Ranchers were on the whole derived from a secular, adventurous stock, uninterested in churches and town life.

The great majority of farmers were members of the familiar large Protestant denominations, but there were also two minority Christian farming groups. In the northwest corner of the region there lived a group of Catholic farmers of Russo-German background, from the Ukraine. These people had come late (after 1910), and consequently were not able to find farms in the better soil areas (the northwest corner of the region was very sandy). Their large families made living difficult, and in addition their farms were generally small—under 1,000 acres. Their religious traditionalism tended to remove them from the agricultural extension network of social activities: 4H clubs, demonstration picnics, horticultural competitions, and the like. Their priest discouraged participation in these functions on the grounds that it was really a "Protestant" culture which good Catholics should avoid. Unfortunately this also separated these farmers from constructive contacts with the Agricultural Representative, who could have helped them with farming problems. This group of farmers had the lowest average per-capita incomes of all farming districts in the region.

The second minority sect group consisted of about 20 families of Plymouth Brethren, a fundamentalist sect of English origin with a few customs resembling those of the Hutterites: emphasis on Pentecost, taboos against mass media, especially radio and TV; and a unique belief that Plymouth Brethren must not eat food in the presence of non-Brethren—a custom which caused continual difficulty for Plymouth Brethren children at lunch time in the schools. In all other respects, however, these people resembled the Protestant farming majority, and their frugality and devotion to efficiency ranked them among the best farmers in the region.

Did the farmers, like the ranchers, establish a cultural tradition? Yes—in the sense that Jasper farmers had distinct ways of operating their enterprises, and of living, and also in the sense that they recall the pioneer days with nostalgia and relish, just as the ranchers remember their own frontier experiences. But in some other ways, the farmers had less distinct traditions. In the first place, the large number of homesteaders and the considerable turnover (the remaining farmers in the 1960's represented less than one-seventh of peak settlement population in the 1915–20 period) meant that a great many kin and friendship ties had been established outside of the Jasper region. Moreover, many farmers had a roving life in the drought-and-depression years when poor crop and prices forced them to take outside jobs for certain periods. Added to this was the outward-facing orientation of farming as an occupation: its concern for national farm policies and markets, for political movements and intervention. Third, the typical farm family viewed its occupation in a more secular manner than the ranchers; with succession less of a possibility due to economic difficulties and frequent migration and turnover, occupations other than farming were viewed as promising possibilities.

THE SOCIAL ECOLOGY OF FARMING

The late settlement in a region of relatively inadequate or variable resources for farming meant that while a few Jasper homesteaders would get choice locations, the majority would not. The traditions of the small, largely self-sufficient family farm were inappropriate to this region of variable resources and low productivity, and these traditions, reinforced by the homesteading settlement laws initially permitting title to a maximum of only 320 acres, led by 1920 to a large number of undersized, economically insecure farm units.

Even though large numbers of homesteaders left the region, especially after 1920, farms did not increase in size as rapidly as one might have predicted. One reason they did not was that much of the abandoned land was impounded for taxes, or put into large tracts reserved by the government for some eventual public use, such as community pasturage. Another was that the conditions of drought and low farm prices made farming of any kind in the 1920's and '30's unprofitable and difficult, and increases in acreage did not help since labor and machinery were too costly to put the additional land into production.

The response to economic difficulties took two main forms: (1) the majority of farmers developed conservative strategies of operation in which much of the small cash surplus was put into family consumption rather than back into the enterprise, since the uncertainties argued against investing in a business which might be wiped out by changes in climate or markets. And of course a large number of farms were literally producing at the bare survival level. Thus for various reasons the farms stayed low in productivity. (2) At the same time, many farmers joined political movements designed to control the financial interests and grain companies responsible for economic uncertainty. Campaigns for direct government aid to farming were also instituted, and these led to the community pastures, the grazing cooperatives, the crop deficiency payments system, and other facilities. All of these movements and campaigns were of province-wide scope, and were general throughout the Canadian prairies and the U.S. Great Plains.

A Jasper farmer, had this to say trying to verbalize farmer habits and compare them to rancher strategies:

The farmer has this quality of thoughtfulness—he thinks, I mean, *plans*. There's quite a difference between him and the rancher, or any stockman. I suppose it has something to do with the fact that the farmer trades with the world. He sells grain to the world, and he buys machinery and a great amount of supplies from all over the world. Now compare this to the rancher, who got his lease land for practically nothing, and buys little more than a fistful, at least until recent years. He needs little and can afford to be completely independent.

Ranchers must be just as "thoughtful" and "plan" just as carefully as the farmer—and of course we recognize that the farmer was expressing his stylized opposition to the rancher. But beyond that, his perceptions of how ranchers and farmers differ with respect to methods of operation, and the implication of how these differences condition their approach to the world, is accurate enough.

While farmers were far more active in politics than ranchers, the ranchers did have dealings with politicians and bureaus in their own interest. However, their strategies were considerably different from those used by farmers. The latter entered directly into the political process: nominating candidates, electioneering, getting up petitions, and in general inserting themselves into the political structure. The ranchers, on the other hand, used the classic techniques of influence and manipulation. That is, while a group of farmers would seek to elect one of their number to office, or to persuade a government bureau to grant a community pasture to a district, the rancher would make a personal, secret call on a government official in an effort to have this official intervene on his—the rancher's—behalf with a bureau. These differences were not invariable, of course—sometimes ranchers combined politically and sometimes farmers manipulated individually—but the tendencies were clear. The difference was related to ideology: the dominant "elitist" outlook and individualism of the ranchers and the egalitarianism and collective spirit of the embattled farmers. But in turn, these ideological differences were related to the differing adaptive postures of the two occupations and to the stability and success of ranching and the precariousness of farming.

As we have shown elsewhere, farmers also responded to increasing economic difficulties by accumulating land from those who left the region in search of better opportunities. During the second generation of operation of the farms, this was really the sole adaptive strategy—farmers were extremely cautious about agronomic innovations and other risky ventures. In fact, due both to lack of money and financial conservatism, many Jasper farmers did not accumulate land in sufficient quantities, or fast enough, to compensate for their difficulties—the conservative management policies while adaptive in many respects, actually worked against them in this context. Their conception of land value was conservative: accumulation was approved, but the concept of investment in land in terms of its future value was not fully grasped. In the 1960's, as prices and the resources-development projects in the region conferred a measure of stability, farmers were beginning to realize the investment value of land, and intensive land-buying became routine. We found by inspecting official records that the number of parcels of land changing hands in two Jasper farming Rural Municipalities doubled between 1952 and 1962. The period also saw the emergence of a social type—the individual called a "land grabber" by local people. Often these men were outsiders—aggressive operators frustrated in their desires in other localities who moved into Jasper to take advantage of the prevailing financial caution that often left desirable tracts of land on the market for a considerable period.

Thus, and although things were changing, the historical economic and ecological situation of farming in the Jasper region, as elsewhere in the Great Plains, was responsible for constraints on economic growth and social stability.

JASPER FARMERS TODAY

The experience of drought and economic difficulty through the years exerted a selective pressure on the Jasper farming population. The results of this pressure (what we call "behavioral selection" in Chap. 10) was most easily visible in the techniques of operating the farming enterprises. We have noted that Jasper farmers became conservative managers as drought and economic depression made farming a very risky undertaking. In addition, we believe that there was a tendency for those men who were conservative in management to remain in the region, and for people with different kinds of management behavior to leave.

The descriptions of the pioneers available to us in the form of letters, newspaper articles, and mimeographed district "history books," as well as interviews with aged survivors, convey an impression of a heterogeneous early homesteader population with good farmers and inept, land speculators and people in search of a permanent home, men who expected to get rich quick on a bumper crop, and men who wanted merely to subsist. Many of these types left in a hurry when they discovered the difficulties of farming or satisfied their speculative objectives. The attrition was particularly severe among the land grabbers, the get-rich-quick people, the subsistence farmers, and the most ambitious, determined professional farmers. The process of elimination continued down into the 1930's, when the accumulated hardships of drought and Depression forced out the last of those who lacked the desire, skill, or funds to make a life on the Plains.

The process of selection also weeded out families who experienced unfortunate coincidences between domestic needs and the needs of the enterprises. We noted in Chapter 4 how certain points in the family cycle might establish needs for higher income, which would lead to enterprise-development activities, such as land purchases, the acquirement of cattle, new types of crops, and the like. But sometimes these pressures would intersect: family consumption needs and wants would coincide with a pressing need for further investment in the enterprise. If drought or unfavorable prices and costs happened also to coincide, the family might well decide to leave. A great many did; of the generation of married homesteaders who came to Jasper around 1910, 38 per cent departed after 1930, when drought and depression hit the west.

Many of the farmers who found it necessary to leave during the drought-and-depression periods eventually returned after finding that their capital and skills had not prepared them for anything other than farming:

In 1936, the grain came up nice in the Spring, but hot dry weather and no rain curled it up in a hurry. I cut my crop for feed. 1937 was the driest year ever, my grain just never even came up. That summer I took all the cattle I had left to Moose Jaw. I had three cows, three yearling heifers and three steer calves. After paying the trucker, I cleared $75 for the lot. Then I went to B.C. to seek my fortune, but there were too many others like me there looking for the same thing. I finally got back to Cowley, Alberta, and I got a job harvesting for $30 a month. I finally came back here after harvest and worked on the dam they were building over on Indian Lake. Then I decided that roving life wasn't for me, and I stuck to farming, thick or thin, mostly thin!

Those who remained, and those who eventually returned, were

the patient ones who were able to contain their wants and ambitions indefinitely in the slow task of building a modest enterprise. We have noted that they did not put every cent back into the farm even when, or if, they had something to invest, because economic and ecological uncertainties made this inadvisable. But they did buy land from time to time, to enlarge their enterprises. They had a high tolerance of uncertainty, and tried to do what was necessary to strike a reasonable average in crop yield—accepting a small but hopefully steady income and avoiding strenuous attempts at "maximizing" yield and income. Reasonably productive methods were retained year after year. Innovative behavior, when it appeared, more often took the form of political participation in movements designed to obtain help from the government, rather than in new and costly methods of farming. That is, the farmer considered that he had less to lose in political action than in cash investments or untried experiments—or, in our terms, the opportunity costs of political innovation were lower than agronomic.

Who were these conservative operators? They were, on the whole, the family men—who were also, in hard times, the people without enough money to finance a new "start" elsewhere. All those who stayed had families on arrival or founded them soon after (the majority of quitters were bachelors or men who had lost their families). Such people also came from villages or country neighborhoods and had extensive experience with farming before their trek to the West. They also tended to be those who continued to follow their sober, frugal habits on the frontier. This does not mean, however, that the men who stayed were the "backward" ones, the less-competent farmers. Many of them had as much skill and ambition to make good money as the get-rich-quick types who left in a hurry. When things began to improve in the post-World War II period, many of these men who had practiced "delayed gratification" for a generation began to move rapidly toward more expansive or innovative policies of management. Their adaptive persistence in the region was thus the result of many factors working together: their obligations to families, and the prohibitive cost of moving large families out of the region; their ability to curb ambition; their strategic patience and frugality.

The people who stayed were thus a relatively homogeneous group insofar as management policies were concerned. Farm sizes did not vary much, due to the homesteading "start" and also to the relatively equal chances of acquiring land from the leavers. This meant, too, that there was no clear social stratification based on opportunity and wealth because these factors were approximately similar for all farmers. The farmers thus constituted a relatively homogeneous occupational group and culture set alongside the ranchers, and all people in Jasper classified the region's country residents into these two groups. (There was a third—townspeople—but this term referred only to the businessmen, very small in number, and not the retired countrymen living in town.)

Within the farming population there were, however, some delicate social and economic prestige differences by country of origin. The Anglo-Americans (people who came from the British Isles, eastern Canada, or the United States) and the northern Europeans (Scandinavians and north Germans) had the edge in number and status; their names were the majority in the leadership categories of town and country organizations, and since most of these people came in the earliest wave of homesteaders, most of them had farms in the better locations. A very few of these families sometimes interacted socially with the group of important ranchers to share the region's social elite category. The eastern Europeans (Ukrainians and other Slavic peoples, and German-speaking groups from southern Russia) came later, had farms of somewhat lower productivity in the poorer locations, and were less prominent in organizational and political life. But there were exceptions to these tendencies, and the status distinctions by country of origin were not as marked as they would have been in urban centers with their teeming immigrant populations in lower-income positions.

The European ethnic cultures of Jasper, like those of other Great Plains areas, were dealt a severe blow by the need to conform to the dominant Anglo-American majority; by marriage to available mates, often not to be found in one's own group, and by the uniform pressures of economic marginality and climatic disaster. For all ethnic groups in the first generation, farming techniques, food habits, interior house decor, a few items of clothing, and churches were established on the Old Country pattern, but nearly all of these specific customs had disappeared by the time the second generation had taken over. For the eastern Europeans, by the 1960's the aging second-generation operators of the farms had also lost most of their feeling of ethnic identity, all but one of the orthodox churches had gone, and relatively few confident speakers of the old languages (Ukrainian, Russian, Polish) were left. The third generation, mostly married to non-eastern European wives, was securely and wholly Canadian-North American. On the other hand, the northern Europeans, with their more secure and "high-status" ethnic identity, clung more successfully to their churches, feelings toward the Old Country, and even made it a point to visit Europe (Scandinavia, Germany) when finances made this possible. But even among these people, ethnic culture was probably weak if compared with the relatively higher rate of survival of old customs and identity in many urban areas.

Since the farms of their fathers and grandfathers were in most cases unprofitable enterprises, the out-migration rate among the eastern European groups was higher than for the Anglo-American and north-central European settler families. The process was hastened, in some cases, by the custom of dividing the already marginal farmland among two or more sons at the death or retirement of the father—an old eastern European peasant custom. This created, in some districts, two or more substandard enterprises that were hardly inviting for the sons to take over or to stay with. In one district that underwent this pattern of devolution, the Hutterian Brethren found it easy to buy up the remaining farms, providing an example of "competitive replacement," as we call the process in Chapter 10.

The kinship networks of ranchers and farmers differed in the extent of their connections. On the whole, the ranchers represented a single interconnected kin network, although, as we noted in Chapter 3, two subgroups—Town and Hill—were more closely knit than the others. But on the whole ranchers, as a small highly intermarried segment of the regional population (not over six hundred people) presented a common front as a kind of kinship society, and were recognized as such by both themselves and the farmers. Farmer kinship, on the other hand, was less extensive on a regional basis. The farming population, being much larger than the ranching (about 4,000 persons), was divided into district groupings reflecting the old solidaristic homestead settlements and the local school districts and villages that cemented local ties. Marriages were more frequently made within these districts than outside of them, forming particular local kinship networks. Ranchers, being few in number and sparsely distributed, had to look farther away for their mates. The practice of ranchers selecting farm girls as wives in districts near ranching areas (whereas very few farmers selected ranch girls) also tied farmers to the ranching families, creating networks that united the two occupational groups in particular localities. These ties were not numerous, however, and when intermarriage did occur, the farm family was considered to be linked to the ranching network, not the other way around. On the whole, ranch and farm kinship networks were separate, and the two occupational groups were largely endogamous. While the regional kin ties of the ranchers helped define their traditions and their intense regional localism, paradoxically the more integral district communities of farmers helped to intensify their tendency to look outside the region for their wider affiliations.

While the ranching districts were ranked on a prestige basis, farming districts were considered to be of more or less equal rank. However, in both farming and ranching districts, individuals were assigned ratings of personal worth or credit based on economic and social behavior. Ranchers thus had district *and* credit-status; farmers had only credit-status, or the qualities of a "good man" in degrees. The factors most often cited in describing a "good man" were: (1) sobriety and perseverance; (2) frugality and cautious investment and management practices; (3) cheerfulness in adversity; (4) cooperativeness and willingness to help a neighbor in need; (5) the ability to provide well for a family; and (6) friendliness and an easy-going tolerant disposition. Few men had all of these qualities, and particularly strong capabilities in some could overbalance deficiencies in other. For example, a man who drank and caroused would be excused if he was a very good farm operator. In addition, a man who had winning personality traits but who was a bad manager and a poor provider could attain a special "character" status: appreciated and laughed at and with, but not taken seriously.

These criteria were used to define what we have called a man's "social credit." A man could accumulate this credit by demonstrating increased capacity and capability as defined by the criteria above. That is, a man who slowly changed from an undependable marginal type to a good manager and friendly person would accumulate credit. Quite often a man's wife would be considered responsible for the change and development, but this did not detract from the credit assigned her husband. Once a man had accumulated social credit, it would be hard for him to lose it. Even if his behavior changed for the worse, allowances would be made for some time, although a complete and permanent reversal would eventually lose him his credit status. Women were judged on a similar basis, although the criteria emphasized homemaking skills. They add up to a factor of personality we might call "niceness": a sweet, tolerant, winning, softly intelligent disposition, often concealing a strong will and a way of getting what a woman wants.

The choice of these particular qualities for defining the credit status of the men was associated with the public atmosphere in which every man conducted his farming (or ranching) enterprise. The farm is open to the view of all who drive by; the conditions of the buildings, crops and summerfallow, the cattle, pastures, irrigation ditches, and many other things are visible and the experienced resident can, with little more than a quick glance, provide a remarkably accurate financial balance sheet for the particular farm or ranch. The society and economy of the farmers, as we have indicated, was remarkably homogeneous, and there were few criteria available for conferring status other than these personal managerial qualities and disposition factors. A man is what he does in Jasper. Although the credit-allocation mechanism is similar, the situation was somewhat more complicated for the ranchers, where a wider range of income and cultural patterns (particularly the rough Bench types versus the Town and Hills ranchers) provided additional criteria for status.

There was a tendency for men with similar (high or low) credit ratings to associate together for purposes of exchanging labor and other things necessary for the successful pursuit of agriculture. We have mentioned these exchange networks in other contexts. In many cases, but by no means not all, families and relatives would be drawn into the exchange relationship and the network would develop into a true social group. If the men were of similar social credit rating, then we would have something that looked like a "social class." However, as often as not the exchange relationship would be confined to the men, and the same families would participate in other types of associative networks for their social life. The reason why men of similar credit ratings *did* tend to exchange or associate was simply that such men would have similar ways of operating their enterprises —hence practical grounds for the association would exist. In our judgment, and in that of informants also, these practical reasons were always more important than any criteria of social status or cultural prestige:

Well . . . now, when I need help I go to the men who'll give it and does it my way. I don't care what kinda clothes he wears or what his wife and kids look like, you know! But when it comes to a good card game or something like that a fella naturally goes to people he feels pretty much the same with.

As among ranchers, a farmer also could gain prestige on the basis of his length of stay. Families who had been in the region from the beginning—that is, who had stayed through the disaster years—could gain approbation: we called it "hardship status." It was analogous to the "settlement status" of the ranchers, based on the date of entry. Since nearly all farmers came about the same time, the prestige was displaced toward the experiences of the drought-and-depression years. However, hardship or settlement status was less important than credit gained through the mode of operation of the enterprise.

In the preceding chapter we mentioned the tendency for paternalistic relationships to develop among larger and smaller ranchers, based on the need to equalize opportunity in a culture of economic differentiation because of differences in resources emphasizing individualism and egalitarianism, but with a degree and skills. A few poor farmers also had these relationships with the big ranchers—in many cases a holdover or continuation of the frontier practice of ranchers hiring impecunious homesteaders as ranch hands. These relationships had the expectable strains stemming from the tension between ranching and farming as competitive uses of resources. Paternalistic inequalities were not found among farmers themselves, because of the prevailing uniformity of farm size and productivity.

The social life of the contemporary farmers was, if we can believe the pioneer reminiscences, less intense than in the early days. On the frontier the loneliness and need for reassurance drove people together, and the memories of the little towns and densely populated eastern North American or European neighborhoods were still strong. In the disastrous periods of drought and depression, apathy and poverty diminished associational life and parties, and the continuing exodus of population was a psychologically depressing experience for those who remained, even though they benefited by obtaining the land of the leavers. In the more affluent 1960's, however, social activities were rapidly reviving, and in a few cases, the old, deserted district schoolhouses were being bought and refurbished for country dances and gatherings.

Visits to Jasper, the region's major and only real town, were far more common than in the past. For many men, women, and whole families this was a regular experience, done weekly and even more often, for good reasons or no reasons, and was a phase of "automobile culture." Window shopping, visits to the two supermarkets, gossip with retired parents and friends, an occasional movie (though most of the patrons of Jasper's one theater were children and teen-agers!) and "just visiting" in the cafes and stores and around the post office, were the common activities. Many farm men were members of some of the big national lodges and clubs, and hence regularly attended meetings in Jasper town. During the winter, most farmers participated in curling rinks (a northern sport, particularly popular in Canada, consisting of "bowling" on ice with large polished stones), and since the rinks were expensive to build, only Jasper town and one other town in the region had them.

Once a month or so most farm families took longer trips, of 60 to 80 miles, to small cities located east and west of Jasper.

Farmers enjoyed the feeling of town and city life more than ranchers, and were more at home with the shopping facilities. The Saskatchewan farmer is not a "hick"; he is usually a confident middle-class–oriented person, adjusted to the outside world with its policies and styles of communication.

The farming pattern of life differed from that of the ranchers. Most of the old ranch houses, sometimes expansions of log cabins or turn-of-the-century frame houses, had a rusty, old-fashioned, though usually well-kept air; a few, especially those of the Hills ranchers, had stylish Western or Indian touches in their interior decor. Farmers lived in small modern bungalows sold by the local cooperative and private lumber companies, or in the repaired and usually enlarged frame houses of the 1910–20 pioneer period. Farm house interior decor often resembled that of the ranch, but more often ran toward an abundance of cheap overstuffed furniture and plastic flowers— stylistically more urban lower middle-class than rural. Articles of aesthetic culture, like pianos, were no more frequent than among ranchers. The symbols of farming culture—4H club trophies and plaques, awards for prize cows or horticultural exhibits, the trade magazines and political papers of organized farming—were far more abundant in farm than in ranch homes. In their place, ranch houses often featured nostalgic regional symbols—old photographs of the pioneer cattlemen or the local ranch in its frontier days, copies of early editions of the *Jasper News,* with its uninhibited accounts of life in the region, or in the repaired and usually enlarged frame houses of the three-generation ranching society (as opposed to the two- or one-and-one-half–generation existence of the farming society).

The dispersed nature of the farming (and ranching) settlement, and the verbal emphasis Jasperites gave to values suggesting a liking for isolation, might provide a false impression of lack of social solidarity and the structure of expectations that control role behavior in human societies. It is true that there is more possibility of physical isolation in the Plains than in any more densely populated society, but nevertheless the social bonds and reciprocities typical of any nucleated society with a small population are just as promiment. Jasper does not lack for gossip, censure, exclusion of transgressors against the norms of conduct, and a general atmosphere of cheerful conformity. "You might as well tell everything, it'll all be known around here anyway," was a typical comment of informants when pressed for information on the system of social control.

For dispersed or not, the Jasper ranching and farming population was one with common origins and common experiences, and a strong sense of historical solidarity. It was one with a long history of voluntary mutual aid and assistance—in the 1960's most Jasper agriculturalists depended upon neighbors and friends for labor and other forms of help in the economy. Moreover, the farming people had common bonds in the agrarian political movements that culminated in the accession to power of the CCF government—a farmer's government if there ever was one. Finally, the very visibility of life in Jasper—the fact that the daily doings, economic standing, and enterprise history of a given farm or ranch was visible at a glance from the highway to an experienced observer, and discussed in detail in the bars and others places of gatherings in town—meant that anonymity was not a concomitant of physical distance.

The following item from the *Jasper Weekly News* is typical of observations made continually by the district correspondents of this paper:

It makes a person feel good to drive by the Walter Standish's place and see the improvements being made. You figure that's one couple that have every intention of staying in the district.

Consequently the important issue was really how Jasperites overcame distance in forging and maintaining the bonds of an intimate rural society. The automobile and the telephone were key factors; others were the ladies' clubs, meeting in the hamlets and towns; the roping clubs and mutual-aid work sessions of the men, and a dozen other occasions for social interaction. These provided constant opportunity for the regulatory activities associated with relatively small societies, and they were used to the hilt. Farmers were more prone to exercise these voluntary associational controls than ranchers, but the extensive kinship network of the latter, covering great distances, served a similar function—while ranch people joined fewer clubs, they compensated by having more kinship picnics and gatherings.

Contacts between farmers and ranchers were not as common as between members of each occupational group's own members. In districts where farm and ranch properties were interlocked, relations would be closer than in areas where the enterprises were separated or simply juxtaposed along a natural boundary, such as the slope of the Hills. Such relations had been growing closer in recent years, as both ranch and farm families discovered common problems in poor roads, lengthy bussing of children to distant town schools, or the need to cooperate on government irrigation projects. But in a majority of districts, the interests of ranchers and farmers were often in competition, especially over leased rangeland. Farmers had succeeded during the 1940's and '50's in acquiring several portions of ranch leases for grazing cooperatives, and pressure by politically minded farmers on the leasing system was strong during the period of our study. In one unusual district—the only one in which both ranchers and farmers belonged to the same social groups, roping clubs, card clubs and the like—the interests of the two occupations nevertheless were still opposed, and a quiet distrust simmered beneath the friendly surface.

Labor- and machinery-exchange relationships were more important in farming society than in ranching, and, as indicated were a major source of socializing among the men. These exchanges were a significant part of farm enterprise economy; we calculated that for the average farmer the value received from help given him by neighbors ranged from several hundred to a thousand dollars a year, although of course his reciprocal exchange of his own services and machines would be equivalent. The extreme shortage of labor in Jasper, as in other North American farming communities, made this sort of exchange necessary and not merely desirable. Jasper farmers and ranchers verbalized their attachment to the system in terms of traditional values: "When a man needs help, it's up to his neighbor to give it to him. That's the kind of country this is. You can always depend on a fella." While these statements give the impression of a kind of frontier altruistic voluntarism, much mutual aid was carefully calculated so as to ensure reciprocity, and, in many instances, actual records were kept. When pressed, farmers would admit that "We keep it balanced over the long run, but

I always like to get the other fellow just a little bit behind me, so I can draw on him when I need it." In other words, while the sanctioning values for labor and machinery exchange were frontier-traditional, the actual practices were all organized and constituted a kind of open, informal cooperative.

The advantages of these informal economic exchanges could be seen in terms of labor opportunity costs. While exchanges were reciprocal, the informality of the system meant that the reciprocal return of labor could be adjusted to periods of slack and leisure; that is, the man who returned the services could do so at little cost to his own operation. Moreover, in some cases the reciprocity was worked out on the basis of an exchange of gratifying experiences for labor: ranchers consistently used urban relatives, or friends not in ranching, as laborers, providing them with good meals and the enjoyable and colorful life of the ranch in return, at very little cost to themselves.

The annual round of activities on the farm both differed from and resembled that of the ranch. The extent of reliance upon grain crops determined the degree of difference. Grain farming in the Great Plains is strictly a seasonal affair: the most intensive work begins with spring planting (in Jasper, April or May), extends through the summer, with a relaxed period in August while the grain heads, then culminates with the early September harvest period, which is a long round of very patient and steady work. The late fall and the entire winter are largely free of agricultural tasks, and time must be spent in equipment or building repairs and work. If a farmer is relatively well-off, he may be free to take a vacation in the winter. While few Jasper farmers relied exclusively on grain, or were wealthy enough to leave, a larger proportion of farmers than ranchers did take one to three weeks off in the dormant season to visit California, British Columbia, Florida, or the Southwestern states (rarely toward the East: the geographical orientation of nearly all Jasperites is Western).

The majority of farmers had cattle as well as grain, however, and the presence of livestock meant that work would extend through the fall and winter. As we pointed out for ranchers, cattle are a year-'round occupation, and this fact helps to explain the provinciality of ranching culture. As farmers move into livestock, they lose leisure time: they trade leisure for greater economic security and the higher prestige of the cattleman.

FAMILY AND ENTERPRISE

Farmers, like ranchers, provide an example of the intersection of kinship and economic roles. The farm family is an entrepreneurial unit supplying its own labor and management out of its nuclear kin, supplemented by other relatives and neighbors. The difference between the Jasper farm family and the Jasper ranch family was not great in terms of the basic categories of roles and social processes, but the differing economic situations did create some significant variations.

The developmental cycle of the farm family, like that of the ranch family, requires the succession of a relative—ideally a son —to the enterprise upon the father's retirement or death. The frequency of succession on Jasper farms, however, was in several senses lower than that of its ranches. In the first place, the great majority of farm homesteaders did not remain in Jasper; consequently the majority of farms did not endure beyond the first generation. In a typical district of homestead townships, there remained only 38 of the original 500 homestead pioneer family units, and about 70 of the original homestead farms. Of course those farm enterprises that remained under the original pioneer family control did undergo succession.

In contrast to the record for farms, the majority of ranches in the Jasper region were in the hands of original families or relatives in the kin group; consequently a higher proportion of all existing ranches underwent succession. A second factor which tended to reduce succession among farmers was the greater opportunity for young men acquiring farms of their own—operated apart from the father's or in partnership, as the case might be. The lower and often marginal economic position of many farms discouraged succession on the part of all sons or relatives, who would leave for town jobs.

Finally, the increasing value of agricultural property in the Jasper area, mentioned in earlier chapters, also was having its effect insofar as many fathers were requiring greater financial returns upon retirement, requiring sons to go into heavier debt to buy the farm from the parent. In addition, the conservative development policies of the fathers often required the son to take relatively large loans in order to push the farm to greater productivity: new machines, new crop routines, the entry into livestock production, and other measures of "intensification" and specialization were becoming more common. It was difficult for many young men to get the financing they needed to make these changes, however, and this opened up the area to outsiders with capital. In the 1960's the region was entering an intense phase of "hand-changing,' in the local phrase.

In Chapter 4 we noted that there was a close relationship between the family cycle, the development cycle of the enterprise, and external factors like drought and economic conditions. A farm operator caught between growing consumption needs of his family, needs for investment in the enterprise, and unfavorable economic or climatic conditions might respond by working harder to increase the productivity of the enterprise, buying more land if he could afford it, taking a part-time job, or selling out and leaving Jasper. Since the majority of Jasper settlers homesteaded during the same period (1910–20), large numbers of them reached similar points in their family and enterprise cycles at the same time.

To illustrate this process, we present a diagram (Fig. 7.1), showing the typical conditions experienced by an unmarried homesteader about age 20 who settled in 1910. These men usually married women from their neighborhoods, and the establishment of the family demanded more income; hence land purchases were made, as shown, soon after marriage. The new acreage required more labor to work, and since the children were not old enough to help out, machinery had to be bought. By this time the farmer had accumulated considerable debt, and a financial crisis was imminent. In one sample township, 28 per cent of the original unmarried homesteader group did leave Jasper during the late 'teens and early 1920's. Intermittent unfavorable economic and moisture conditions encouraged this departure.

Those settlers who managed to stay, accumulated additional

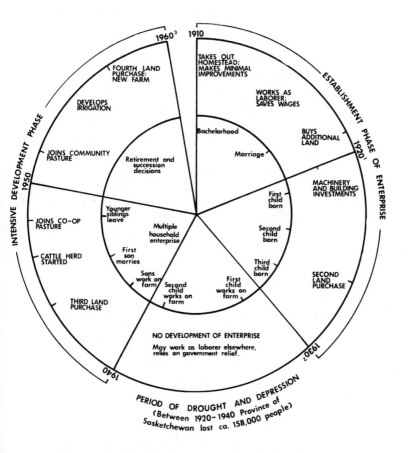

Figure 7.1. Family Cycle and Enterprise Cycle—
1910 Homestead Farmer, Age 20

IN ONE TYPICAL SPECIMEN FARMING TOWNSHIP:

[1] In the period 1910-1920: 28% of initial homesteaders and their families left permanently.

[2] In the period 1920-1930: an additional 34% left; thus, from 1910-1930, 62% of initial homesteaders left.

[3] Of the remaining farmers, 63% retired between 1940 and 1960. Of these, 52% were succeeded by sons.

land. By the late '20's and the entire decade of the 1930's, both drought and depression lowered levels of living to a bare survival point, and another 34 per cent of the original group in the specimen township departed. Some took jobs elsewhere, returning only to put in a crop and harvest it. Others became ranch laborers. The availability of grown sons did not help much, since the climate did not permit crops; hence many sons also worked away from the farm.

The decade, 1940–50, with better moisture conditions and much available land at bargain prices, permitted a return to enterprise development activity, with the sons helping out, and lowering the cost of labor. In the 1940's or 1950's, however, the sons would be ready to take over the enterprise from the aging father. If the farm had to support a married son and his children, new stresses would arise, and again the families would have to decide whether to stay or make some other decision. Figure 7.1 shows the father buying enough land to create two units, one of which the successor son would take over.

Thus the relationships of the family cycle and the enterprise cycle can be generalized as a series of economic crises or pressure points, affected at intervals by external conditions. The principal pressures arose at the time of marriage, when the children were born, before the children were old enough to contribute their labor, and when the older son or sons were marrying and beginning to contemplate succession or staying in the region and buying a new farm with the father's help. During the 1930's, the 1910 homesteaders had some help from their older children, but the disastrous drought and economic depression made it difficult to survive. On the other hand, conditions of relative prosperity during World War II and after eased the situation somewhat. However, the rather slow pace of development of the enterprise meant that much had to be done to launch the sons who wanted to take over or start a new farm. At the same time, the parents had to get enough out of the enterprise to retire on a decent income. Thus in spite of the growing prosperity of the 1940–60 period, the undercapitalization of the farms meant that there would be continued need for deferred gratification.

Figure 7.1 suggests that under conditions of uncertainty and marginal resources, the developmental cycle of the enterprise is stretched out farther than it would be in a more fortunate environment. Thus the full development of the farm is delayed and frequently its needs intersect with the needs of the growing family group. This sets up repeated pressures for economic survival.

The relationship of father and son in farming society resembled that in the ranching, but there was a greater tendency for father and son to consummate formal business agreements on the future takeover. Farmers were generally more business-oriented—"secular"—in their approach to the running of the enterprise, and succession was regarded less as the maintenance of a traditional continuity of ownership, more as a working business arrangement. This fact tells us something also about the nature of kinship roles in the family. In ranching families the father-son relationship was almost always strained, and to convert it into a contractual arrangement would require a considerable transformation. The emphasis on the traditional and prestigeful nature of ranching, and the corresponding moral responsibility of inheritance, tended to generate considerable anxiety in both father and son. In farm families, with less of a traditional sense of the family and its land, and a more business-oriented conception of the enterprise, it was somewhat easier for the father and son to discuss openly and to arrive at suitable agreements on financing and payment of the debts assumed on takeover. As noted earlier, the basis of this is the money the son pays the father for the farm, which becomes the aged parents' income after retirement.

We noted that the ranch sons had few alternatives but succession. Since the number of ranches in the Jasper region was restricted by the grazing lease tenure regulations, only one son could take over. The others were required to find ranches elsewhere, become cowboys or manual laborers, or leave the region. While the costs of remaining in farming were higher than for ranching, actually the farm sons had somewhat more numerous alternatives. In the first place, there was a greater emphasis on education among the farmers, and more boys were being encouraged to complete high school than were in ranching families. This was beginning to equip them more adequately than ranch boys for employment opportunities. In the second place, the continual sale of farm properties provided greater opportunity for a farm boy to acquire (with the financial help of his family and kin group, if he could not obtain a loan) an old farm and start out on his own. This procedure also was encouraged by the financial situation described previously: often a father would prefer to help his son get started on a "new place" and then sell the family farm to the highest bidder. In this way the retiring parents would extract the enhanced value from the farm, and at the same time the son would also be taken care of. One common pattern was for a father to buy an additional section or half-section of land by purchasing a farm from an aging man without succession possibilities, and then to operate this in conjunction with his own, making an agreement with his son to let the latter take it over as his own after his son married. The father and son thus became business partners on two cooperatively operated farms until the father's retirement, at which time the two places were merged as one farm unit. The land acreage of the second "farm" often would be marginal, and the son would have a hard struggle, but sooner or later the father retired, and then the son had one large farm. Such arrangements were extremely rare in ranching, since there were so few ranches available for sale. During the period of our study (1962–64), only one case of this occurred in the ranching community, while at least 25 were noted among farmers.

The role of the farm girls was similar to that of the ranch daughters. They were prepared for migration by education (nearly all finished high school), and ultimately for feminine occupations: nursing, secretarial work, school teaching, and the like. A few married ranchers, but far more married farmers. To marry a rancher was the fulfillment of a dream for some of these girls, who knew that the venture would give them a certain status, although many discovered later that their husbands had doubtful "social credit" status. Invariably these girls threw themselves into ranch life with vigor, wearing the costumes, competing in the horse shows, and participating in the social side of the community brandings.

Growing up on a farm is less romantic than on a ranch, but probably involves just as much hard work. The boys are encouraged to take responsibility at an early age, and the fathers will seek to educate them in the techniques of management—perhaps a little more conscientiously than the ranch father, who usually displayed a curious unwillingness to treat his son as something more than a hired hand. Jasper farm boys and girls were incorporated into 4H club activities at an early age, and this served to train the growing farm child in the world view of professional farming (4H clubs existed for some ranching communities also, particularly the Town and Hills groups, but these clubs usually did not solicit the help of the agricultural extension agent, and concentrated on horsemanship). The farm clubs were intimately associated with extension work and its ideals, and the larger percentage of farm boys who went to agricultural college as compared to ranch sons although both were small) was due in large part to the proselytizing activities of the extension agent.

The Agroecology of Farming

W. A. Mackintosh in *Prairie Settlement: The Geographical Setting* (1934) wrote:

Climatic information is customarily stated in terms of averages and normals. The agricultural settler, however, does not live by averages, annual or seasonal, but from day to day and season to season. He deals with climate as a matter of probability. He is affected not only by the normal occurrence of rain but by the departures from normal. The variability of climate conditions is more important than their average occurrence. It is possible for crops to be frozen three years out of five in an area which has an *average* frost-free period longer than the required growing season. Dry farming may be a paying business in one area with an average warm-season rainfall of 10 inches and not in another. Life in the Prairie Provinces adapts itself not only to certain climatic normals, but to the degree of climatic variability (pp. 17–19).

While climate—rainfall and temperature—were without doubt the key factors for the farmer and rancher, most natural resources (and prices as well) needed for agriculture also displayed considerable variability. A certain amount of control of economic fluctuation has been made in the past 20 years, in ways already described, but most of the problems associated with variable natural resources have remained. The farmer, with his relatively small properties and dependence on field crops both for grain sales and cattle forage, operates on very close margins, and fluctuation in yields means corresponding fluctuation in income, thus creating difficulties of financing the crop in the following year.

All natural resources—soils, wind, precipitation, topography—require careful attention and experimentation in order to maximize, or to strike a reasonable average yield. Among these, moisture was the principal preoccupation. During the period of our research, the average farm family could finance its economic operations and provide for modest consumption needs if—using wheat as a model for analysis—the farm, of around 1000 acres, 50% in crop at any one time, yielded about 10 to 15 bushels to the acre. Obviously the yield varied considerably—from 6 to 17, depending on moisture. The farmer therefore had to do everything possible to save moisture for his crops because he could not be certain of precipitation in the following year.

In order to raise a crop of around 15 bushels, the wheat needs a minimum of 11 inches of moisture—11 inches measured as one would measure rainfall. The mean annual precipitation for the grain-growing districts north and south of the Hills in Jasper (see Figs. 2.2, 2.3) is around 11 inches. However, the annual variability is great enough so that the farmer cannot rely on the annual rainfall to provide all the moisture he needs. Therefore ways must be found to store moisture in the soil, to add to the amount that might fall as rain or snow.

The technique of summer-fallowing is the most important of several means to do this. The technique requires that the farmer keep part of his land out of crops each year (most Jasper farmers held out one half, alternating yearly), with the surface loose and free of weeds, thus creating conditions which favor the retention of soil moisture (but also soil blowing). In the following year this saved moisture is supplemented by rainfall (and perhaps a little from snow, if the snow will melt and soak in during the winter) and thus hopefully will add up to at least 11 inches. Bumper grain crops in Jasper often are produced not just with very heavy rains in the current crop year, but with saved moisture *plus* rainfall. There have been bumper crops in years with very little rainfall if the previous fall and winter precipitation, saved by summer fallow, was abundant.

The precise origins of the Great Plains summer-fallowing system are obscure. Some form of fallowing—letting lands lie idle at intervals to regain fertility—was practiced from ancient times in New Eastern and European agriculture, but the system of permitting land to lie fallow in order to accumulate moisture was developed or reinvented in North America in the nineteenth century (no one is completely certain of its precise history). Summer-fallowing was being practiced systematically in eastern Saskatchewan by 1885. In Jasper the technique was being recommended as early as 1900 by government agricultural agents, but many farmers seem to have worked it out for themselves on the basis of accidents. For example, farmers would leave Jasper in drought periods to take jobs elsewhere, returning the following year to put in a crop. Some of them found that the next-year's crop was better than would be expected—this as a result of the accumulated moisture in the fallow land.

Thus the basic strategy of "dry farming" in the northern Plains involves looking ahead one or two years and preparing for all eventualities. It is not a daring, risk-taking strategy, but a cautious one, requiring careful attention to detail and the need to plan ahead.

Various writers on the Great Plains have mentioned the tendency for farmers to swing from moods of optimism about a basic change in the moisture cycle, to deep pessimism. Jasper settlers were no exception. The homestead influx in 1910 coincided with a wet period, and the myth of a permanent change in the weather was born at that time. After the droughts of the late 'teens and '20's, the conviction of drought as an abnormal condition did not die, but after the decade of the 1930's, the violent swings in mood had ceased. By the 1960's, Jasper farmers displayed (on answers to special questions on our schedules) an even-tempered, calm recognition and appraisal of the inherent variability and unpredictability of Great Plains weather—an attitude born not only of experience, but also of the stabilizing influences of the livestock industry they were all entering to greater or lesser degrees.

Soils in the Jasper region vary greatly, as a result of extensive alluvial action during the glacial period, and from runoff from precipitation in the Hills. The heavier the soil, the greater its moisture-retentive power; hence the heavier, clayey soils representing old lake and pond bottoms were best for field crops, especially wheat. Rye and barley could be raised more successfully on lighter, sandier soils. Alfalfa and grass forage crops could be raised on almost any soil, providing irrigation was applied, although the heavier soils were best in the long run. The very sandiest soils were gradually being retired from use for field crops and returned to pasture grasses.

In the earlier days of farming, the distinctions between soils was not appreciated, and grains were raised everywhere. By the 1960's, the process of "resources specialization"—including the placement of crops on suitable soils—had made progress, though was not complete. The variability of soil types was especially great in districts at the foot of the slopes of the Hills, and farmers could expect everything from heavy clay to pure sand in a quarter- or half-section of land. This variability in soil type constituted the principal ecological problem concerning soils. Exhaustion of fertility was begining to be a problem in districts that in the 1960's were going into their third human generation of cultivation, and artificial fertilization was just beginning. Farmers typically showed considerable caution and skepticism, owing to the high cost of fertilizer and its doubtful results in a dry country; to be effective, fertilizer needs adequate moisture.

Hail, torrential thunderstorms, and high winds were enemies of Jasper farmers, and could destroy a crop in minutes. There appeared to be fairly regular pathways for hail and thunderstorms, and farmers in these areas had to learn to live with the associated risk. Various types of insurance could be bought to reduce this risk, but these policies—even those offered by the provincial government—were relatively expensive, and the conservative Jasper farmers were inclined to avoid them unless their sense of probable occurrence told them it was time to take out insurance. Most farmers believed they had a fairly good "feeling" for when these disasters would strike, and would delay taking out policies until they thought they were about ready for one. They were often wrong. Many farmers (and their fathers) kept records of climatic phenomena, however, and one farmer interviewed had determined that he could expect a bad hailstorm about once every decade. He also found that at this frequency, hail insurance would not pay, and he had learned to live with the expectation that his crop would be wiped out at least once every 10 years. His method of managing his farm was adjusted to this eventuality in that he tried to save a certain amount of cash regularly to accumulate enough to cover him during the hail year.

Grasshoppers, one of the plagues of Great Plains farming, strike in enormous numbers about every seventh year, due to the breeding cycle of the main species. Various methods developed on experimental farms were used by Jasper farmers to protect their crops, but as with the recurrent hail, there was really little that could be done. Careful business management, with regular savings, was the best protection against these eventualities.

Equally important to summerfallowing in permitting Jasper farmers to make their fields bloom with grain was the development of the relatively drought-resistant varieties of hard red spring-planted wheat that have since made the Canadian plains famous as the producers of the best bread wheats in the world (when moisture permits!). These grains provide a good example of how externally invented or supplied factors aided adaptation in regions like Jasper. Farm machinery and many other items of technology furnish additional examples.

The problem to be solved in the development of adapted wheat seed (similar problems existed for the other grains as well) was the need for a plant that would grow very rapidly soon after planting, in order to catch the brief early spring moisture season; and then mature during the dry late summer, ahead of the occasional fall rains. Wheat is especially susceptible to "rust"—fungus diseases—when moisture is too abundant or comes at the wrong time. The first wheat to meet these needs to some extent was *Red Fife,* originating in a handful of seed sent from Scotland to David Fife, an Ontario farmer. The seed apparently originated in the Baltic region, from whence it spread to Scotland. This wheat then spread from Ontario into the U.S., and then back from the U.S. into Manitoba, where it triggered the first wheat boom of the Canadian plains.

However, it was found that *Red Fife* was a little late in maturing, and hence was frequently caught by the late frosts so common in the northern plains. By 1911 a new, early-maturing variety had been developed by the infant Canadian Department of Agriculture: *Marquis.* It was the wheat used by Jasper homestead settlers exclusively after 1915, and it dominated the plains until 1935. Beginning about then, a whole new series of wheats, each adapted to a different set of conditions in various parts of the plains of the U.S. and Canada, emerged to replace *Marquis* and *Red Fife.* One of the most important of these, used especially in areas with a good chance of excess moisture, is *Thatcher,* an unusually rust-resistant variety. Since new types of rust fungus are constantly evolving, the agricultural scientists are required to create new varieties of grains, and a new type emerges nearly every year. In this, as in many other things, the agricultural extension agents are important in disseminating information, although the ultimate experimentation and decision-making must be done by the individual farmer.

Also of great importance in developing the grains agriculture of the plains was the development of suitable methods of milling or grinding the grain. The hard red wheats make the best bread (and the northern barleys the best beer!) but they are resistant to ordinary methods of milling. Consequently special technology had to be devised, and many agricultural historians regard these methods as the critical factor in making the Canadian plains one of the world's great breadbaskets. The roller process, originating in crude form in the Ukraine, where hard red spring wheats also probably originated, was improved in Hungary in the 1870's by introducing porcelain and steel rollers, and it was this equipment, brought into Canada and the U.S., that made it possible to grind grain efficiently and in large quantities rapidly—and ultimately, permit Jasper farmers to make a living.

These external factors provide the frame and much of the

means for Jasper farming: it is Jasper farmers themselves who provide the practice and the outcome. Over time, Jasper farmers have probably learned more from each other than they have learned from experts, although the expert is essential as a communicator of administrative rules and regulations, new techniques to be tried, and new products. But Jasper farmers themselves must put these things to test, and in the words of one farmer, they "watch each other real carefully" to see how the experiment works out. Often the man who decides to try a new thing has been urged to do so by his neighbors: the innovator in Jasper is not necessarily a "leader," only a farmer who happens to have a little extra cash and who agrees to be the "goat," as one of them called himself.

Thus, the evolution of adaptive strategies of farming in Jasper, was a dominantly trial-and-error operation, supplied and assisted by knowledge and technology communicated by agricultural extension agents and experts from the experimental farms. Periods of intensive trial-and-error experimentation were: (1) the pioneer farming era when the homesteaders and the few farmers who preceded them lacked knowledge of the peculiarities and variability of the natural resources, and had to find ways of raising crops and livestock. The homesteading process itself was a huge trial-and-error social experiment, and its results have already been described. (2) A second major period of experimentation occurred in the 1930's and 1940's during the drought and after, when government agencies first took an interest in the problems of the Western farmer and began to institute irrigation, community pasturage, and other cooperative arrangements. These experiments were often only partly successful: irrigation was often poorly done, and the consequences have been severe in some localities. (2) The third period of innovation began after World War II, with increasing prosperity and hence greater ability to invest, and also with more massive government inputs. This period also saw the emergence of more specialized knowledge and the communication of this to the farm and ranch operators—modifying somewhat the trial-and-error character of the innovation. Therefore it is only in the recent period that a degree of rational planning for predictable outcomes has been a part of the Jasper agrarian regime. Until this period, Jasper agriculturalists have, in the main, been on their own; what they have done has been done largely on the basis of their own ability and mistakes.

The future of Jasper farming, despite the evident hazards and uncertainties, is fairly bright. The expansion of cattle-raising facilities has introduced a balance into the failing grain regime, and the out-migration of marginal operators has permitted the remaining farmers to acquire more land. Diversified cattle-grain production, sometimes including a few hogs and sheep, was proving viable in the 1960's and there was little doubt that it represented the future stable pattern. As this occurs, many Jasper farmers gradually convert to a species of small, intensive rancher, or cooperative rancher, as in the case of the grazing cooperatives.

This change in mode of production has also meant a cultural change: many though not all of the farmers were beginning to assimilate the rancher attitudes toward private entrepreneur-ship and cattle sales, wear the distinctive Western costumes, and participate in the roping and horsemanship sports. The occupa-tional cultures of farming and ranching are not entirely matters of tradition but are based on the particular activities and interactions characteristic of the modes of production. Horse-manship is not simply a hobby, but develops naturally out of the fact that a man with cattle needs a horse to manage them. The costume and the romantic attitudes, of course, are rein-forced by the mass media, and the general prestige of ranching in Jasper regional culture also encourages the farmers' cultural-ecological shift.

However, while *farming* is in Jasper to stay, the *farmers* have constituted a fluid and unstable population. This apparently paradoxical situation comes about through the changing oppor-tunity costs of farming. In every respect, these costs seem high: the farmer could make more in occupations that his usual educational level would make possible; and his investments in the typical undersized farms would provide him with higher income if he transferred his money to urban businesses, or even to the relatively risky but remunerative specialized agro-businesses like cattle feeding and purebred cattle raising. (One farmer almost doubled his annual income when he sold his farm and went into purebreds; and four years later he sold the entire farm-ranch for nearly twice what he paid for it.)

Thus the opportunity costs of the traditional cattle-grain type of farming are clearly higher than for ranching, but some of the same qualifications we noted for ranching apply to farming as well. First, not all farmers are equipped to handle urban businesses; second, not all farms are bad investments, especially in an era when government has begun to provide pasture and irrigation facilities and opportunities for expanding the live-stock business. This is what we mean when we say that farming is a viable industry and a permanent feature of the Jasper economic scene. It is simply that farming must be conducted by the implicit rules established by the climate and the national economy, and that means efficiency of operation and enlarge-ment of the land area and capitalization of the farm units. Hence more farmers will leave, and those dedicated to the farming way of life and the natural environment of Jasper will benefit in their preferred way.

BIBLIOGRAPHIC NOTES

The Saskatchewan homesteading frontier was the last large home-stead area opened in North America, and the land agents of the Canadian Pacific Railway made special efforts to attract settlers from the United States. The phrase "last best West" was coined by these agents as a catchy inducement. The whole story has been told by Paul S. Sharp in "The American Farmer and the 'Last Best West,' " *Agricultural History*, Vol. 21 (1947), pp. 65–74, and Karel D. Bicha, *The American Farmer and the Canadian West*. Lawrence, Kan., Coro-nado Press, 1968. Incidentally Bicha shows on the basis of analyses of census and migration data that although 600,000 people from the United States eventually moved to the Canadian West, only about one-third actually stayed for more than from 3 to 5 years! Most of the 600,000 came from western Midwest and eastern Plains states, with a sizeable contingent from western Washington state—thus the migration simply followed plains-prairie country northward. Indications of this pattern were found for Jasper: 95 per cent of the rancher and farmer families with U.S. origins were from plains or mountain states. In addition, the homestead reminiscence literature in Jasper mentions a fair number of families from eastern Midwest origins, like Wisconsin and Michigan, but nearly all of these families left Jasper before or during the drought of the 1930's. That is, the westerners, while they also left in droves, were also more likely to stay, having pre-adapted skills for the environment.

The Canadian West farm frontier and country life has produced a number of interesting specimens of belles lettres and autobiography. Particularly revealing are Sinclair Ross, *For Me and My House,* Mc-Clelland & Stewart, 1957, a portrait of a Saskatchewan church minister and his disillusioning experiences in the prairie towns; W. O. Mitchell, *Who has Seen the Wind,* Macmillan (Toronto), 1960, a novelized auto-biographical account of growing up on prairie farms and towns; J. G. McGregor, *Northwest of Sixteen,* Tuttle, 1968, the story of the author's family's pioneering experiences in Alberta; Wallace Stegner (the author of *Wolf Willow*), *The Big Rock Candy Mountain,* Duell, Sloan & Pearce, 1938, a novel which contains important sections on Canadian and U.S. northern Plains homesteading and small-town experiences; Carlyle King, ed., *Saskatchewan Harvest,* McClelland & Stewart, 1955, a fine collection of stories, essays, and other pieces dealing with life on the prairies; Helge M. Ingstad, *Land of Feast and Famine,* Knopf, 1933, concerned with U.S. and Canadian Plains life; Vera Lysenko, *Men in Sheepskin Coats,* Ryerson Press, 1947, a classic description of the Ukrainian settlers in Western Canada. Perhaps the best novel of Plains pioneer life, and with a North Dakota setting, is O. E. Rolvaag, *Giants in the Earth,* Harper, 1927 and other editions. A sequel, *Peder Victorious,* has attracted less attention.

For a sensitive study of the small-town culture of the majority of Jasper settlers (those with British Isles backgrounds who had settled for one generation or less in eastern Canada), see John K. Galbraith, *The Scotch,* Houghton-Mifflin, 1964. One of the few community studies for Western Canada was done by Jean Burnet (*Next Year Country,* University of Toronto Press, 1951). S. M. Lipset's *Agrarian Socialism,* 1951, also contains much information on the culture of Saskatchewan farmers, as does Stegner's *Wolf Willow,* 1962. Partial studies of Saskatchewan farming towns and districts have been made by the Center for Community Studies of the University of Saskatchewan—see, for example, Richard Laskin, *Organizations in a Saskatchewan Town,* 1961. The definitive study of rural Saskatchewan as a whole is to be found in the 12 reports of the Royal Commission on Agriculture and Rural Life, Province of Saskatchewan, issued in 1956. Report No. 12, *Service*

Centers, contains information on population dispersion in semiarid environments, and the effects of the pattern of agricultural development on society.

For information on ethnic cultures of Canada and their fate, see *Citizenship, Immigration, and Ethnic Groups in Canada: A Bibliography of Research.* Economic and Research Division, Department of Immigration, Ottawa, 1962. See also Marlene Stefanow, "Changing Bi- and Multi-Culturalism in the Canadian Prairie Provinces," in C. C. Zimmerman and S. Russell, *Symposium on the Great Plains of North America,* Fargo, 1967, and F. G. Vallee and others, "Ethnic Assimilation and Differentiation in Canada," *Canadian Journal of Economics and Political Science:* 23 (1957), pp. 540–49.

Some aspects of North American social stratification are exemplified in the farming society of Jasper. See, for example, Joseph A. Kahl, *The American Class Structure,* Holt, Rinehart & Winston, 1957, Chaps. 2, 3. Specifically, we refer to the effects of homogeneity of income and visibility of status criteria, both of these tending to blur status lines and make the concept of class or stratification ambiguously applicable to these rural societies. See an illuminating analysis of the same thing in a European community: J. A. Barnes, "Class and Community in a Norwegian Island Parish," *Human Relations,* Vol. 7, pp. 39–58, 1957. The classic study of Canadian social stratification, but particularly emphasizing eastern Canada, is found in John Porter, *The Vertical Mosaic,* University of Toronto Press, 1965.

For a study of the social functions of exchange of services among farmers, see Solon T. Kimball, "Rural Social Organization and Cooperative Labor," *American Journal of Sociology,* 55 (1949), pp. 38–49. A detailed study of exchanges among Jasper farmers and ranchers and their various functions is found in John W. Bennett, "Reciprocal Economic Exchanges among North American Agricultural Operators," *Southwestern Journal of Anthropology,* Vol. 24 (1968), pp. 276–309.

For studies of kinship organization in North American society, see David M. Schneider, *American Kinship: A Cultural Account,* Prentice-Hall, 1968; Melvin Kohn, "Social Class and Parent-Child Relationships," *American Journal of Sociology,* 68 (1963), pp. 471–80; David M. Schneider and G. C. Homans, "Kinship Terminology and the American Kinship System," *American Anthropologist,* 57 (1955), pp. 1194–1208; Millicent R. Ayoub, *American Children and their Relatives: The Kindred in Southwest Ohio,* Fels Research Institute, Yellow Springs, Ohio, 1959; Leo A. Despres, "A Function of Bilateral Kinship Patterns in a New England Industry," *Human Organization,* 17 (1958), pp. 15–22.

For studies of father-son relationships, the succession process, and the family as a business in other cultures see George K. Park, "Sons and Lovers: Characterological Requisites of the Roles in a Peasant Society," *Ethnology*, Vol. I (1962), pp. 412–424; Robert Hunt, "The Developmental Cycle of the Family Business in Rural Mexico," *Essays in Economic Anthropology*, American Ethnological Society publ., pp. 54–79, 1965. A useful review of the relationship of family and kinship to economic change is provided in William J. Goode, "Role of the Family in Industrialization," in *Social Problems Urbanization, Science, Technology and Development*, Vol. 7, of U.S. Papers Prepared for the United Nations Conference on Applications of Science and Technology for Benefit of Less-Developed Areas, U.S. Government Printing Office, 1963. Studies of family cycle and its relationships to property in Africa are found in Robert F. Gray and P. H. Gulliver, *The Family Estate in Africa*, Boston University Press, 1964.

Attitudes of Great Plains farmers toward drought and other natural disasters have been studied extensively. One of the more colorful episodes was the period in the late 1920's and 1930's when self-proclaimed "rainmakers" stalked through the dried-out communities offering to induce the heavens to rain for a fee, with indifferent results but with a good deal of entertainment! A popular and amusing Broadway play, later made into a movie with Katharine Hepburn, celebrates the flamboyant personalities of the rainmakers. Aside from these instances of folklore, some serious studies have been made of how farmers confront the uncertainty produced by recurrent drought. Thomas Saarinen, in his *Perception of Drought Hazard on the Great Plains*, University of Chicago Press, 1966, presents the results of a detailed attitude survey on this problem. He found that: (1) perception of drought hazard varied significantly with the degree of aridity of the locality; (2) less so with the amount of experience with arid conditions; and (3) also less significantly with respect to personality (the more perceptive individuals were also somewhat more inclined to have high achievement-orientation scores on Thematic Apperception Tests). Saarinen also got a tendency toward optimism as a characteristic of arid-adapted agrarian behavior. E. Z. Vogt, in his study of New Mexico bean farmers (*Modern Homesteaders*, Harvard University Press, 1955), emphasized this optimism factor, finding that it was the key value in what he called the "gambling orientation toward the farming enterprise" (p. 99). The Jasper data agree with Saarinen's first two points (perception varies with degree of aridity and of experience with it), but we did not obtain much evidence of the optimism factor. The reasons for this disagreement with Saarinen's and Vogt's data may lie in the facts that (a)

Jasper farmers had managed to diversify their production and did not rely exclusively on wheat or beans, as did farmers in the other studies; (b) Jasper farmers had been settled longer than Vogt's recent homesteaders and consequently had had a longer time in which to work out an adapted perspective and strategy. We should also distinguish between attitudes or values concerning optimism-pessimism and the actual behavioral strategies of adaptation. In this study we regard attitudes more as rationalizations or accompaniments of action, not as causes. Jasper farmers had well-developed techniques for coping with drought; their attitudes toward aridity and variability were either idiosyncratic or adjusted to the existence of these techniques.

For references to the Cooperative Commonwealth Federation (CCF) and other Saskatchewan farmers' movements and organizations of a cooperative nature, see the notes for Chaps. 4 and 9.

EIGHT

The Hutterites

In the late winter of 1951 a bearded Hutterite elder, accompanied by a non-Hutterite real-estate dealer from Alberta, arrived in Jasper town to talk to the local agricultural extension representative and a few farm equipment dealers. A quiet tour of the district west of town followed, and calls were made on a number of farmers in that area who were known to be interested in selling their land. This was the first word the community had of the impending migration of Hutterian Brethren. In March the highway north of town carried three large trucks loaded with young men, furniture, farm implements, and construction tools, heading east out of Alberta, to occupy the site bought during the winter in Jasper. Just a year later, there were more trucks and carryalls on the highway, and the women, children, and old people arrived to take up residence in the new houses. This was the start of the first colony. In eight years, five more colonies found sites in the region (see Fig. 2.2 or 2.10 for locations). Thus came the Hutterites: Jasper's final large settlement of agrarians.

Hutterites are one of the three major surviving sectarian groups of Anabaptist Christians; the others are the Mennonites, who have been at least partly assimilated into the Protestant order of sects, and the separatist Amish, a semicommunal and extremely conservative wing of the Mennonite faith. The Hutterites are the only group among the three who have rigorously insisted on the communal frame of existence, which requires that all important property be shared by the entire community, and that the children be raised mainly by the collective institu-

246

tions of the colony. The economy is that of a large, diversified agricultural enterprise, and all Hutterites are farmers since no satisfactory way has been found to exist communally in an urban-industrial setting. Hutterian beliefs include strong injunctions against extensive involvement with the "outside"—that is, the majority society—since to Hutterites, the "outside" is not only tempting and corrupting in its pursuit of money and personal gratification, but also unChristian, having fallen away from the original teachings of Christ. There is therefore a basic paradox in Hutterian ideals: while the world must be avoided, because it is a defiling of the true Christian way, it also must be dealt with successfully in order to preserve the Hutterian faith and further the mission of Christ.

The Hutterian settlement of the Jasper region also represents the most economically successful human settlement in the region's 70-odd years of Euro-American settlement in terms of range and diversity of use of natural resources and indices of productivity. In general, it is also the most successful in terms of combining high productivity with a conservationist program for resources—Hutterites usually take good care of their land and water. The Brethren are efficient farmers not only because of their skilled management and intensive use of machinery, but also because of their ability to control consumption in order to fulfill their ideal of austerity, which incidentally provides them with substantial investment capital. The combination of a relatively large labor force with quantities of machinery and tools, plus investment in nearly all branches of agriculture, provides them with a balanced "economy of scale." This response to the built-in uncertainties and high risk of a specialized natural environment is hard to beat.

HISTORY

The European sixteenth century was a long and complex period of social and religious protest and revolt. Three events stand in the background of Hutterian history: the Peasant War of Germany; the Protestant Reformation; and the second, and much less-well-known religious "reformation": the Anabaptist.

The Peasant War of 1524–25 was an armed revolt of the farmers of central Europe who had reached the limits of their toleration of heavy taxation and political misrepresentation. Economic development had changed the medieval social polity, and growing urbanism required new forms of government. The translation of the Scriptures into German had made available to the common people the egalitarian message of fundamental Christianity, and this was perceived and accepted as a blueprint for social reform. The armed revolt of the peasants was suppressed, but the religious revolt continued throughout the century, and on into the seventeenth. The emergence of Anabaptism was related to the Peasant's War, and was in one sense the prolongation of that revolt by peaceful means.

Anabaptism was not a highly organized movement, and it possessed no towering ideologists and theologians of the stature of Luther and Calvin. It was, nevertheless, a pervasive and consistent doctrine, with adherents in every country of Europe. It advocated a return to the doctrines of the Church of Jerusalem under Jesus, as implied in the Book of Acts of the Apostles: egalitarian social relations, a sharing of possessions, charity and brotherly love for all, and a life of austerity and simplicity. These doctrines were perceived by both the Catholic and the orthodox Protestant churches as radical and revolutionary, since they challenged the authority of all established churches and denied the ascendancy of the emerging bourgeois order as well as the clergy and secular aristocracy. Early Protestantism had shared some of these beliefs, but the acceptance of the Protestant movement by established governments led to persecution of Anabaptists by the Protestant leaders.

The socioeconomic basis of Anabaptism was apparent in the character of its adherents. The great majority were peasants, a substantial plurality were small-town tradesmen, laborers, and merchants, and a minority, professionals. The center of gravity was rural and small town, and the opponents were conceived as the corrupt and wealthy townsmen and aristocracy who had fallen away from Christ's teaching by pursuing self-gratification and incidentally squeezing the poor and the peasants. There is no need to obscure the revolutionary meaning of the Anabaptist movement: it was the sixteenth-century version (or really the beginning) of the proletarian revolts that culminated finally in the secular socialist and communist movements of the nineteenth and twentieth centuries. That it took a predominantly religious form is a reflection of the importance of religion in the sixteenth century—and also of the fact that armed revolution was hopeless against the superior forces of the state. Even so, a partly Anabaptist faction seized control of the city of Münster in 1532 by force of arms, and controlled the city for three years, establishing the first political commune in European history.

The point of origin of Anabaptism is considered to be a meeting of three religious protesters, followers of Zwingli, in Zurich in 1525, who formed the Swiss Brethren. (Zwingli later denounced them.) Within a few years, dozens of similar groups arose in various parts of Europe, and by 1530, persecutions of these groups led to their flight from most parts of central Europe. The immediate antecedents of the Hutterian Brethren were loosely federated Anabaptist groups in the Austrian Tyrol, who, fleeing from persecution there, entered Moravia (now part of Czechoslovakia) at the invitation of local lords who respected the sobriety and efficiency of these people and wanted them to help them run their country estates. On the way to Moravia, these groups decided to federate, and to accept fully the custom of communal sharing of property, which, they believed, on the basis of the Book of Acts, to have been the practice of the early Church. This group eventually became the Hutterites—named after one of their early ministers who was instrumental in allaying factional disputes and enforcing their communal doctrines and practices.

With only one brief interruption, the Hutterites enjoyed patronage and prosperity in Moravia until 1622, when the Catholic Church persuaded the Moravian lords to drive the Brethren from their estates. There followed a period of persecution and wandering through southeastern Europe, culminating in 1767 with a determined attempt by Hungarian officials to stamp out the sect once and for all. The Brethren fled to Rumania, and now reduced to a small cadre, were saved by the intervention of Russian officials, on the scene because of the Russo-Turkish War. The Russians, in particular the General Sametin, acting on the advice of Catherine the Great, who wanted the Brethren to settle in southern Russia to serve as a model for the backward Russian peasantry, assembled the remaining Brethren and brought them safely to the Volga. There they joined other German-speaking religious protesters and Anabaptists like the Mennonites, and became part of the substantial German minority in the agrarian population.

The Russian period lasted until 1870, when the Czarist government attempted to draft the Hutterites into the Army. Hutterites will under no circumstances accept military service, since they renounce all war and violence, and so they prepared to move. American land agents, scouring Europe for likely settlers for the Western frontier, persuaded the Hutterites and other German-speaking groups to make the trek to the New World. The Hutterites came in three waves, from 1871 through 1879, and finally settled in South Dakota. There they remained until 1918, when the American government tried to draft them into the Army, and local patriots mistakenly harassed them as German enemies. Canada invited them to settle in the Prairie Provinces, then still short of settlers. Their South Dakota colonies were abandoned, but taken in trust by the state government, which later sold them back to Manitoba Hutterites in the 1920's. Most Hutterites today live in Canada, but a substantial and growing number are found in both of the Dakotas and Montana. The Province of Alberta has the largest number of colonies.

The recent move into Saskatchewan was prompted by difficulties the Brethren had with the Alberta provincial government. Throughout their history, the Brethren have experienced oppression and harassment, not to mention outright persecution and martyrdom. Alberta, like some United States state governments, has attempted to restrict the number of colonies, and the practice of establishment of new colonies. The Hutterites divide their colony settlements in two when the population reaches from 125 to 130 because they have found that communal social life is difficult to manage with larger numbers, and that economic conditions in the northern Plains make it hard to support more people on the land available to them at the desired level of consumption. While the Alberta attempts to prevent this budding process have been revised and partly rejected by the courts, shortages of land added to the need to move elsewhere. Saskatchewan has been more cordial; it has established a special commission to assist Hutterites to find colony sites, and incidentally to work with them to prevent saturation of particular districts. A number of colonies have been persuaded to move north to the forest frontier to help develop this pioneer region of the Province. The group of colonies in the Jasper region were the first Hutterites to appear in Saskatchewan.

BELIEFS

The principal doctrinal difference that sets Anabaptists apart from most other Christian groups is the rejection of the practice of infant baptism. "Anabaptism" means re-baptism, which is a distorted label applied to them by their detractors, who saw them baptizing adults—a "second" baptism in terms of sixteenth-century conditions. Anabaptists spurned the practice of baptizing infants as unfair and contrary to Christ's teachings and the practices of the early church, which only accepted adults into the faith. Infants and children are conceived by Anabaptists to be too immature to understand the meaning and significance of Christianity. While this issue generated much heat, it is now fully accepted insofar as the regular Baptists are regarded as part of the Protestant order. (The Baptists were English analogs to Anabaptism, but appeared in a different social setting and lacked the Anabaptists' social revolutionary zeal.) In any case, no Hutterite is baptized until he or she is about 20 years old and "voluntarily" requests it.

In all likelihood the real issues behind persecution concerned other Anabaptist beliefs. The sects seriously proposed to establish the Golden Age in the guise of true Christianity, and rejected the official churches as corrupt. They regarded the State as evil; war as intolerable; taxation as unfair and for the Devil's purposes; contemporary culture as sinful and tempting: "Love not the world, neither the things that are in the world. If any man love the world, the love of the Father is not in him" (John 2:15–17). Modern Hutterite beliefs continue in this pattern, but show a number of compromises which mirror the Brethren's own remarkable ability to flourish in the world when conditions permit. Hutterites refuse to take political office or legal oaths, and are supposed not to vote—but they *have* voted in local elections when their interests are involved. While they believe that the State is corrupt, they enjoin their followers to obey its laws and pay its taxes (although occasionally they complain about taxation supporting war). They continue to resist military service and in the United States Hutterite boys now serve in conscientious-objector conservation camps (the Brethren refused even this in earlier years). They avoid non-Hutterite society but are taking an increasing part in charity activities in local communities, and are mingling with the local people in informal contexts. They continue to practice consumption austerity, since this is Christ's way, although the collective level of living of the colonies has been rising in recent years. The Community of Goods—the term Hutterites use to refer to their communal property system—still functions effectively, although covert individual accumulation of possessions often appears in many colonies. The Brethren forbid themselves to engage in usury or profit-making industry, but sell agricultural products for whatever they can get and drive a hard bargain for anything they want to buy.

Thus the basic Hutterite beliefs are really a blueprint for a particular way of life. Their purely religious ideas are not exceptional: they use Luther's translation of the Bible, and their general Christian dogma is for all practical purposes identical with that of most fundamentalist or Pentecostal sects—all of whom are really modern representatives of the tradition which began with the Anabaptists, and before them, in the medieval communal sects. But the important thing about Hutterite beliefs is the fact that they are all qualified either by "yes, but" statements, or by modifications of practice, as indicated in the foregoing paragraph. This is a reflection of the basic paradox in Hutterian life pointed to earlier: while the Brethren must avoid the World, they must also learn to use its rules and procedures in order to survive. Hutterites are especially good at this, probably because they established a compromise form of Anabaptist withdrawal at an early date during the Moravian period when they accepted the patronage of the aristocracy.

The Hutterian acceptance of modern technology is another instance of this compromise policy. Machinery, power equipment, refrigeration, central propane heating, the very latest farming implements, large modern workshops, station wagons (usually only one to a colony, however, to control trips to town), are the stock in trade of every colony. Jasper Colony Number 6, isolated on the crestal plateau, even owned a snowmobile and was part of a two-way radio system linking the ranches in this remote area. Another colony owned four latest-model grain combines with air-conditioned cabs; another had a shower room with stainless-steel walls. Most had central propane gas heating systems. These are all cases of "collective consumption," not individual, and thus the Hutterites preserve their basic personal austerity. The acquisition of expensive equipment is defended on the grounds that the colony system must compete in an increasingly high-cost agricultural economy that emphasizes capital requirements over labor; consequently the utmost efficiency of operation is sought. There is truth in this view, since the Hutterites do support a much larger number of people on given units of land and other resources than individual farmers— "We *have* to be good," remarked one of the young agricultural managers.

Hutterites have very large families and have the fastest rate of population increase of any social group in North America. Population growth, and the press toward enterprise efficiency, forced them to adopt modern machinery in the 1920's, like other Great Plains farmers. Stainless steel shower rooms may seem extravagant, but the Hutterites' need for large quantities means that the ability to buy surplus material and large bargain lots make such purchases economical. In a way, the Brethren's own sobriety and efficiency make them prisoners of prosperity—at least collective prosperity.

THE JASPER SETTLEMENT

When Hutterites establish new colonies, they do so with great efficiency and skill because they have a conscious blueprint for domestic and farming institutions. The colony is a world in itself, a kind of portable village, with essential equipment, funds, and labor force. The Brethren usually have enough cash to buy most of the land they need for the first decade or so of colony existence, and these large land purchases have the effect of providing a more adequate share of natural resources in this exceedingly variable environment—that is, the larger the land area, the greater the chance of finding some good soil, adequate water supplies, good pasture, or level topography.

Hutterites believe that colonies should not be too close together, since this tends to encourage resentment and opposition among non-Hutterites and also creates competitive relationships among the colonies themselves in their local sales of farm produce (the Brethren sell vegetables, eggs, chickens, and other products locally as well as selling their cash crops on the national market). The six Jasper colonies were located at varying distances from one another (see Fig. 2.2), but those west of Jasper town are very close together—most of them have joint land boundaries. These four were too close together by Hutterite standards, but this happened because of the availability of land. In other words, when land is available in large quantities in a particular district, the Brethren will locate their colonies there regardless of proximity. This situation has developed in recent years as large tracts of land have become much harder to find. In many parts of the northern Plains, Hutterite colonies have reached a saturation point.

The population of the six Jasper colonies in 1964 was about 559 men, women, and children, or about 7 per cent of the total population of the Jasper region. This represented an average per-colony increase of 42 per cent over the population of each group in the first year of its settlement. Demographers have found that the Hutterite population doubles every 16 years, and since colonies split when the population reaches about 150, the maximum population of the Jasper colonies would be about 900.

This will probably never be reached, because colonies are dividing at increasingly lower population levels. In any case, we could assume that the Hutterian population will probably level off at about 10 per cent of the total regional population, assuming no important additional growth in the non-Hutterian. As we shall see later, the economic productivity of this small segment of the regional population is extremely high.

A total of 55 farms were sold to the Hutterites in order to acquire the land for their colonies, but most of the former owners retired into Jasper town. Considering the fact that between 1946 and 1960 a total of 685 Jasper farming enterprises disappeared from the census totals, the fraction purchased by the Brethren was small, and would not justify the oft-heard criticism of the Hutterites as a major factor in driving out local farmers.

However, the local impact of these sales can be great: in the area west of Jasper town, the four colonies there bought 44 farms in an area approximately 162 square miles, or about one third of all farms in this district. At the time of our study, the land purchases of the four colonies were not complete, and additional farm sales could be expected. Eventually about one half or more of all the farms in this district could be expected to go to the Hutterites. By 1965, the colonies controlled about 4 per cent of all land in any form of agricultural production in the Jasper region.

The locations of the colonies as shown in Figure 2.2 were not due to accident. In each locality, land was available because of some adaptive defect in the individual ownership system of farming enterprise. (It should be obvious that Hutterites compete with farmers, not ranchers for land, since in Saskatchewan the Brethren are not permitted to obtain grazing leases, hence have to buy "deeded" land—in private tenure.) West of town, the majority of farmers were Eastern Europeans who had settled this region of sandy soils and rough topography after the better areas had been taken. Some of these people also practiced division of their property upon retirement, thus leaving a number of substandard farms to their sons, many of whom refused to take over. For these and other reasons, the district had many abandoned farms and farms operated by aging people ready to sell in the 1950's. The Hutterite offers—the Brethren often offer cash, and prices above the going rate—were taken eagerly.

Colony Number 6 was located in the "Bench," as this section of the plateau is called, where the non-Hutterite population was reduced to a few hardy ranchers. The area had been the site of a substantial homestead farming settlement, the homesteaders attracted by the deceptively long grass on the plateau. But the impossibility of farming the area, with its short growing season and general isolation, had driven away this entire settlement by 1950. Therefore much land was available, and the Hutterites bought it. Colony Number 5, east of Jasper town, took advantage of a series of large tracts of farm land that had been sold by their former farmer-owners to outsiders on a speculative basis. About 3,000 acres were available, and by buying this, the Hutterites encouraged adjoining farmers to sell also. Thus in these, and the other cases, the Hutterites located their colonies where large tracts of land were available because the land was not being used, due to tenure arrangements, or to difficulties of managing the specialized resources on a small-farm basis. The Hutterites therefore represented a case of "competitive replacement," a term we shall define in Chapter 10.

Hutterites frequently were accused by Jasper people of causing an increase in land values in the region which made it difficult for young farmers to get established. This is a serious accusation, and we made an effort to investigate it. We found that while land prices did jump rapidly when Hutterites began buying, this was due partly to the sellers, who often met together and agreed to jack up the prices, knowing that Hutterites were often willing to pay bonus prices. The Brethren were continually solicited by farmers anxious to sell. Secondly, we found that the price eventually reached for land after the Hutterite settlement was no greater than price rises in another and similar region in Saskatchewan that had no colonies. What happened is that the Brethren simply caused a sudden jump in prices that would have occurred normally a few years later in the speculative land market of the 1950's.

The six Jasper colonies in some respects formed a region within a region, insofar as the Brethren had more to do with each other than with non-Hutterites. However, the amount and kind of relationships among the colonies was influenced by several factors. The first we shall consider is the branch of the sect a particular colony may belong to. All Hutterites are divided into three branches based on the three groups or waves of immigrants coming from Russia to North America in the 1870's. Two of these branches (or *Leute* as the Hutterites call them)— the Darius and the Lehrer—were represented in Jasper: two colonies of Lehrer and four of Darius. Hutterites marry only inside of their Leut, and the customs of the Leute differ slightly (for example, Lehrer men use buttons on their clothes; Darius men have hooks and eyes). Other things being equal, Brethren of the same Leut associated together more than with members of the other branch. Where, however, two colonies of different Leute are very close together, they will tend to have more relations with each other than with their fellow-Leute colonies located at a distance. Hutterites exchange machinery and labor, jointly plan and design new agricultural ventures, attend each other's weddings and funerals, let their young people associate together for courtship, and have other associations of a type to be expected between what are, in effect, farming villages of a European type.

FAMILY AND MARRIAGE

Hutterites respect the nuclear family of parents and children, and provide private apartments of two to four rooms for each such unit in the row houses they customarily build. Marriages are expected to be love matches, and considerable care is taken to bring young people together in order to find compatible mates. At marriage, each couple is provided with such basic necessities as furniture, a clock, and a sewing machine for the wife to make the family clothing. Children are usually born in the local hospital—Hutterites greatly respect the need for professional medical care (in the sixteenth century they had their own doctors). The children are raised wholly by the parents and older siblings until the age of three, when the colony school system takes over, but even so, children always sleep in their parent's apartment. Children also attend the public school, built by the colony on its premises, and taught by a local school teacher from town. Schooling stops at the 8th grade.

The most important kinship grouping in Hutterite colony society is the group of male siblings of each nuclear family. These boys retain their affectual ties on into adulthood, and often they may constitute a kind of brother-clique which can have considerable importance in the operation of the colony, since a group of such brothers may have managerial positions in the various agricultural activities, and can function as a voting block in colony assemblies. This brother group is, in fact, the only important clique-like structure in Hutterite society: friendship ties are not highly developed, and age-groups, with the exception of the unmarried young girls, are weakly developed.

Each Hutterite is also a member of an extended patrinomial family, which always cuts across two or more colonies because of the fission process. Often such an extended family will constitute the entire population of a colony, although most colonies have representatives of two or three families of this type. Relationships among the relatives of these big families were about the same as one finds in non-Hutterite farming or ranching society in Jasper; for example, when visiting another colony, a Hutterite will be given a bed in his relative's apartment.

Each of the three Leute consists of a large number of these extended families linked by marriage—thus the Leut might be likened to an endogamous "lineage" in anthropological terminology. The reasons for the lack of marriage across the Leute is given by Hutterites themselves as entirely practical: the differences in customs, though slight from an outsider's viewpoint, are sufficient to cause trouble when a person from one Leut marries into another. For example, there was one marriage in a Jasper colony of this type, and the wife got into difficulties with the elders because she insisted on making her husband's clothes on the model of the other Leut. Hutterites live by hundreds of meticulous rules that must be observed or carefully and consciously changed when the need arises.

The basic problem of kinship in Hutterite colonies stems from the collective and communal way of life. The most important group in Hutterite society is not the kin, but the communal village. Hutterites work together, go to church as a group, eat at tables segregated by sex, and raise their children communally. Kinship therefore must not be allowed to become a rival to this collective entity. (The groups of brothers, for example, can become a threat to colony unity when they become too cliqueish and attempt to control decision-making processes.) Various means have been developed by the Hutterites to control kinship and other forms of factionalism: manipulation of functional job and task assignment, such as rotation of jobs, in order to break up cliques; discouragement or prevention of nepotism (a son following in his father's job); and discipline by the minister.

COLONY ORGANIZATION

Figure 8.1 diagrams the instrumental structure of a typical Jasper colony—and for Hutterite colonies everywhere, since there are no significant departures from this chartered plan. It is a complex type of organization for a relatively small group, but communal life and big enterprises require complex organization. The plan is moreover identical—save for some of the titles given the functionaries—with the structure of the Moravian colonies in the sixteenth century. Hutterites found out early how to organize their large diversified enterprises, and the people in them, and they have never changed. The content of their economic activities, and the emphases placed on certain of these, naturally change depending upon resources, and on the nature of the external society, but the structure has remained without alteration. This is of course due not only to the Hutterite reliance on dogma, but also to the fact that the plan is actually an extremely efficient way of operating a combined group of diverse agricultural activities. The Israeli *kibbutz,* a modern communal agricultural enterprise, is organized in an almost identical fashion. The *kibbutz* did not copy the colony—it is simply that there are really a limited number of ways of organizing a communal agrarian system.

In Figure 8.1 one can see that colony leadership has two principal levels: the Elders or Executives at the top and the Managers just below them. Two positions combine both levels: the

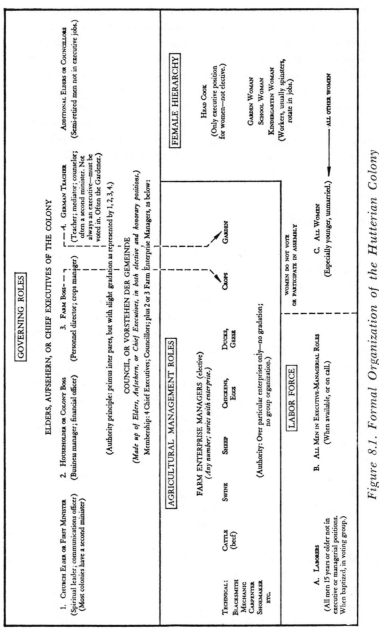

Figure 8.1. Formal Organization of the Hutterian Colony

All adult males take part in the Assembly—the colony's group-decision body. Women do not participate or vote.

Farm Boss and the German Teacher. The former is in charge of the field crops on the managerial level but, because of the large amount of labor expended on crops, he is also a general personnel director and task organizer on the Executive level. The German Teacher (not always an Executive) is usually the Garden Man on the managerial level. This is so because the garden is always close to the buildings and is worked by the women. The Teacher also directs the women who run the nursery school and kindergarten and is around the colony premises all day long. There is also a Council that functions more or less on the Executive level, although usually one to three Managers may be members. The Council discusses important issues to be brought before the Assembly, which consists of all baptized male members—in effect, all men 20 years or older.

The labor force consists of all members of the colony, male and female, although Executives and Managers may be excused from ordinary labor when they must perform their assigned tasks. In every colony there are a number of men who are neither Executives nor Managers, but usually these are the younger men. One reason for the practice of colony division is to give all men a good chance at becoming leaders, so as to maintain commitment and a feeling of responsibility. It has been found that the majority of men who leave Hutterian life permanently (actually the number is very small) are those who have not been elected to leadership positions and who believe they never will be.

The women constitute a separate category in Hutterian society. Hutterites believe that women are subordinate to men, although men have an obligation to cherish and defend them. Actually women can play an important informal role in Hutterian life, often exercising considerable influence on their husbands. The Head Cook is the only woman with what might be considered managerial responsibility, and she is also the only woman who is elected to office. In most of the Jasper colonies the Cook was the wife of the Householder or General Manager, since this facilitated the technical and financial planning involved in the commissary. The women who worked in the kindergarten and nursery school were often spinsters, of whom each colony had two or more. Women are not forced into mar-

riage, and the Brethren recognize the advantage of having a
spinster or two for performing certain kinds of tasks.

The Executives are graded in authority as represented by the
numerical order of the roles at the top of the chart. The Church
Elder, or chief minister, is the most important figure. His duties
are not only to conduct church services (often with the assistance
of a second minister) but also to maintain communications in
the colony, discipline offenders, maintain the faith, and in
general function as a paterfamilias. The Householder, or manager and financial expert, is second in authority, and in some
contexts of colony affairs is superior to the minister. He manages the entire economic operation and also represents the colony
in its dealings with outsiders. We have already discussed the
Farm Boss and the Teacher. The retired Elders are older men
who are no longer in executive or managerial positions, but
whose advice and counsel is frequently sought. In a church
service or a colony business assembly meeting, all the Elder-Execu-
tives sit on a bench behind the table which serves as an "altar"
and face the entire congregation. Thus the functional operation
of the colony, and its religious identity, are merged in the
arrangement. This is, perhaps, the most fundamental fact of
Hutterian life. Religion and daily life are blended: religion
defines this way of life, and its conduct is a manifestation of
religion.

The activities of the Hutterian colony are organized on the
basis of what we have called "managed democracy," meaning by
this term a combination of egalitarian group decision and
patriarchal authority. It is hard for the average North American
to conceive of this combination, since by definition the two are
supposed to be opposites! However, human beings can adapt to
almost any amount of contradiction if they want to. Hutterites
have no secular *theory* of "democracy" or "patriarchy," but simply carry on the business of a Christian brotherhood with ideas
developed in the sixteenth century. It is the description of the
egalitarian church of the apostles and disciples which brings
egalitarian elements into their social order, and it is this same
source, plus some Old Testament ideas, that brings patriarchal
arrangements (and the subordination of women) into the picture.
Thus, Hutterites elect every man to office in an assembly meet-

ing, but they believe that such election is the will of God, and that therefore once elected, a man has considerable authority. Every man is supposed to be treated alike so far as possessions go, but the Executives have a few more privileges and of course much more authority. All issues are supposed to be openly discussed and fairly voted on by all the men (the women do not vote), but most issues are thoroughly thrashed out in informal caucuses by the leaders before being brought to a vote.

The development of the farming enterprises is in the hands of the Managers, who are expected to run their operations with considerable autonomy. In order to get the equipment they need, however, or to make improvements, they must present a sound case to the Executives and the Council, and eventually to the Assembly. They must be able to take failure without complaint or resentment. The managers are in a de facto competitive situation, but are not allowed to openly compete or scheme against each other or against the executives. A degree of competition is covertly acknowledged by Hutterites, and is known to be a spur to accomplishment, but this must never be admitted since it is against the tenets of an egalitarian brotherhood. There is always some temptation for managers to run their activities for their own profit, and one type of "sick" colony is one where this begins to happen. However, the small size of the colony makes clandestine dealings very difficult, and the communal conscience is a strong deterrent.

Another process difficult for the outsider to comprehend is the presence of high motivation to achieve on the part of most Hutterite men in the absence of the usual incentives to such motivation in the majority society: competition and material rewards. The process is difficult to explain, because there is a *degree* of marginal or covert competition, differential rewards, and recognition of a man's need to "rise" in responsibility, as we have described. Nevertheless, Hutterian society manages to obtain great efficiency and dedication to hard work from its men and women with only minimal development of the kinds of incentives common to the "outside." The most general answer to the question of "how?" is simply the intensive socialization of every Hutterite in the principles of group welfare, and in the religious ideal of brotherhood as fulfillment of the mission of Christ. An individual Hutterite gains the respect of his brothers if he works well and hard—this is his principal reward, and he has been taught from early childhood that this is a very important one. Moreover, if a Hutterite lives up to the rules, he automatically is guaranteed equal and fair treatment, and this, too, is a considerable reward. Basically the Hutterite system modifies the workings of the personal prestige factor in status, the factor so common in an individualistic society; in its place, the colony system substitutes the opportunity to serve the group and exemplify the teachings of Christ as the Hutterites define them.

ECONOMIC ADAPTATIONS

Originally Hutterites lived as much by their craft manufactures as by agriculture, but beginning with their Russian sojourn, agriculture came to be the dominant economic pursuit. This was strengthened in North America, since the Hutterites found it necessary to keep up with growing commercialization and mechanization in order to support their communal settlements. Their built-in traditions of efficiency and rationality also assisted. The Jasper colonies were all intensive agricultural enterprises of great diversity (as suggested on Fig. 8.1, where some of the activities supervised by the managers are listed; some colonies had several more than shown).

The introduction of Hutterites into Jasper meant a cash gain to the area of about $1.5 million, the amount paid to the farmers whose land they bought. Their agricultural production made a substantial boost in the total production of the region: in wheat alone, 14 per cent of the total Jasper production was sustained by the colonies in 1963, and the gross income of the colonies was $400,000 over that for all the farms the Brethren replaced. Such increases in production occurred on only 4 per cent of the total agricultural land area. Not all of the cash went into the Jasper economy, of course, since much of it was saved for colony fission and also used for bulk purchases from urban outlets of needed commodities such as surplus metal or bolts of cloth (Jasper lacks such sales outlets). Farm equipment

and automotive dealers had substantial increases in sales due
to the Hutterites, however, and Hutterite traffic in vegetables,
eggs, poultry and other commodities accounted for a substantial
gain in sales in these things to regional customers. Hutterite individuals had only a few dollars allotted to them as spending
money, and of course the retail merchants did not gain much
from this. However, in many ways, Hutterites raised the income
and productivity of the Jasper region.

In their traditional practice of diversified farming, the Hutterites can be said to have been "preadapted" to northern Plains
agriculture, which has always suffered from too much reliance
on grain and cattle. With their much larger land areas and
large gross colony incomes (the average was about $75,000, with
the median closer to $100,000), they can afford many farming
activities that would cause the small individual farmer to go
broke. Hutterites can sustain deficit enterprises because their
income is large enough to cover them. When prices pick up in
these spheres, they can benefit from the sustained skills and
facilities. The ideal of Hutterite diversification is a sensible,
though always slightly shifting, balance—the Brethren criticize
a colony that seeks to overexpand in one temporarily profitable
sector.

The Jasper colonies showed variations in their production
schedules in accordance with particular patterns of resources,
and particular levels of skill and interest. Egg production varied
from 10,000 dozen annually to 90,000; cattle sales brought from
$11,000 to $70,000; number of swine sold ranged from 430 to
1,800. The colony on the Bench greatly emphasized livestock
over grain crops, due to the altitude, but most of the other
colonies reversed this pattern. While these differences were significant, it should be emphasized that all colonies were highly
diversified as compared to even the most diversified individual
Jasper farm, where the costs of operation and family consumption required intense concentration on the most profitable cash
crop—usually grain. Studies of crop yields, livestock weight at
sale, and other indications of efficiency of production were not
conclusive, since many factors (moisture variability and pasture
conditions, for example) affect these. However, the data did appear to indicate that the Hutterites were as good as the best

farmers, and far better than the worst. Nevertheless, differences were noted that correlated with the age of a colony: very young colonies generally had less productive or efficient regimes due to their inexperience and problems of starting. The rapid transfer of information between colonies, however, usually results in a leveling-off of these differences after a few years in a region.

Consumption austerity as practiced by Hutterites constitutes a genuine saving, and makes an important contribution to their economy. The average colony will have about 13 nuclear families of parents and children. There will be just one passenger vehicle (in Jasper, always a large truck-type station wagon) for all of these families, whereas in non-Hutterite society, each nuclear family unit would have its own. Production of food in the garden alone was worth about $10,000 at retail prices for the average colony, and all of the work was done in the garden by the women, which thereby permitted the men to concentrate on large-scale production. A typical Jasper farm family of four persons spent $2,500 in a typical year on recreation and entertainment of all kinds; a colony of 74 persons spent $1,500.

Craft activities still existed in the colonies, although crafts lack the economic importance they once had in Hutterian economy. All Jasper colonies made most of their own clothing and shoes, most of their furniture, built their own houses and farm buildings, wove rugs and mats, and constructed a number of their farm implements. With the exception of construction work and farm implement manufacture, most of these crafts were traditional, or were carried on in order to keep people busy and occupied. Some colonies engaged in new crafts, like the making of stainless steel kitchen equipment, sold or bartered to other colonies. Hutterites also love hand-made gadgets—in the sixteenth century they were famous for devising simple machines like comb-cutting devices, book binders, noodle-makers, and the like. Today things like these would be bought, but colony mechanics enjoy tearing them down and improving them. Many Hutterites realize that some of these craft activities probably cost more in labor than they are worth in income, but they also know that it is important to continue to engage in crafts because of their morale-building value. One Jasper Hutterite remarked to the writer that when the Elders permitted the Brethren to have radios, he was going to make sure that they built their own!

We spoke earlier of the conservationist practices of Hutterian agriculture. Many of the large farmers and a few of the ranchers in Jasper did abuse their resources in order to sustain or increase income—although we have noted that a conservative and conservationist philosophy tended to prevail. Hutterites can afford to conserve more easily than many farmers because of their economy of scale. For example, they can take bad land out of production for a few years to convert it to other uses, while most farmers could not do this without suffering a serious drop in income. Hutterian water resources were usually more adequately developed than on the average Jasper farm since the Brethren had more capital to put into the expensive facilities— although in this respect most of the ranches did equally well. Hutterian production of forage crops was large enough to permit most colonies to avoid extensive grazing and to feed the cattle with hay and grain. Summer-fallow practices were careful and carried out with blade implements—often too expensive for the average farmer, but far better for the light Jasper soils.

Hutterian farm management techniques were basically similar to those practiced by most farmers and ranchers insofar as the Brethren did not make detailed economic studies of their enterprises. They farmed according to a sensible trial-and-error approach, and rarely made anything other than simple cost and price computations. Their engineering and mechanical skills were usually more highly developed than their financial management, a common pattern in Great Plains agriculture. Hutterites do not make sophisticated management analyses, not only because their limited educational level would not sustain them but also because they resist outside experts probing into their life and economy. Moreover, these studies often require detailed accounting of the productivity of different agricultural activities and the labor of individual workers. This is taboo in Hutterian society because it would tend to establish criteria for differential prestige, and also provide temptation to alter the traditional ideal of diversified balance. In any case, the large scale of Hutterian agricultural economy makes such studies relatively unimportant, since it covers mistakes and relatively unproductive episodes.

Relations with the Jasper Community

Hutterites are seldom welcomed by the local inhabitants of Great Plains communities, who fear their powerful competition, irresistible ability to buy land, and alleged failure to spend money with local merchants. We have shown that most of these accusations are misleading, since essentially Hutterites add greatly to local productivity, buy large quantities of special equipment, and at least in Jasper, do not artificially inflate land values. Their presence in an agrarian community has about the same effect as large corporative farms might have. There is a grain of truth in the criticisms, but there are also plenty of compensating factors.

But the non-Hutterites in Jasper had other criticisms as well. They noted that the Hutterites stood aloof from the rest of society and social relations, and refused to take part in the churches and in politics—hence were not fully participating members in the community. This was a source of considerable anxiety in Jasper, where great store was set on friendly, neighborly interaction on the basis of old frontier values. Hutterites seemed to belong to another race, another world—their presence meant just so much less social interaction in a region already concerned with a felt loss of the satisfying social life of the old days.

Hutterites were not only aware of these criticisms, but recognized that their sectarian apartness did indeed create a barrier to participation. Most of the Jasper colonies were making special efforts to find ways of interacting in Jasper society without compromising their principles. They were also insatiably curious about the non-Hutterite world, and sometimes a Hutterite would become a good source of local gossip. The Brethren liked to wander around town during their frequent business trips, talking to merchants and dealers and local government officials, taking an occasional drink in the beer hall, or visiting the homes of acquaintances. Some Hutterites tried to become experts on local history and traditions in an effort to identify with the community and be able to interact with the community leaders, most of whom were preoccupied with such matters. The colonies made occasional cash contributions to a few of the local charities and the regional hospital. All of the colonies made an effort to help their small-farmer neighbors, and lent a hand whenever it was needed. Farmers and ranchers in the vicinity of the colonies were generally accepting of the Brethren, and even enjoyed their company, although those who felt they were ticketed for absorption by land purchases often showed marked resentment.

There is one pattern of Hutterian behavior in relationship to the non-Hutterian community which is repeated in all of the Plains communities. It is a source of hostility toward the Brethren, and is difficult to control. Hutterite children are confined to the colony premises most of the time, but occasionally get taken to town or on a visit to a local farm or ranch. On such occasions, they discover a rich world of possessions they barely knew existed, and sometimes the temptation to appropriate an item is too strong to resist (even young adults succumb occasionally). The attitude is probably reinforced by the Hutterian self-imposed isolation from the external society, which may then be seen as fair game. In any event, the Elders are vigilant, and whenever thefts occur that can be traced to colony members, redress is made and disciplinary procedures instituted.

In the Jasper community there was a small group of men and women who over the years had developed close relations with the colonies, or with a few families and individuals in them. A proprietor of a local restaurant, the manager of a grocery store, a school teacher, a local farmer-rancher, and a few other people had found occasion to become intimate with the Brethren. Economic ties usually started the relationship: sales of produce, exchanging labor, an occasional cash loan to or from the Brethren, and from these relationships there could develop warm personal ties. The Brethren appreciated these friendships and contacts, but at the same time they were anxious about them, because frequently they turned sour. The restaurant proprietor mentioned was a good customer and even a friendly drinking companion with the young Brethren, but from time to time he would develop strong hostility to the Hutterites, whose ways appeared to frustrate him, or induce deep feelings of guilt. Similar ambivalent relationships developed with ranchers and farmers near the colonies; after repeated exchanges of labor and machinery, dinners at the colony, guest status at weddings, and similar evidence of friendship, a man could turn on the Brethren, accusing them of breaking his fences, stealing his cattle, and other false or distorted things. The strain of having to live and deal with these "foreign-like people" in a gregarious and clannish North American society was simply too much for people with strong feelings of alienation from that society: their only friends, the Hutterites, were symbols of their alienation, and this could induce considerable guilt.

The Future of the Colonies

When Hutterites divide their colonies they usually split the population down the middle of the age pyramid so that the new colony—or "new farm" as they like to call it—is a virtual duplicate of the parent. The new group is chosen by lot after the new land and site has been located, necessary buildings constructed, and the first crops planted. The new colony never has as much machinery or equipment of all kinds as the parent, since Hutterites believe that there is no point in depriving two settlements of the tools necessary to sustain the economy. Hence the new colony struggles to become established and grow. The parent colony usually supplies the new group with a cash grant —often as much as $200,000, which is just about enough to buy the land—or gives it a series of loans over the first few years. But most colonies can obtain bank loans with little difficulty, due to their reliability and collective wealth.

The Jasper colonies would begin to fission in the late 1960's, and the question in everybody's mind at the time of our study in Jasper was whether they would establish daughter colonies in the region. The issue was one of concern to the provincial government as well, since the Hutterites and a special government committee had collaborated on an agreement to avoid saturation of settled districts. We have also noted that Hutterites themselves are concerned over this matter, though because land is getting so scarce they often take sites where they can find them.

Our own study of the ecological situation in the Jasper region revealed that there was only one location that was ripe for Hutterian entry: an area south of Colony Number 6, on the Bench. Land was available there for reasons already described, and it would be sufficient to permit establishment of a second colony in that district. In all other districts, farming and ranching were well established, and unless general economic conditions changed drastically, there would be no possibility of large land sales. It was therefore with considerable interest that the writer learned in 1967 that a colony had selected the district south of the bench for establishment, exactly where we had predicted.

It is therefore probable that the seven colonies in the Jasper region represented the permanent settlement. These colonies will of course remain indefinitely—one is inclined to say "forever," because Hutterites think that way. There is a timeless quality to Hutterian culture since they have never really changed their outlook or charter—only their technology. When they buy land it is with the intention of establishing a permanent settlement, and their economy permits them to experiment, alter their procedures, and do what is necessary to survive.

Hutterites have made the most productive economic adaptation to the resources of the Jasper region, and to the conditions of the national agricultural economy that affects Jasper. The things that make them so are the very arrangements that the non-Hutterite farming population is gradually moving toward —although with different techniques, and in adjustment to an individual enterprise system. Community pastures, grazing cooperatives, community irrigation schemes, and other things do for the farmers in some measure what communal agriculture does for the Hutterites: absorb risks, increase capital, and create social organization that permits a more efficient use of labor and human effort. We cannot say that the farmers have learned from the Hutterites, because their movement toward these things is an independent one based on government encouragement. But the results are very much the same. Clearly the overriding concern of economic development in the Jasper region is to permit a larger population to be supported on the specialized and variable resources. Barring a major population decrease in North America, the current trend of depopulation of rural areas must be halted, and cooperative-collective institutions can help greatly. They already have, as shown on Figure 2.5, where the population of farming districts served by community pastures and other organizations were beginning to show stabilization at a higher level than areas without these facilities. The same principle works for Hutterites: they are able to support a considerably larger population on the available resources than are individual farmers and ranchers. And they do it in a way generally more conserving of these resources.

Hutterian economic success is helped, not hindered, by their separatist policies with respect to the majority society. Since Hutterites end their formal education at the 8th grade, they are barred from possible employment in higher-paying jobs in the towns of the general region; such jobs usually require high school diplomas. On the "outside" most Jasper Hutterites could expect to get only the most menial positions, paying no more than $6 a day. Their labor in the colony was therefore worth far more than anything they could get on the outside, or in economic terms, their labor opportunity costs were low. The situation was different for those farmers and ranchers with more formal education or special skill training. Their labor opportunity costs tended to be high—so high that they lost money by remaining in agriculture. The situation resulted in a very limited out-migration of productive Hutterite men—the colonies kept most of their best and most intelligent workers. Their self-teaching made up for the loss of formal education, so they received the best of both worlds: low opportunity costs but relatively good practical education. There were, however, some signs that the lack of high-school level knowledge was beginning to hamper agricultural decisions and practices.

Opportunity costs of Hutterian investment in farming were also low, considering the capitalization of the colony farms and the religious charter which prohibits any change in the status or sale of the enterprise on the open market. Hutterites "have to be good," as the Brother quoted earlier noted, because they have no alternative. When there is no choice of alternatives, opportunity costs remain low: what you do is what you do best, and if you improve your performance, the "best" is good indeed.

As time passes, will the Hutterites change their ways? We have commented at various points on Hutterian attitudes toward change, in particular how they are able to modify their "instrumental" (economic and technical) culture while preserving their dogma, customs, and social organization. They are able to do this because the instrumental side of life is defined as a means to an end: maintenance of the Hutterian social system and beliefs. (Among the Amish, instrumentalities become part of the ends, and consequently the Amish strive to maintain their literally— horse-and-buggy way of life and economy.)

However this may be, living in a rich, individualistic world is a constant source of temptation, and Hutterites, especially the young, are by no means immune. Even more important is the fact of prosperity: the efficiency of these people can create financial problems in reverse: too much money, and corresponding inducements to increase the level of living. The latter has unquestionably been inching upward in recent years, just as it has to an even greater extent in the kibbutz of Israel. During four years of field work in Jasper, the writer witnessed many improvements in comforts and conveniences in the six colonies. Most of these were of a collective nature, but individuals too, were beginning to accumulate possessions, however secretly.

Perhaps more important than the question of culture change is the one of expansion. Land is disappearing, and sooner or later the Hutterites will have to find ways of either losing people by defection and education, or controlling their reproduction. It is not difficult to see colonies like those in the Jasper region becoming permanent settlements which no longer divide when population grows, but which send out some of their young people into the outer world to find their own way, and to carry a modified version of the Hutterian beliefs into secular society. New forms of colonization may be attempted; the Hutterites have considered Latin America and rejected it (the Mennonites accepted it, and have flourishing communities there), but they can always reconsider. The Canadian North is now being entered tentatively, as we noted earlier. There are other possibilities. In any case, Hutterian traditions will not perish: for 500 years, the sect has survived, despite (or because of) persecutions, wars, famines, internal decline, and other disasters. Their most vital trait is economic and technical adaptability, stabilized by their unchanging traditions and social organization, and this accounts for their success in Jasper.

BIBLIOGRAPHIC NOTES

This chapter is based on my book on the Jasper colonies, *Hutterian Brethren: The Agricultural Economy and Social Organization of a Communal People,* Stanford University Press, 1967. For additional general studies of Hutterian culture, see John Hostetler and Gertrude Huntington, *The Hutterites in North America,* Holt, Rinehart, and Winston, 1967; Paul S. Gross, *The Hutterite Way,* Freeman Publishing Co., 1965; Victor Peters, *All Things Common: The Hutterian Way of Life.* University of Minnesota Press, 1965.

For histories of Anabaptism and the Hutterites, see George H. Williams, *The Radical Reformation,* Westminster Press, 1962; Roland H. Bainton, *The Reformation of the Sixteenth Century,* Beacon Press, 1952, Chap. 5; John Horsch, *The Hutterite Brethren, 1528–1931,* Goshen College, 1931; Robert Friedmann, *Hutterite Studies,* Goshen College, 1961. An account of Hutterite beliefs is also found in Robert Friedmann's book. The basic Hutterian catechism is Peter Rideman, *Account of our Religion, Doctrine, and Faith,* 1565, translated by K. Hasenberg and published by the Bruderhof movement, Plough, 1950. The Bruderhof movement founded by Eberhardt Arnold, is a voluntary Hutterian convert group, organized in England and operating with chapters in New York and South America. For an account, see Emmy Arnold, *Torches Together: The Beginning and Early Years of the Bruderhof Communities,* Plough, 1964.

For a recent account of the difficulties Hutterites have had with North American governments, see Victor Peters' book referred to above.

Information on the economic rationality of Anabaptists generally, and Hutterites in particular, can be found in Peter Klassen, "The Economics of Anabaptism," unpublished dissertation, Department of History, University of Southern California, 1962; Donald Sommer, "Peter Rideman and Menno Simons on Economics," *Mennonite Quarterly Review,* Vol. 28 (1954), pp. 205–23.

Craft manufacture is part of the self-help theme in all communal or utopian sectarian groups, whatever the historical tradition. The custom leads to decorous, sparsely furnished interiors, with an emphasis on natural finishes and materials. A pictorial study and analysis of Shaker crafts is found in Edward D. Andrews and F. Andrews, *Shaker Furniture: The Craftsmanship of an American Communal Sect,* Dover, 1950.

Interpretations of Hutterian cultural and technical change are found in Chaps. 10 and 11 of my book mentioned above, and in Joseph W. Eaton, "Controlled Acculturation: A Survival Technique of the Hutterites," *American Sociological Review,* Vol. 17 (1952), pp. 331–40. For a study of Hutterian personality, with implications for change, see Joseph W. Eaton, *Culture and Mental Disorders,* Free Press, 1955.

The incentive theory in industrial society is outlined in Chester I. Barnard, *The Functions of the Executive,* Harvard University Press, 1950.

Studies of Hutterite population appear in Robert C. Cook, "The North American Hutterites: A Study in Human Multiplication," *Population Bulletin,* No. 10 (1954); Joseph W. Eaton and Albert Meyer, *Man's Capacity to Reproduce: The Demography of a Unique Population,* Free Press, 1954.

For accounts of the kibbutz permitting comparisons to the Hutterites, see H. Darin-Drabkin, *The Other Society,* Gollancz, 1962; Eric Cohen, "Progress and Communality: Value Dilemmas in the Collective Movement," *Informational Review of Community Development,* Nos. 15, 16 (1966); Yonina Talmon, "The Family in a Revolutionary Movement: The Case of the Kibbutz," in M. Nimkoff, ed., *Comparative Family Systems,* Harper, 1965.

NINE

Cooperation and Competition in Agricultural Production

In the last two chapters of this book we intend to discuss aspects of our study that bear on problems and processes of agrarian development. This chapter will supply additional data on cooperative and competitive strategies and relationships in the Jasper economy, viewed as a problem in the allocation of resources and the accomplishment of desired ends. The next (and last) chapter is a summary of the entire book in the sense that it brings together all previously presented materials dealing with the processes of change and adaptation, and concludes with some recommendations for further developmental steps in Jasper and regions like it elsewhere.

Underlying our approach to agrarian development in these chapters is recognition of the role of the external society in Jasper's economic affairs. The important role played by both private and governmental agencies in local society in North America can scarcely be exaggerated, although often enough the role is misunderstood. It is essential that bias be avoided here, because the issues are important and the processes leading toward interdependence of all sectors of modern societies are irreversible, at least in some respects. Perhaps most essential is an understanding of, first, that most rural North Americans have never rejected involvement in the nation, but have actively sought it as part of their desire to be incorporated in the national entity; second, that their involvements almost always entail manipulation of the external agencies and forces, both in terms of local modifications of government regulations, and also direct political action to get what they want from government and big business.

This chapter is concerned with aspects of both of these features of the relationships of the Jasper society to the nation. Our practical interests are highlighted by an analysis of the strategies used to mobilize local social organization and also to manipulate the government-sponsored programs. Our theoretical interests are concerned with the role of cooperation and competition in the social systems of agrarian societies.

The latter topic properly begins with a recognition of the close relationship between cooperation and competition. These are seen not as opposites, as they sometimes are in popular discourse, but as closely related forms of social relationships. Cooperation generally refers to strategic activities involving two or more persons carried out jointly for mutual benefit. Competition refers to separate efforts to accomplish identical goals on the part of two or more persons, in accordance with certain rules. Thus there is in competition a component of cooperation insofar as the persons involved agree, in effect, to carry out their goal-seeking behavior in a certain way. Competition is the socially ordered version of rivalry, and it is not open combat or unrestricted aggression.

Moreover, both cooperation and competition usually involve an element of social exchange. This refers to the fact that when one person performs a certain act, the other is expected to respond in a predictable way in order to realize a gain for one or both. The actions are not random or unpredictable, but are ordered in some fashion—the particular patterns being influenced or shaped by prevailing institutions in the society. This means that in Jasper cooperation and competition are not carried out primarily for idealistic reasons, but are significant means of goal-accomplishment.

Thus, in the practical vein, we note that cooperation and competition have strategic significance in Jasper agricultural economy because they are useful. Cooperation is necessary in relatively small-scale agricultural societies the world over because the costs of production are usually so great that without some local cooperative sharing and assistance, income or consumption would be lower than desired. This is true not only for obvious cases like peasants in the emerging nations of Africa, Asia, and Latin America, but for North American farmers as well. The Hutterites have built their entire agrarian scheme on this principle.

Competition is useful in Jasper agricultural society because it is a method for distributing resources, spurring effort, and increasing productivity. Jasper ranchers and farmers are private entrepreneurs competing for prices in the open market, a pattern of behavior that often results in effort to improve yields and efficiency. Land, water, loan capital, and other things needed in agriculture are not automatically distributed to everyone, but must be bargained for, negotiated, and redistributed by local people in interaction with government bureaus. Competition for resources can result in their acquisition by the most efficient operators, who thereupon increase the productivity of the resources.

Specialists distinguish three principal forms of cooperation in agriculture: cooperation in the actual production of crops and livestock; cooperation in the marketing of the products; and cooperation in the buying of commodities needed in farming. The last-named is a specialized undertaking—really a matter of farmer-owned factories and distribution networks. Cooperation in production involves the pooling of some or all of the factors of production: land, tools, and labor. Cooperation in marketing involves the pooling of the product and the agreement to accept uniform prices based on the grades of quality of the products. The most extensive form of cooperation in production is the cooperative farm, in which all the factors of production are based on collective property. This type has proven to be difficult to organize in societies where private ownership of land and other resources are well established, which is to say most agrarian societies the world over. However, forms of production cooperation involving less than this drastic pooling of all property can flourish where the need is felt.

Marketing cooperation—a specialty of the western Canadian farmers, as it is of the fruit and vegetable-growers of California —emerges when there is reliance upon one or a very few crops that have a history of price fluctuation. In this situation farmers often trade their individual search for profits for the security of a guaranteed uniform price. In commodity cooperation, as in ordinary consumer cooperation, there is no risk at all to the institutions of private property or profit, and therefore these types of cooperation are the most widespread and popular forms.

FARMING AS A CAPITALISTIC ENTERPRISE

We may now describe the economic institutions that provide a framework for agricultural activities in North America. Like other aspects of North American economy, these are capitalistic; that is, they are organized on the basis of (a) private property, or private ownership of the means of production (land, water, tools, machines); and (b) private entrepreneurship, or the operation of the individual farming enterprise as a capitalistic venture by the owners.

Excepting the large, company-type farms which seem to be increasing in some parts of the United States and Canada, the majority of farms are owned and operated by single families who have clear title to their land, or, as in the case of Jasper ranchers, enjoy long-term, relatively secure government leases which can be used much as if they were private property. The combination of entrepreneurial operation and private land tenure means that the individual farmers and ranchers are expected to conduct their operations as if they were small private companies, relying upon their own acumen and skill in order to make a living and a profit.

In the classical terms of nineteenth- and early twentieth-century economic thought, this mode of operation is conceived as taking place within the context of a free market economy in which prices and costs are expected to find desirable levels in the normal process of competition. The individual operators thus are ideally expected to compete indirectly with one another for rewards by producing more and better farm products for sale to the market. In classical economic terms, their economic relationships *with each other* are viewed not as part of this market system, but as local, personalized phenomena of interest, perhaps, only to the rural sociologist or anthropologist making community studies.

In the broad terms of tenure and operation, Jasper ranchers and farmers adhered to this system. There were no cooperative farms (although there are some elsewhere in Saskatchewan), and all of the farms and ranches of the region were owned by local families and operated by them for their living and profit. Jasper agriculturalists rejected conceptions of agrarian economy in which all land would be owned by the state, or all products produced and marketed under government regulations. As devotees of private property and supporters of the freedom of the individual to produce, Jasperites would tolerate government regulations and invasions of the property sphere only if these were of direct benefit to their enterprises.

However, if we inspect the pattern of Jasper agriculture, we discover a number of significant practical modifications of capitalistic institutions. In the first place, part of the "free market economy" is actually carefully controlled, with administered prices and much political involvement—as in the Canadian grain marketing system. The Jasper farmer sells his grain and much of his livestock to the farmer-owned Wheat Pool, a giant marketing co-op, which in turn sells it to the Canadian Wheat Board, a federal government organization that sells the grain abroad. The farmer is thus to a large extent guaranteed prices—or at least their fluctuation under a free market system is leveled off. (In the United States, control of prices for the farmer is accomplished or attempted by government subsidies of various kinds, a very expensive system, since it frequently operates by paying farmers *not* to produce.)

Second, farmers do not operate their enterprises in isolation from one another. Although machinery has lessened neighborly cooperation, farmers and ranchers in Jasper as elsewhere assist one another with their needs for labor, machinery, and supplies on the basis of informal but well-organized district and inter-farm exchange systems. Thus, underlying the individualized, competitive entrepreneurial system at the local level are various types of diffuse cooperative networks that help reduce risks by lowering labor opportunity costs. That is, by using each other, Jasper farmers and ranchers lower the cost of labor and rentals and thereby reduce the amount of risk capital needed to operate their enterprises.

Third, agrarian people in North America, and especially Saskatchewan, have also accepted and even advocated various schemes for spreading scarce resources more evenly by cooperative and collective action. In effect, this means taking quantities of natural resources—land, water—out of private ownership and making them available to a larger number. In Jasper, about 18 per cent of the agriculturally used lands were held in various forms of government or cooperative tenure; this represented a substantial increase over the distribution as it existed from 1910 to the 1930's. Even ranchers, ruggedly individualistic as they were, were favorable to collectively used irrigation schemes.

These cooperative measures arose out of the need to reduce the risks inherent in small-scale capitalistic agriculture operating with marginal resources. Jasper agriculturalists—especially farmers who were most vulnerable—saw the need for modification of the idealized institutional pattern, and managed to get these felt needs translated into a variety of institutions. These arrangements did not conflict with entrepreneurial agriculture but in fact were designed to strengthen it by making it more prosperous.

JASPER VALUES

The traditional values used by Jasper farmers and ranchers to sanction and justify their economic activities were variants of the familiar North American pattern. This pattern has an individualistic emphasis based on the institutions of property ownership and the unique experiences of a relatively recent frontier. The frontier however, was also a cooperative milieu in which the settlers, all equal in their poverty, were required to help each other in order to survive.

The traditional Jasper value system thus had two sides—an individualistic side in which people are supposed to make their own way without assistance, and an affiliative side in which people are supposed to help one another when need is evident. The following quotations from our interviews illustrate and define the dual pattern:

"Everything we did here, we did by ourselves; we didn't get no help from nobody!"

"You need good neighbors in this country—a fella who won't help out when it's wanted is no kind of neighbor."

"Nobody that has anything is socialistic at heart—only the fellas that have nothing but want something, and those who will take anything they can get for nothing."

"We don't expect handouts, you know, but in the drought you need some kind of help. These deficiency bonus payments for grain, that's a good thing, but they overdo that too. Too many of 'em around here just depend on it."

Translating into more direct language, we find the following credo:

1. It is good to do things by yourself, without help;

2. . . . but when you do need help, it is good to have someone around to give it.

3. People who can't make it on their own should be helped;

4. . . . but those who take help from the government tend to be lazy . . .

5. . . . although, the government should help out in time of need.

These statements seem contradictory, or at least mutually qualifying: they stress the individual and his single-handed efforts, but also, at the same time, the value of neighborly assistance to people who cannot make it on their own. Individualism is honored, but so is reciprocity; the strong, rugged loner is idealized, but then the weak and the failures are not rejected, either. Local society should remain free of government help, and provide its own assistance to unfortunates, but it is, after all, the duty of the government to help out in time of need. In this way Jasperites have begun to acknowledge the role of government in cushioning the shocks of a fluctuating capitalistic economy.

These values include individualistic and cooperative elements, but Jasper people are silent or indirect on the issue of competition. This is in contrast to the explicit competitive theme in North American business culture. Competition as a theme or value is played down in Jasper culture because it seems to violate the frontier spirit of open-handed assistance and mutual aid. The value system is thus only a partial representation of the actual pattern of behavior: its elements of individualism and cooperation are accurate, but it fails to portray the competitive spirit and forms of interaction—although one might argue that competitiveness is *implicit* in the individualistic component as a consequence of the individualistic search for success.

We did collect a number of statements on competitive behavior in our field work, although we found it difficult to do so. Jasperites seemed to prefer silence on this issue. The few comments recorded were negative, such as this typical example: "He's the kind of a fella who'd kill his grandmother in order to get a piece of land." The remark was one of several referring to a particularly famous elderly man who had amassed a large farm largely by competing for land with his own relatives. While there was condemnation of his behavior, the man was also regarded as a solid and successful citizen and was given public awards as a pillar of the community and the older generation. While occasionally condemning competitiveness and never praising it, Jasperites indirectly sanction it since it plays an important role in the economy, as we shall see.

We shall now describe several types of cooperation on the tasks of production as practiced by Jasper agriculturalists, including the Hutterian Brethren. We present these in the order of degree of their formal organization, starting with the most informal:

RECIPROCAL ECONOMIC EXCHANGE

All Jasper farmers and ranchers assisted each other by exchanging labor on regular tasks, commodities and tools needed in farming or ranching, machinery, and information on new crops, cattle breeds, and procedures. Among ranchers, haying operations and the annual branding and inoculating of calves was usually performed cooperatively. These various exchange activities were important economically, as the value of all forms of exchange for a typical farmer averaged about $600. Since his average cash operating costs were about $2,000, the neighborly exchanges constituted an important savings.

We found three types of exchange: (1) dyadic (that is, two-man) exchange partnerships between neighbors or relatives. This was the most common type of exchange, and consisted mainly of reciprocal exchange of labor on routine tasks. (2) Exchange rings consisting of more than two men (groups of neighbors and relatives). The rings functioned principally for work on special tasks, especially planting and harvesting. Therefore their work centered around the use of the large, expensive machines used by crop farmers. (3) District cooperation on livestock. These consisted of large groups of neighbors in the same district sharing the special tasks of branding and inoculating the spring calves.

Jasper ranchers and farmers regarded these forms of exchange as illustrative of the "frontier spirit" of the region. They emphasized their informal, friendly basis, and did not recognize, or were unwilling to acknowledge, the economic value and necessity of the work. The reason for this attitude was found in the fact that the exchanges were voluntary, and all of them were bound up in social relationships. Friendships, kin-group ties, the district picnic, and other social functions were associated with the exchanges, and in many cases the exchanges served to provide the major opportunities for social relationships among these relatively isolated farmers and ranchers. While the money values of the exchanges were sometimes recorded so that reciprocal exchange could be calibrated, the majority were not, and the reciprocity was simply "kept in mind" and automatic adjustments made over time. A man's attitudes and friendliness were factors included in the exchanges—one who played the game with a surly disposition risked exclusion. To make purely economic aspects of the exchanges more obvious, and thus to organize them formally, would tend to reduce the important social functions to monetary values, and this would violate the tradition of voluntary, friendly assistance.

Participation in cooperative exchange was governed mainly by the scale of a man's enterprise. Neither the very small and impoverished enterprises, nor the very largest ranches and farms participated in the regular exchange partnerships and rings as extensively as the majority of medium-sized enterprises with comparable patterns of production. Many of the smallest farmers and ranchers would slip into a paternalistic relationship with a nearby big rancher, who would help them in various ways and expect docile labor in return. The biggest ranchers would almost always participate in the district brandings, and some of them got together among themselves for machinery and breeding experiments, but they were usually not included in the regular neighborhood rings because of their large size: reciprocation was difficult and embarrassing.

The importance of economic differences in governing reciprocal exchanges highlights the involvement of the system in social status. Jasperites like to believe that everyone is equal, has equal opportunity, and equal skill. Of course, there is less economic differentiation in Jasper than in larger urban societies, so their belief in equality is by no means a myth. But the existing differences create a need to try to make the system "come out right," to use a favorite Jasper expression. Paternalistic relationships between large and small ranchers, or between large ranchers and very poor farmers, are often represented as ordinary dyadic exchange partnerships, and the routine observer will probably not be aware of the hierarchal nature of the relationship, in which loyalty, docility, and hard work are given in return for favors and patronage. In any event, paternalism illustrates still another social function or social setting of cooperation in Jasper society and economy: bridging gaps between economic statuses.

Our emphasis on the economicity of informal neighborly exchange in Jasper should not be taken to imply that the system was adequate in itself. There was no question that Jasper operators could benefit greatly from more formalized cooperative arrangements in several contexts. The most important of these was machinery: we studied the number of expensive powered farm machines, like the big grain combines, and found that there were more than were actually needed to get in the total crop, although Jasper farmers defended their practice on the grounds that the frequent need to harvest rapidly because of unpredictable weather made personal ownership of a complete set of machines necessary. However this may be, the cost was considerable, and the farm machinery cooperative, in which a group of farmers get together and buy and use these expensive machines cooperatively, could be a desirable innovation.

However, reciprocal economic cooperation among Jasper agriculturalists was an open-ended, diffuse cooperative organization, functioning so as to reduce costs, and also risk, by reducing the amount of capital needed to operate the enterprises. This is an important function for relatively small agricultural enterprises, and similar practices are found in all small-scale agricultural societies the world over, regardless of cultural tradition.

Hutterites exchanged labor, commodities, machines, and information among the various colonies, just as farmers and ranchers did. This practice accorded with their communal philosophy, but it was also a highly practical activity and was informally organized—there was no formal intercolony cooperation body. Colonies in which the executives were engaged in an intercolony quarrel would display considerable intercolony cooperation at the managerial level of the separate farm activities if such interchanges were useful.

Hutterites did not exchange labor and other things with ranchers and farmers to any great extent. Sometimes ranchers or farmers would let the Brethren pick berries on their property, in which case the Hutterites would pay for the privilege with fresh vegetables or chickens. Often Hutterites would help a neighboring small farmer in need of labor or machinery, but in these cases reciprocity was not expected. The same lack of reciprocity was found in the case of large ranchers assisting small ranchers or farmers in their vicinity. This type of action was regarded as proof of the spirit of friendly helpfulness of Jasper culture. Hutterites, too, liked to emphasize this spirit, and thus to identify with the region. Their exclusionistic policies made it difficult for them to blend with the local society, and they often seized on the possibility of helping a neighbor as proof of their integration with the community.

In none of the cooperative activities described to this point was there any modification of property rights. The exchanges took place between approximate economic equals, each owning his own land and tools. If he lacked certain implements, or the time to complete a task by himself, he was helped by neighbors and relatives. Cooperative exchange was, in fact, facilitated by equality: if a man had too small, or too large an enterprise, he did not participate fully in the cooperative activities. The same applies to the Hutterites: while their society is communally organized, each colony is a separately owned enterprise, and exchange between them has the same informal basis, practical needs, and functions as that between farmers or between ranchers. And one reason, aside from ideological exclusionism, that Hutterites did not exchange with neighboring farmers was that the colony enterprises were so much bigger.

Organized Cooperation for Livestock Production

In the early frontier period of ranching, before the grazing lands had been subdivided into leases, all of the ranchers who used the free pasturelands in a given creek basin were organized into a Roundup Association or "Pool" that functioned each year as a means of collecting the cattle, branding, and sorting them out into the respective, privately owned herds. The Association hired a director and a rider, who kept track of the animals during the year. Dues were paid, special assessments levied from time to time, and regular meetings held. This system of cooperative management of grazing in the open-range type of cattle production disappeared with the leasing system, but its echo persisted in contemporary Jasper in the form of the gatherings of neighboring and district ranchers for branding and inoculating cattle.

As a livestock industry developed among farmers as a means of cushioning their fluctuating grain economy, special mechanisms were developed by the government to facilitate the move toward cattle. There were two systems: the community pasture, and the grazing cooperative. The difference between these was the difference between resources used collectively and managed by government for collective benefit (the pasture), and a grant of grazing land given to a corporate group of farmers organized as a cooperative.

The community pasture consisted of a large tract of land (see Fig. 2.2) purchased by the government from failing farmers, or taken over from municipal bodies that had seized the land for nonpayment of taxes during the drought-and-depression period of the 1930's. The pasture was managed by a staff of two or more men who maintained fencing and corrals, and cared for the animals during the summer grazing season when the farmer patrons kept their cattle in the pasture. Applications for membership were received by the government bureau—the Prairie Farm Rehabilitation Act agency—located in the provincial capital. Membership was granted to those whose economic needs for the additional pasture were demonstrable on the basis of specified criteria.

Thus the group of patrons, as the members were called, did not form a "natural" cooperative group, but were assembled *ad hoc,* so to speak, on the basis of universalistic criteria. In some cases, of course, the patrons were mostly from the surrounding district, and consequently did have some socioeconomic unity. Moreover, in several cases, the political maneuvering required to obtain the pasture was performed by a group of farmers of the locality. However, on the whole the pasture members were not cooperators since they simply paid fees for the privilege of pasturing their cattle.

The pasture manager did hold meetings of the patrons, and practical matters were—or at least were supposed to be—discussed and voted upon. These meetings often dissolved into arguments, however, and decisions had to be made by the manager. Moreover, individual patrons often made private deals to obtain memberships for friends or relatives, and sometimes favors would be maneuvered, such as getting a larger share of the excess hay raised on the irrigated tracts of the pasture. The use of the pasture was thus marked by considerable dissension and competition, although the basic philosophy of the pasture system was phrased in cooperative terms.

The grazing cooperative was an entirely different institution. The members were required to organize for the purpose of obtaining a lease, consequently the group always consisted of a "natural" social group of neighbors, relatives, and friends already accustomed to the informal modes of economic exchange described previously. Success in acquiring the lease and receiving other benefits of the cooperative laws depended upon the efficiency and harmony displayed by the group. Once the lease was acquired, the cooperating group managed its lands as a unit, doing its own work, keeping its own books, and making its own decisions. Each member, of course, kept his own private farm and pasture as well. The grazing cooperatives of the region had a history of remarkable harmony and efficiency, and were regarded by cooperative officials in the provincial government as models of the cooperative movement. The spirit and practice was in marked contrast to the dissension and individualism displayed by the community pasture patrons.

Yet the people involved in these two types of organized cooperation were of similar outlook and status, or in some cases, actually the same persons. In many instances men who had fought bitterly with each other while pasture members were able to cooperate smoothly when they were among those successfully obtaining a cooperative lease. The difference was created by the fact that the cooperative fitted into the basic institution of private property ownership: in effect, the group of farmers became joint owners of a piece of land. Since they were required to manage this land for their own profit, they had incentive for performing efficiently and harmoniously. In the pasture system, lacking title to the land, and with the facilities under government financing and control, there was no incentive for true cooperative management and decision-making. *Thus we see in these two cases how the same institutions of private property and individual operation, in differing settings, can promote competition in one instance, cooperation in the other.*

While the Indians were not agricultural, they did practice a form of "cooperation" among themselves that deserves a note. Their economy consisted largely of the government dole, plus whatever they could pick up in the way of cash, by legal or illegal means. This activity was not such as to foster a sense of property ownership or the concept of capital to be used for investment. Consequently it is no surprise to find that the Indians lacked the kind of cooperation described for the other groups. Instead, Indians simply used each others' property without asking—"cooperation by informal appropriation" might describe the process. If an Indian family deserted their government-built plywood house for a week or two, they would be sure to find another family in it upon their return to the reserve—and they would simply look for another vacant house to appropriate. Food was not really shared, but simply given or taken, with no particular thought or rule of reciprocal exchange. The reciprocity was there, but not acknowledged or recognized, since the general poverty meant that the continual practice of appropriation would balance out automatically.

We turn now to a discussion of more openly competitive

forms of interaction in agricultural production and resources utilization.

COMPETITION OVER WATER

Water was the Jasper natural resource in shortest supply and the most unevenly distributed by nature. Its chief economic use in the region was to provide irrigation for the raising of forage crops for livestock—wheat and other grains are not very responsive to irrigation, and, in any case, the region lacked sufficient water to permit any large-scale program of grain irrigation. Small tracts of land will produce substantial amounts of cattle feed under irrigation: for example, a ranch with a herd of 200 animals, requiring 10 square miles of native pasture for summer use, could provide all or most of its winter feed on about 75 acres of irrigated land.

The irrigation projects of the Jasper region were as follows: (1) a large number of private schemes, each based on a "water right" assigned by the provincial government to the particular ranch or farm unit in historical order, and transmitted with the unit to subsequent owners. These schemes consisted simply of a main ditch coming out of the creek bed, with subsidiary ditches carrying the water to small fields where forage crops were raised. The oldest of these water-right–based schemes, on a ranch, dated from about 1887. (2) Community irrigation programs, financed and managed by the government, based on large reservoirs constructed along creek watersheds, to store water during the spring snow melt from the hills for use in spring and summer for the irrigation of plots of land rented to individual farmers and ranchers. (3) Special irrigated areas connected with the community pastures and using water from the community projects. (4) A large variety of private schemes on farms and ranches involving small dams along drainage areas to impound water in pools used for irrigation and stock watering. (5) Sprinkler irrigation involving the use of special pumps to obtain the water from ponds or creeks, and sprayed on forage crops. Many of these were illegal.

The first thing to note about this program of irrigation is

that it operated mainly on the basis of individual ownership and operational principles. The water-right system is a nineteenth-century development out of the Western doctrine of "prior appropriation," a legal convention that replaced the humid-lands concept of "riparian rights." Riparian law was inapplicable in the arid West since the streams did not flow all the year, and when they did so, had a limited amount of water, hence could not be used indiscriminately. The water-right system was based on first-come-first-served; that is, the first man on the creek got Right No. 1, and so on. A Jasper water right entitled a man only to so many acre-feet of water during the period specified, usually during the spring flood resulting from snow melt. If he did not take his water then, he could not take it later.

Moreover, the government-developed community irrigation schemes were not cooperative organizations, but simply tracts of land subdivided into individual plots rented by the government for a fixed fee to applicants. These applicants, like the community pasture patrons, had to prove their need for irrigation facilities in order to secure a plot.

Since the entire irrigation system was dominated by private property concepts, and since water was a scarce resource, it is not surprising to find considerable competition. The water-right system was essentially competitive in that anyone with a water right of his own might feel justified in taking as much water as he needed, using it any way he desired, and taking it at any time, regardless of the laws. Complaints were constant, and the government water bureau was engaged in continual informal adjudication of quarrels. In all cases these did not become open between neighbors, but involved a man complaining, usually by indirection in the form of an ambiguous letter or a casual remark to the supervisor, of abuses somewhere on the creek: "I think you oughta know that someone—I won't mention names—is taking more than his share there above me." The bureau or the local project supervisor would then be duty-bound to look into the matter and persuade the malefactor to mend his ways, with ultimate threat of legal action. It was never difficult to find the culprit, if it was more than just a rumor, mistake, or malicious report, since the officials knew the water users and their habits with great intimacy. The fight could thus be resolved without open confrontation, a necessity among neighbors who depended on each other for mutual aid and friendship. A better example of the mingling of competitive and cooperative inter-actions could hardly be found. The same two men who were engaged in a protracted competitive battle over water could also cooperate continually on labor and machinery exchange, and the "water fight" would often not interfere with their mutually profitable and socially satisfying relationship.

The sprinkler irrigation device had resulted in an intensified version of these individualized competitive struggles. While laws governed the use of sprinklers—they required a separate water right—their simplicity and efficiency tempted many operators to obtain them and use them clandestinely, usually at night. Re-duced water flow in the creek—something every man along the creek watched closely—might indicate the use of a sprinkler, and people would stay up late at night and listen carefully for the tell-tale sound of the pump.

The community irrigation schemes had their share of com-petition as well. The plot users often did cooperate with each other in a neighborly way on the labor needed in planting and harvesting the forage, and preparing the ditches, but surrepti-tious stealing of water existed in the form of plot holders taking more than their allotted share. The plot holders for one of the schemes were organized with government encouragement as a water users' association, and the government attempted to get them to make their own rules and take over some of the financ-ing of the works, but these attempts were no more successful than comparable attempts to consider the community pasture patrons as a cooperative. The basic reason was the same: lack-ing title to the scheme as a whole, the water users were dis-inclined to take the responsibility, and were content to let the government pay the bills and regulate the scheme. In addition, their assembling was not voluntary, with roots in existing "neigh-boring" practices, but *ad hoc,* based on plot rentals.

COMPETITION FOR LAND

Land, like water, is a scarce resource, but one of finite rather than fluctuating supply—hence its scarcity is largely a function of its productivity measured in terms of the costs and prices in agricultural production. In Jasper, land had rapidly increased in value in the period since World War II due to increased prosperity and new ways of using even submarginal soils for livestock production. Many Jasper ranchers and farmers had discovered that land was cheap at any price, since cattle prices were high and almost any kind of soil could produce pasture. This situation bred competition for available properties. We studied a sample of all land sales taking place in a 5-year period and determined that nearly all the properties had gone to the most efficient operators. These were, in a few cases, also the most abusive operators from the standpoint of use of their resources, but they were not a majority.

There was equally strenuous competition for grazing leases, but here the competitive struggle was not a simple matter of attempts to find and buy available land but was bound up with the government's third-party interest in controlling lease assignments. Grazing leases, like the community pasture and irrigation project memberships and plot rentals, were not granted to just anyone, but only to those who could qualify as serious livestock producers with evidence of residential stability and on the-spot management. When a ranch was sold the government had to certify the lease transfer arrangement before the deal could take place. The former leaseholder could sell his own land, if he had any, and also the "improvements" made on the lease, which usually added up to the market value of the land.

Whenever a ranch was up for sale, or was known to be close to this status, severe competition among possible buyers developed. This competition took the form of attempts to make sure of who the government would decide was qualified for the lease transfer. Ranchers sometimes applied for the lease before the ranch was publicly announced for sale, and this practice was regarded as treachery by the ranching community, and would be met by social ostracism. More open competition was displayed

by the farmers, who regarded ranching as an outdated and unproductive way of using valuable land. Farmers would use all
their political skills and connections to get advance information
and influence the parties to the sale, including government
agents. In several cases, they used the grazing cooperative law
as a vehicle, petitioning a transfer of all or part of the ranch
up for sale to their group as a grazing co-op. This technique was
successful in two important cases in the decade preceding our
study.

Competition with ranchers for land was not confined to the
occasion of a ranch sale, however. Especially determined farmers
were capable of mounting a campaign to obtain a particular
ranch lease by attacking the efficiency and legality of its operation. For example, in one successful case the ranch was in the
hands of a fading family and was operated only on a token
basis. Farmers persistently called the abuses of the lease regulations to the attention of the land bureau, usually by the indirect
methods noted for water disputes, and were eventually successful
in having the lease removed from control of the family and
transferred to themselves. There were many other examples of
the strategic manipulation of legal rules in a competitive
atmosphere.

Farmers also competed in the open market—again by forming
cooperative groups who prepared bids for the ranch property,
sometimes topping the next largest bid by an established rancher.
Ranchers were incapable by tradition and custom of forming
such combinations but they usually used all the personal influence they possessed, as individuals, to stop these groups of
determined farmers.

In spite of farmer activities, the majority of grazing leases in
the region remained in the hands of the grazing ranchers.
Farmers had made inroads, particularly in the form of the grazing cooperatives, but their failures were more numerous than
their successes. Still, they were determined to obtain a greater
share of grazing land, and ranchers knew that the attacks would
not cease. The farmers obtained a considerable amount of solidarity from their combined attempts to seize ranch land, and
since many of these attempts were organized around efforts to

obtain leases for a grazing cooperative, we find another instance of the intertwining of cooperative and competitive mechanisms.

Hutterites were devastating competitors in the "land game," as it was frequently called in Jasper. The colonies were well aware of the fact that local people did not welcome them, and that both resistance to their coming and, conversely, eager attempts to sell them land at bonus prices, would be made. Hutterites, since they are large operators and live frugally and save money, always have cash to buy land, and are willing to pay higher prices than non-Hutterites. This makes them difficult to compete with. They also cleverly seek land in districts with marginal resources that are not suitable for small-scale individual farming or ranching, and where the existing operators are often eager to sell out. Once a colony has acquired the bulk of its land in a given locality, the remaining individual operators will soon sell to the Brethren, since they become isolated or even surrounded by colony property. The structure of the situation—the Hutterites' pressing need for land and their need for it in very large tracts, plus their ability to pay high prices—makes it virtually impossible to compete with them. The only instance in recent Jasper history where farmers successfully outbid a colony for a large tract of land occurred when a group of farmers got together and bought two large farms and made them into a grazing cooperative. Only by this combined action could the individual operators amass sufficient cash and power to compete with the colonies.

Colonies also competed with each other for land, as did the individual enterprisers, although the competition was usually *sub rosa* because of the political need for the colonies to present a united front. They also competed for services: two colonies in the Jasper region had a prolonged struggle over who would control the telephone line coming into both colonies. One colony wanted to construct this line to serve a wide area, and the other colony wanted it as a virtually private wire. Colonies also competed in the door-to-door marketing of vegetables and fowl in the local area. These forms of competition between communal cooperators are inherent in the basic structure of their enterprises: the separate colonies are operated not as combined co-ops

but as private agricultural businesses owning their own land.
The situation also shows how Hutterites are not completely able
to avoid being influenced by the outside world.

RELATIONSHIPS WITH EXTERNAL AGENCIES

In all of the cooperative and competitive relationships described, an important element consisted of external agencies
and forces affecting the distribution of rewards and resources
within the Jasper agricultural community. In other words,
cooperation and competition are not always simple or local, but
usually involve a "third party": government agencies, the market economy, and other external institutions. Jasper ranchers
and farmers compete and cooperate with each other, but often
over facilities provided by the outside, in accordance with ground
rules established by the agencies, and modified by Jasperites.
   Thus to get what they want and need for their enterprises,
Jasper farmers and ranchers need to use the existing facilities
in the larger society: the banks, private sources of funds, government agencies that control access to and allocations of water,
land, and financial resources. Much as Jasperites like to emphasize their individualistic competence and pioneering self-help,
they are part of the larger network of facilities and institutions
of the North American agrarian economy and its political representatives. Various methods are used to keep in contact with
these outside sources of help. The local Agricultural Representative, a provincial government agent, provides them with information on financial and commodity benefit programs of many
kinds, and helps them design management programs tailored to
take advantage of these benefits. The local supervisor of the
irrigation programs sponsored by the federal government,
through its Prairie Farm Rehabilitation Act, gives them similar
assistance on water development, assigning rental plots on the
big schemes and providing shared-cost aid on their own private
schemes. Ranchers, and particularly, farmers, make it a point to
keep in touch with the central headquarters of the agencies
involved in all of these matters, and sometimes bypass the local
representatives if the issue is important enough, or if they have

personal acquaintances in the main offices. Both farmers and ranchers do not hesitate to contact their legislative representatives in the provincial capital when they are seeking favors, although the farmers tend to do so oftener as groups, or by open petition, than ranchers, who seem to prefer individual contact. The establishment of the several community pastures, irrigation schemes, and grazing cooperatives in the Jasper region has a background of political activity of this kind.

These methods of intervention must be carried on with certain rules, lest they take the form of open competition among neighbors. That is, the seeking of favors and benefits nearly always carries an implication of competition: the farmer who wants to dam a drainage pathway must consider what this might do to his neighbor's property down the line; the rancher who wants a lease up for expiration must consider who among his neighbors also wants the lease, since if the need is greater elsewhere, in the interest of neighborly cooperation and friendship he might better stay out of the competition; the man who covets various government financial benefits must think carefully about this lest he be accused by his colleagues of "freeloading," and thereby lose social credit. There is, therefore, a constant interplay between the local social network and its cultural values and standards, and the external resource agencies. The local people do not simply openly seek all the benefits possible, but control their seeking in accordance with local standards; hence the community has informal means of modifying the allocation of resources by these external sources. The system is intricate, and requires considerably study before an outsider can begin to grasp its nuances.

Conclusions

We have seen, first, that cooperative and competitive relationships in the Jasper region take their form from existing property rights and forms of enterprise management. That is, they should not be understood as the simple result of human nature, but as the activities of men in a particular type of socioeconomic framework. This is exemplified by the fact that while men may

compete bitterly over water and land as individual entrepreneurs, the same men will cooperate constructively in a grazing cooperative or where a legal change in property rights (and
economic necessity) make it expedient and desirable to do so.
Two men can write secret accusatory letters to government
agencies about each other and yet share their respective tasks
and machinery. Even Hutterites, conditioned from infancy to
sharing and cooperating on everything, can compete for land
and services on an intercolony basis and yet cooperate extensively on the tasks of production.

At the same time, cooperation is not the sole solution to
Jasper's economic problems. *Competition* is a useful strategy
in several senses. First, it is a spur to individual effort in an individualistic society—even one with a respectable quotient of
dedication to cooperation. Jasper agriculture was for four decades a retarded or at least undercapitalized enterprise. Increasing farm prices after World War II, and greater availability of
loan capital, ushered in an era of relative prosperity. Competition itself became a psychological spur to greater effort and
innovativeness.

Secondly, competition functioned to provide a more equitable
and certainly more productive distribution of resources. In spite
of government regulations that aimed at a fair distribution to
all, the rules of property ownership and the tenure period of
leases made it difficult for farmers to get land. By organizing
competitively against ranchers, farmers were able to put the
regulations to use and acquire grazing lands. In the free competition for land available on private sale, the more efficient
and aggressive operators generally won out, thus raising the
productivity of the land. This has not always meant that land
went to the most conservation-minded operators, but after years
of experience with this risky habitat, most Jasper farmers and
ranchers developed a closer adherence to a conservationist ethic
than farmers in other parts of North America and the world.

The successful competition displayed by Hutterites for land
acquisition unquestionably increased the productivity of the
region. In this case, however, the competition is at the expense
of the non-Hutterite farmers who are displaced by the colonies.
Hutterian willingness to lend assistance gratis to their smaller

neighbors is in part an attempt to compensate for this consequence—a case where cooperation or at least altruism is one result of competition.

With respect to water, the role of competition is probably always negative. Competition for land in Jasper has resulted in a more equitable distribution and increased productivity without serious loss of substance. Competition for water, however, has resulted in a diminution of the supply and considerable hostility among neighbors, however cleverly they may divert the hostility from the locality to a third party—the government bureau. It would seem that cooperative mechanisms are more efficient in allocating a natural resource in fluctuating supply, and of course all water distribution schemes in all societies eventually have developed along cooperative lines. Jasper agricultural operators need to develop water cooperatives, and during the period of our study the government was beginning to encourage the formation of such organizations.

The forms of cooperation and competition described in this chapter are not random actions, or individual adjustments, but constitute an organized system of adaptive strategies. They are carried out with definite rules and expectations, and Jasper operators follow these rules with little deviation. It is understood in Jasper that when men have no joint title to and responsibility for resources it is their duty to do their best individualistically, and to compete with each other for these resources. The extent of the competition is governed by rules that arise in a small, face-to-face society—one in which mutual survival is dependent in part on mutual assistance. Consequently competition is regulated by these needs to preserve its constructive features, discourage its divisive features. Only rarely will a rancher violate the rule that application for a lease rumored to come up for sale must wait until the official announcement—and when the rule is violated, the individual must suffer a form of ostracism and can no longer expect favors from his colleagues. Struggles over water and land rarely reach the stage of open combat; the rules require the use of the government as a mediator, and the dangers in surveillance are muted by secret reports to the authorities.

Cooperative action has its own rules. Economic exchange and

mutual assistance between neighbors operates by the principle of reciprocal equal exchange, with the partners keeping mental tallies of the progress of the relationship. A man who takes too much without reciprocating soon finds it difficult to obtain help. The organized forms of cooperation have their own explicit rules, usually defined for Jasperites by government regulations. Conformity is encouraged by the benefits that result from adherence to the rules. An efficiently run grazing co-op can expect to obtain government financial aid for corrals, water development, and other facilities.

Cooperation and competition in Jasper contain some implications for agrarian development. The Jasper system is, first, a mixed system, one that extracts benefits both from cooperation and competition. It is not a blueprinted ideal program invented by economists, engineers or politicians, but a naturally developing system that recognizes various potentials in complex human relationships. It is founded on the institutions of entrepreneurship and private property, but it finds it possible to modify these arrangements when need dictates. While Jasper agriculture has had its unproductive periods, the potential for change and growth is always there, based on its essential eclecticism and flexibility.

One major weakness of the North American agrarian system, however, is its tendency to overuse or abuse natural resources in the quest for greater production and profits. Some effects of this can be observed in Jasper: too much light soil still is in cultivation, causing blowing. Early irrigation was poorly engineered, and salinization has resulted. But neither of these have been excessive, and the current direction of agrarian development has been to modify them; more and more marginal soil areas are going back into pasture, and contemporary irrigation schemes are properly engineered, with some of the old, salinized projects under reclamation. Perhaps Jasper people are more conservation-minded than others because of the great hardships they suffered in attempting to build an agrarian community in this specialized environment. And then, too, Canadians have been more conservative, less "progress"-minded than U.S. citizens, more willing to take a little less and build more slowly toward a secure future. Unquestionably these diffuse but very important cultural emphases play a role in agrarian development —in modern North America as in the emerging countries of Asia, Africa, and Latin America.

But the Jasper case illustrates another important point: that the scope of cooperative and competitive relationships in a local agrarian society is importantly influenced by the relationship of the society to the national bureaucratic structure. We have seen how this structure establishes conditions for the interactions of the local agricultural operators. Laws facilitating organized co-operative institutions can be seized by farmers to implement their own cooperative interactions, sometimes in the context of their competition for land with ranchers. Where government-sponsored organizations like the community pasture and the community irrigation schemes avoid modifying property rights, and control access to the resources, cooperative relationships are difficult to establish. These effects are, of course, specific to an agrarian economy organized on capitalistic lines, but they also show that outside interventions play their role in the development process, and can modify the social relations of the local community.

BIBLIOGRAPHIC NOTES

Anthropologists have been concerned with agrarian development from the standpoint of the problem of change: how traditional cultures either resist change or accept it. Examples of this approach are found in all of the following works: Arthur H. Niehoff, *A Casebook of Social Change*, Aldine, 1966; Charles J. Erasmus, *Man Takes Control*, University of Minnesota Press, 1961; George M. Foster, *Traditional Cultures and the Impact of Technological Change*, Morrow, 1956; Edward Spicer, ed., *Human Problems in Technological Change*, Russell Sage Foundation, 1952. A generalized discussion in the form of a handbook for technical aid specialists is found in Conrad M. Arensberg and Arthur Niehoff, *Introducing Social Change*, Aldine, 1964. The approach used in the present volume would tend to place greater emphasis on objective conditions of risk and insecurity, and less on cultural traditions.

For a modern definition of the economic model of North American agriculture and its contemporary situation, see Edward Higbee, *Farms and Farmers in an Urban Age,* The Twentieth Century Fund, 1963. Also valuable for defining the whole broad picture of American agriculture and rural economy and society is the 1962 Yearbook of Agriculture, *After a Hundred Years,* U.S. Department of Agriculture. Walter Goldschmidt's *As You Sow,* Harcourt, Brace, 1947, though now rather dated, contains some excellent basic analyses of socioeconomic process in American farming life.

For general studies of cooperation and competition see Robert A. Nisbet, "Cooperation," *International Encyclopedia of the Social Sciences,* Crowell-Collier-Macmillan, 1968; Edward W. Bakke, *Bonds of Organization: An Appraisal of Corporate Human Relations,* Harper & Bros., 1950; Mark May & Leonard Doob, *Competition and Cooperation: A Report,* Bulletin No. 25, Social Science Research Council, (1937). A specifically comparative, anthropological treatment is found in Margaret Mead, ed., *Cooperation and Competition among Primitive Peoples,* Beacon Press, 1961 (original ed. published by McGraw-Hill, 1937). A classical socio-psychological study of cooperative-competitive relations in small groups is Morton Deutsch, "The Effects of Cooperation and Competition upon Group Process," in D. Cartwright and Alvin Zander, *Group Dynamics,* Harper and Row, 1960. Deutsch found in an experiment that while the amount of knowledge learned by a group organized cooperatively was about the same as that learned by a group organized in a competitive manner, they approached the problem of learning differently. For example, the cooperative group experienced greater ease of communication; the competitive group, however, had the more spirited discussions. For general presentations of social exchange theory, see Peter H. Blau, *Exchange and Power in Social Life,* Wiley, 1964, and George C. Homans, *Social Behavior: Its Elementary Forms,* Harcourt, Brace, 1961.

For specific studies of cooperation in the agricultural sphere, see Wilson Gee, *The Social Economics of Agriculture,* Macmillan, 1954 (various references); Ward W. Fetrow, *Three Principles of Agricultural Cooperation,* Farm Credit Administration, Circular No. E24, 1948; Donald F. Blankertz, *Marketing Cooperatives,* Ronald Press, 1940; Walter Preuss, *Cooperation in Israel and the World,* R. Mass, 1960; Raymond W. Miller, *A Conservative Looks at Cooperatives,* Ohio University Press, 1964. Analyses of agricultural cooperation in Saskatchewan with special significance for this chapter are Cooperative Union of Saskatchewan, *Agricultural Production Cooperatives in Saskatchewan,* 1964; A. F. Laidlaw, "Cooperatives in the Prairie Provinces," in *Yearbook of Agricultural Cooperation,* Basil Blackwell, 1962. (See also notes for Chap. 3.)

For descriptions of mutual aid and informal, reciprocal cooperation among North American farmers, see Solon T. Kimball, "Rural Social Organization and Cooperative Labor," *American Journal of Sociology,* 55 (1949), pp. 38–49; Herbert Lionberger, "The Relation of Informal Social Groups to the Diffusion of Farm Information," *Rural Sociology,* 19 (1954), pp. 233–43; Charles P. Loomis and J. A. Beegle, "Informal Social Systems," Chap. 4 of *Rural Sociology: The Strategy of Change,* Prentice-Hall, 1957. A more detailed analysis of economic exchange in Jasper is provided in J. W. Bennett, "Reciprocal Economic Exchange among North American Agricultural Operators," *Southwestern Journal of Anthropology,* 24 (1968), 276–309.

The field of economic anthropology has become involved in the issue of informal cooperative exchanges among farmers and peasants in a peculiar way. For some time certain anthropologists have held that modern economic theory and methods of analysis do not apply to economies that lack a formal market with monetary rules of exchange— or, for that matter, to any segment of modern economy that happens to operate on the basis of reciprocity and informal exchange, rather than money and the impersonal market. An example of this point of view can be found in George Dalton, "Economic Theory and Primitive Society," *American Anthropologist,* Vol. 63 (1961), pp. 1–25. The opposing position, which holds that economic theory *is* applicable to these non-market kinds of transactions and exchanges, is represented by S. Cook, "The Obsolete 'Anti-Market' Mentality: A Critique of the Substantive Approach to Economic Anthropology," *American Anthropologist,* 68 (1966), pp. 323–45. I stand with the opposition on the issue, since the reciprocal economic exchange in Jasper is thoroughly "economic," in addition to its important social and symbolic functions, and also takes place in a society completely dedicated to market economic principles.

The issue of the relationship between private property and forms of cooperation in agricultural production (discussed in the chapter) constitutes an example of how practical economic matters get wound up in ideology, and how the pressure of external institutions may shape local ideas and practices. Thus in the case of the cooperative veterans' farms in Saskatchewan, there was real dedication to the principle of cooperation and willingness to make the farms a success, but since the entire outside society defined security and success in terms of ownership of property, member after member of these farms found it difficult to accept a role in the cooperative farming organization without some guarantee of property, at least as something he could count on if he decided to withdraw from the farm, or something he could live on after retirement. The story is recounted in Henry Cooperstock, "Cooperative Farming as a Variant Social Pattern," in B. Blishen and others, eds., *Canadian Society*, Free Press, 1961. Only the Hutterites and the kibbutz communalists of Israel have succeeded in overcoming the ideals and pressures of an individualistic, property-owning society. For other discussions of cooperative and communal peoples, see the various books of H. F. Infield; for example, *Cooperative Communities at Work*, Dryden Press, 1945. Infield tends to be highly idealistic about the possibilities of success of such communal experiments.

For a pioneer study of the problems of the riparian rights concept of water law in the arid West, see Walter Webb, *The Great Plains*, pp. 435–52. A summary of the development of Western water laws away from riparian conceptions and toward prior appropriation and other variations is found in Betty Dobkins, *The Spanish Element in Texas Water Law*, University of Texas Press, 1959, Chap. 1. Texas water law is unique in that cooperative elements based on the old Spanish village *acequia* or cooperative irrigation district are built into it.

For some references to the conservation problem in North American agriculture, and agriculture generally, see the notes for Chap. 3. The following study by sociologist Walter Firey develops for the conservation issue a position somewhat similar to the one explored in this chapter for cooperation: that conservation does not usually emerge spontaneously out of ideological motives, but rather as a practical idea and set of practices conferring definite advantage on an individual or group: Walter Firey, "Patterns of Choice and the Conservation of Resources," *Rural Sociology*, Vol. 22, pp. 113–122, 1957.

Problems of relationship between the local community and the national macrocosm are dealt with repeatedly in this book and have been summarized for Jasper in a theoretical paper: John W. Bennett, "Microcosm-Macrocosm Relationships in North American Agrarian Society," *American Anthropologist*, Vol. 69 (1968), pp. 441–54. This paper takes the general position that the influences of the majority society on the local agrarian community have by no means been entirely destructive. That they *have* been so is implied by Maurice R. Stein in *The Eclipse of Community*, N.Y., Harper, 1960.

For some studies of relationships of local agricultural societies with external institutions, see Ernestine Friedl, *Vasilika: A Village in Modern Greece*, Holt, Rinehart, and Winston, 1962; Michael Kenny,

"Patterns of Patronage in Spain," *Anthropological Quarterly,* Vol. 33 (1960), pp. 14–23. These and other studies of peasant communities have stressed the role of the "cultural broker," or functionary who intervenes with outside agencies for the benefit of the localite—like the Agricultural Representative in Jasper.

TEN

Adaptation and Change

In this final chapter we shall summarize the patterns of agrarian and social development in the Jasper region with the use of concepts based on our adaptational approach. Our objective is to suggest how such concepts permit a level of generalization embracing both market agrarian societies and those not fully accommodated to market conditions. Therefore we believe that the differences between farming and peasant societies sometimes have been exaggerated by economists and anthropologists because both have neglected to study certain fundamental ecological and economic processes.

ADAPTIVE POSTURES

Let us consider first the general pattern of adaptation to Jasper natural and socioeconomic resources exhibited by each of the four principal groups in the population. The postures are presented as types, emphasizing the positions of the four groups in the Jasper economy.

The Indians represent a group that has no productive relationship to natural resources, hence cannot survive agriculturally. Their reserve is too small and its resources too refractory to permit a viable utilization, and the government agency responsible for their welfare failed to provide the capital that might have helped to some extent. Sources of income involving "legitimate" labor are no longer available to the Indians due to the mechanization of agriculture and to their deteriorating

306

social relations with whites. Consequently Indians have turned to the available *social* resources, establishing manipulative strategies in order to obtain what they need. In this manner, the Indians resemble thousands of marginal communities the world over who lack control over the resources permitting productive activities of an agrarian or industrial type, and whose supply of cash is too small to permit investment.

The Hutterian Brethren represent an adaptation that emphasizes a combination of the savings and profitability of an economy of scale, with techniques of social exclusion that provide very low opportunity costs for their labor. By buying very large amounts of land and developing their water and soil resources, the Hutterites can use machinery and advanced agrarian routines efficiently, and profit by the lowered costs and high yields these permit. By keeping the level of formal education low and their culture exotic, they exclude themselves from the local job markets and thereby gain by increasing the value of their own labor. The very scarcity of local job opportunities other than in agriculture works to their benefit. This adaptive posture is relatively unique in its combination of large economic scale and low opportunity costs, since all other cases of large-scale diversified enterprise usually function within a general cultural milieu involving considerable labor competition. Hutterites also know how to wheel and deal; they are shrewd manipulators of the business world of farming. Thus they are able to utilize the resources of the region and the market economy to their own best advantage. Their success illustrates how a human group can operate profitably with resources considered inadequate by others who lack the requisite organizational traditions.

Perhaps even more dramatic from the standpoint of adaptive strategies is the ability of the Hutterites completely to accept the conditions of individualistic capitalism in their economy—insofar as they must deal with the outside world—and yet preserve their own internal "communistic" or communal system with a set of values markedly divergent from those characterizing the rules of capitalistic society. As one pre-publication reader of this manuscript remarked, "This is adaptation with a vengeance." The ability to balance or juggle conflicting systems is an old Hutterian strategy: it is the basic reason they have survived for so long and in so many, from their standpoint, basically hostile social and natural environments.

The ranchers represent a successful adaptation based on a highly specialized use of minimal resources. That is, by mainly using resources in their natural state, with minimal development, and by paying low grazing fees, the rancher cuts costs. Moreover, he uses resources—natural grass and water in the hills, where droughts are rare—that are least affected by the vagaries of the plains climate. He does not have to depend on the variable and refractory soils. The rancher is a pastoralist, and as such bears close comparison with other pastoral peoples. His adaptive success, helped by government supervision and control of his leased lands, has led to a stable population and a traditionalized cultural style and social organization. The rancher is as much of a capitalist entrepreneur as any North American industrialist, however; he simply plays the role in a different—perhaps an old-fashioned—way.

Farming is an adaptation based on a relatively specialized use of refractory natural resources that consequently must be changed or improved in the process. This means relatively high costs and great dependence on these resources, and consequent economic difficulty when variability lowers yields. Farmers have variable and fluctuating adaptability: there is no sure way to level it out so long as the farm units remain relatively small. Various measures—resources development, government provision of additional resources, loans of capital, the PFAA bonus payments to farmers whose crop yields are low due to drouth, and other devices—have controlled fluctuation to some extent, especially in districts with development projects, but the only reasonably certain cure in the context of the present market economy is the enlargement of the land area of the enterprises, which is done at the expense of a decreasing population.

Three of these groups—ranchers, farmers, and Hutterites— all function within the same general economic context: the agrarian market economy of Saskatchewan, Canada, and North America. The things they produce, and the markets in which they sell them, are adjusted to the needs and vicissitudes of these external economic forces. However, each of the three groups operates within this common economic frame with a different cultural style. The cultural traditions and social organizations of the three require differing uses of particular resources, and these factors are continually reinforced by the relatively successful functioning of the different modes. The importance of the reinforcing process can be seen in a negative sense in the case of those farmers who shift to livestock production: in doing so, they begin to take on some of the cultural style and identifications of the ranchers.

Figure 10.1 summarizes some key differences and similarities in the three modes of operating within the market economy. Some of the more important patterns revealed by it are:

1. Innovation is a specific, not a general response. The most consistently innovative operators in Jasper were the Hutterian Brethren, whose large economic scale, extensive diversification, and single-minded devotion to agriculture as a way of furthering and securing their traditional sectarian culture encouraged continual experimentation with new technology and agricultural procedures. Ranchers, also operators on a relatively large scale, were the least innovative as a group. Their relatively secure economy, modest level of living, and culturally sanctioned mode of operating led to satisfaction with current income. Farmers had no consistent pattern of innovation as a group: their innovativeness often depended on the scale or prosperity of the individual farm: where these were positive, innovation would likely be present—although other factors might impede it. Farmers illustrated the rule that an operator will remain conservative so long as uncertainty is high and risks are perceived as significant. This means also that their cultural style was relatively pragmatic; their conservatism was more a matter of an instrumental adaptation than was the ranchers'.

2. Relationships to the external world and to government vary considerably, although all three groups were required to deal routinely with external agencies. Hutterites remained aloof, and dealt with the agencies at arm's length, so to speak, but their imposing economic scale forced the external society and governments to recognize and deal with them. Ranchers resembled the Hutterian pattern insofar as they disliked intimate relations with the outside and with government, but they did not hesitate to deal with politicians and attempt to influence govern-

	Cultural Style: Emphasis on Tradition or Nature of Expressive Solidarity	Orientation to External Society	Relations with Government	Technical Innovativeness	Use of Natural Resources	Economic Scale	Opportunity Costs	Susceptibility to Economic Fluctuation and Environmental Variability	Level of Living
HUTTERITES	Unchanging sectarian culture	Exclusionistic; withdrawal; largely independent	Distant; manipulative	Very innovative	Intensive and extensive; conservationist	Large	Low	Reduced greatly by diversification and scale	Collectively high; individually low; but probably rising in both categories
RANCHERS	Traditional western and localized culture	Reserved; mixture of independence and dependence	Distant; manipulative; on individual basis	Very conservative	Extensive; minimal; specialized; conservationist	Large to medium	Low; variable	Reduced greatly by resources use pattern, plus high prices	Modest, varies by income rising slightly
FARMERS	Weak traditions; secular viewpoint	Open; dependent on outside to large extent	Participative; directive; on group basis	Conservative and innovative—depends on situation or scale	Intensive; conservation difficult due to small scale	Small	High; variable	Considerable vulnerability	Modest, probably rising

ment policy if it was in their interest to do so. They also depended on external help for grazing leases, pasture development, and irrigation. Farmers, with the weakest economic position, were the most aggressive participants in government and viewed the external society simply as a projection of the local scene. They were dependent on external agencies and markets for nearly all of their capital. Thus, on a scale of intimacy of participation with and dependence on the outside, the Hutterites were the most aloof and the farmers the least, with ranchers in between.

3. We have emphasized the concept of opportunity costs as a device to analyze the relationship of the Jasper economy to the larger market economy. Opportunity costs can be computed for two aspects of the agrarian economy: labor or occupation, and capital investment. In the case of the former we noted that among the three groups involved in production, farmers had the highest labor opportunity costs, since technically they could earn more by using their formal educational training to secure jobs with higher or more stable remuneration than farming. Hutterites had the lowest labor opportunity costs, since their low formal education and their religious taboos against permanent outside employment, plus the very evident benefits of remaining in the colonies, effectively barred or discouraged them from leaving. Ranchers also had generally low labor opportunity costs, since, somewhat like the Hutterites, profitable enterprises and cultural traditions keep them in ranching. We also noted, however, that for both the ranchers and farmers the situation is complex, and the individual operator must make his own decisions as to whether to pursue agriculture or try his hand at other occupations. Moreover, job opportunities in fields other than agriculture are extremely scarce and not very remunerative in the Jasper region, and entrance into urban occupations is difficult for rural-trained people.

With respect to the opportunity costs of capital investment, we are confronted with the problem of rising values in agricultural properties. Essentially the question here is simply: can a man earn more by realizing his capital value in his farm or ranch and investing it in some other business? With respect to farms, again the answer tends to be "yes"; the opportunity costs of investing in farming are high, due to the undercapitalization of so many farms. Ranching has lower costs, due to the relative profitability of ranching and to the immense capital appreciation of ranch properties; they are extremely secure investments, even though they may provide relatively lower returns than some other business. Hutterite investment opportunity costs are of course low; by their own rules the Brethren cannot sell their colonies, and they realize relatively high rates of return. But we must again qualify the results by pointing out that many farmers and ranchers, aware of the inferior position of their enterprises, prefer to accept lower rates of return on their labor and capital investments because they like the life. The concept of opportunity cost must, therefore, always be qualified by cultural preferences.

The concept of opportunity costs also aided in the understanding of choices of strategies made by farmers to gain a better economic position. We noted that while they almost universally rejected costly agronomic experiments and innovations, and were even cautious on land accumulation, they were much more inclined to engage in political activity designed to obtain resources or stabilize prices and markets. The opportunity costs of innovation were too high—the risk of losing income in these marginal enterprises was too great. On the other hand, political participation entailed no risks—its opportunity cost was low— and one stood only to gain. In this sense politics can be seen as a resource alternative grasped by farmers when the need arose and the cost was low.

Similar mechanisms were at work in the various types of informal economic exchange practiced by Jasper farmers and ranchers. While these exchanges were reciprocal, reciprocity was adjusted to periods of slack or leisure, or people were used as laborers who were content with a few days or so of life in the farm or ranch as their "pay"—while the operator received the benefit of their labor. Thus the cooperative exchanges operated in large part on the basis of low opportunity costs.

4. It can be seen in Figure 10.1 that several key continua run parallel: (a) the continuum of scale; (b) relations with external society and government; (c) opportunity costs; (d) degree of

traditionalization of the cultural styles. In all four continua, the Hutterites and the farmers are at opposite poles, with the ranchers more or less in between. This suggests that economic security plus cultural isolation reinforces traditionalism (and also demographic stability and kinship connectedness), reduces the need for dependence on external agencies in order to obtain needed resources, and lowers opportunity costs, since the better-established enterprises can afford not to exploit local job opportunities in fields other than agriculture.

North American agricultural societies had no place to go but "up"; that is, starting from a polyglot undeveloped frontier, they could move only in the direction of more ramified social systems. Clearly, economic development has been associated in this case with increasing social development. On the other hand, many studies of peasant and tribal societies have shown that economic or agrarian development is associated with the opposite result; namely, social disorganization and breakup of the traditional groupings and relationships. While these results are expectable, considering the differences in the history of North American frontier and established peasant-tribal societies, there is still something incomplete about the record. For disorganization can be a passing phase; as the agricultural innovations take hold in peasant societies, they, too, develop socially, although certain changes in the traditional social forms are required.

It should be noted that in spite of differences, all three Jasper entrepreneurial groups seek the same basic objectives: economic security, stability of residence and social ties, and a favorable position *vis-à-vis* the market economy. Their consumption standards are relatively modest, although it is possible that all of them may be rising with the slowly growing prosperity of the 1960's. A mingling of the consumption styles of farmers and ranchers accompanies the shift to livestock production on the part of the former, showing the dependence of some features of cultural style on the market economy.

TIME AND DEVELOPMENT

The economic achievements of the Jasper ranchers and farmers described in this book required approximately three human generations to evolve to their present state. The Hutterites entered the region recently with an agricultural regime perfected in Alberta under generally similar environmental and resource conditions, although minor changes had to be made to cope with Jasper peculiarities—principally lighter soils and less rainfall. For the ranchers and farmers, agricultural development has consisted primarily of building enterprises of sufficient size and diversity to handle the inherent variability and risk. This was accomplished with the help of government interventions of several types, described elsewhere.

Ranching enterprises benefited from the allotments of grazing leases which were, in most cases, sufficiently large to permit the ranches to operate as "economic units." As costs have risen and standards of production improved, however, ranchers had to add to their pasture land and develop their forage production. Thus adjustments have been made steadily, largely at the expense of the smallest ranches, whose leases are sold to the larger when the land bureau approves. Development of an improved irrigated forage system of about 60 acres in extent on an average ranch requires approximately seven years; a rancher will therefore have the energy and time to develop three or four of these installations, depending on suitable resources, in his period of tenure. Only four or five ranches out of the 50 or so with the requisite resources had completed their irrigation regimes by 1963.

The development of a superior breed of beef cattle may take from 10 to 15 years, depending on the type desired. The refinement of an existing strain of straight Herefords to produce a "name line" of standard cattle associated with the particular ranch was the favorite regime in those ranches interested in breeding. A few were developing an Angus-Hereford hybrid, and a very few were entering the Charolais-Hereford-Angus breeding regime in the mid-1960's. All breeding projects and experiments were still in their early stages during our study.

Thus after three generations of ranching, the irrigated forage production and cattle breeding projects still had a long way to go. Only recently had Jasper ranchers begun to feel the necessity for intensive development.

The needs, possibilities, and rates of development in Jasper farming were more complex than in ranching. The farmer, starting with undersized enterprises from the standpoint of both land, water, and capital, was required to pay attention to a great many separate projects. Farming also requires much more machinery and generally more buildings (especially granaries) than ranching. A change in cropping patterns or types requires careful attention to timing, soil types, cover crops, fertilization, and a number of other things that makes the date when the innovation will pay off uncertain and usually long-delayed. We have already described the disinclination of most Jasper farmers to engage in complex development schemes because of the high risks due to uncertainty.

It required, on the average, two full human generations or about 50 years to build a cattle-grain farm from the original 160- or 320-acre homestead to about two sections, or around 1200 acres—a reasonably viable "economic unit" in the 1960's. In a typical case, the first-generation operator would have been able to add about three-fourths of the total land area in his lifetime, and establish the basic cropping pattern, adjusted to soils and topography. The second-generation successor or buyer would typically add the remainder of the land, buy the necessary powered machinery, build adequate structures, and introduce the new forage crops needed for livestock. The third-generation operator would complete the livestock part of the regime, and of course would continue to add land when available. Thus in Jasper a farm unit considered to be sufficiently diversified by the standards of the 1960's, and with its natural resources adequately developed, would require a minimum of two and a maximum of three human generations—from 50 to 75 years—for completion (see Fig. 7.1).

Due to the influence of the external agricultural economy for which Jasper people produce, however, farms—and ranches to an increasing extent—were never really "finished." Since the values in North American agriculture and living standards are constantly changing, the definition of economic viability for one generation is out of date by the next. This poses a problem for the social scientist insofar as the rate of economic change is often faster than the rate of culture change; the values that sanction a particular pattern of production and level of living may persist into a new successor generation, which then experiences pressures for change in these values. This situation requires, for economic survival, a remarkably adaptive approach to both culture and economic activity.

Jasper farming-ranching culture was based on two traditions: the open-range, adventurous ranching, and the eastern and British-European small-town–oriented subsistence-farming. The difficulties created by refractory natural resources and national economic conditions, plus the lack of capital, reinforced the conservative management traditions associated with these styles, and therefore for two generations tended to reinforce the pioneer cultural values. We have shown how Jasper cultural values and status definitions tended to focus on conservative management: the cautious, modest operator who saved his money and avoided conspicuous consumption had become a kind of ideal type in the ranching and farming population. While those who stayed in the region knew they had to accumulate land and develop some of their resources, these ventures were relatively cautious. By the 1960's, the region was close to the "take-off" stage of development, to use a term introduced in a recent work on the theory of economic development. The changed conditions, requiring more capital investments and greater innovativeness and daring, were a challenge to the young successors to the ranches and farms of the region, but not all of them were responding. Often it was the outsider, buying farm and grazing leases, who showed the objectivity and determination needed to move to a higher level of productivity and more intensive development of resources. These people were free of the inhibiting cultural strategies of conservativism and modest investment.

The innovative process was always at work in the region, however. The second generation was generally more innovative than the first, and the problem of refinancing the enterprise on takeover or purchase was necessary even in the earlier years. Jasper operators, allowing for the limitations of their resources

and capital, were as flexible as most North American agriculturalists, and cultural traditions were probably no more inhibiting than in many other regions of Canada and the United States.
We are suggesting that the entrepreneurial agricultural tradition, though it can manifest conservative, peasant-like phases,
has a tradition of response to economic opportunity that can
become manifest when conditions permit or demand.

Many anthropologists who have studied peasant societies have
explained their economic conservatism by cultural factors. For
example, some peasant societies may have patterns of ritual that
channel productive resources into nonproductive uses, as in the
case of the accumulation of livestock for use as dowries; or
others may be found to devote only a minimal amount of labor
to particular crops, using the balance of their time in social
activities or ceremonials.

As explanations of economic "backwardness" these cultural
patterns are not wrong, since unquestionably the behavior involved does divert attention from productive economic activity.
But the cultural explanations ignore the ecological and economic roots of the customs themselves. If the term "peasant"
means anything, it refers to agriculturalists who for *very long*
periods of time have had to cope with extreme shortages of
capital, exploitative practices by landlords and governments that
inhibit their opportunities, and weakly developed national
economies. Over time, peasants learned that attempts to increase
or rationalize production will fail, or would subject them to
additional risks and exploitation. Hence they developed customs
that used the available resources in ways that provided a modest
local existence, savings to cushion against the recurrent bad
times, or devices that consumed economically productive resources for social rituals. The situation breeds an attitude resembling the "zero-sum game" of the experts on game theory:
resources are fixed and finite, and any use of them tends to
reduce the supply, hence they must be saved and used for social
ends. Economic uses tend to be too risky, and the possibility of
loss is high.

However, this attitude is not peculiar to peasants. We have
shown that Jasper operators shared in it as well as a response to
the difficult economic conditions of the past. And in the chang-

ing present, many Jasper operators have not been sufficiently flexible to change their behavior toward a more productive pattern. But throughout the history of Jasper agriculture there always were a few who did see and seize opportunity, and in the contemporary period an increasing number were doing so. Because of external help, their participation in a market economy, and their basic entrepreneurial traditions they were perhaps more able to make this change than the typical peasant. But at the same time we must remember that many peasant societies respond in similar ways: in spite of cultural customs suppressing investment and development, there are always a few peasants who strike innovative postures.

Moreover, time really may be the critical variable. The longer an agriculturalist has to put up with high risk and exploitation, the greater the chance for his conservative strategies to become embedded in cultural reinforcements. The difficulty is that much of the surface appearance of peasantry can obscure some of these reinforcement differences: two peasant groups, similar in style, may respond very differently to changed opportunity because in one case there are fewer cultural reinforcements of conservatism, due to a shorter time period. In North American communities there is an additional factor: the general underlying commitment to pragmatism and instrumentalism created by the relationships to the external institutions.

Government aid is not the only force in agrarian development. The pace of development in the Jasper region can be regarded as "slow" if we compare it with other parts of North America that have enjoyed better resources and more external support, but the rate is "fast" if we consider it from the standpoint of how Jasper people were required to do it largely on their own resources. We have shown how Jasper ranchers and farmers used their own social system in such a way as to spread risks, increase scale, and allocate resources. This process is reminiscent of peasant agriculturalists who have been found to manifest considerable rationality and competence in using their own social and economic resources to promote survival under hard conditions. It would seem that agrarian development must always proceed from this dual standpoint: how it can be furthered by intensive use of available resources and styles of operation, and how it can benefit from external support and assistance.

Conservation of Resources

The basic approach of farm management and agricultural extension services in North America has been characterized by strong emphasis on production, but relatively weak stress on conservation. This has led in the United States to the problem of agricultural surpluses, although Canada has not really yet suffered from this particular hazard of success. As a consequence of the punishing droughts and dust storms of the 1930's, however, the people of the Great Plains have been more conscious of conservation than those in other parts of North America.

But in the context of capitalistic agriculture, the desirability of conservation is not enough to ensure its practice. Conservation of soils and water resources can mean, under given demographic magnitudes and pressures to produce, a limiting and inhibiting force. This is true especially in the early stages of a conservationist regime, before the new agronomic strategies have had a chance to pay off.

The best conservationists in Jasper were the operators of enterprises of large scale, particularly the bigger ranchers and the Hutterian Brethren. They were able to take care of their resources and keep some of them out of use only because their incomes were sufficient to cover the losses entailed. This is resources conservation by default, so to speak—although the people involved were usually cognizant of conservationist values. The small farmer, forced by income needs to keep his land under intensive cultivation, was often aware of the possible abuse, but had no choice in the matter. Canada has had no "soil bank" system, no subsidies for nonproduction, and fewer of the conservation experiments that have served the conservationist goal in the United States.

The conservation issue is bound up with population, and the question of the level of population that Jasper resources are able to support at given or desired consumption levels. This population level is of course influenced by the destruction of resources through carelessness or ignorance. Bad engineering in the early days of Jasper irrigation has eliminated several thousand acres from cultivation, since poor leveling resulted in ponding of the water and subsequent rise of salt to the surface. In one district, the population might double if these lands could come back into cultivation.

This is an issue with two sides, however. If we consider the Jasper region from one conservation standpoint, it can be argued that under present economic incentives, which tend to encourage exploitation of resources, the region is better off with fewer people, since larger enterprise units tend to be more conserving of their resources. However, in this sense, and ironically, a little spoliation, like the salinized irrigation plots mentioned above, might actually be desirable, since it removes land from cultivation (it can always be reclaimed, though this is usually too expensive at present cost levels), and thereby reduces population. We do not formally recommend abuse of resources as a means of controlling man's exploitation of the land (!)—only point out in this way that cultural-ecological processes are usually very complex, and simplistic conservationistic programs and ideology often do not take into account all the factors.

Abuse of existing resources is not only a matter of how particular enterprises are operated, but also where they are located. The homestead farming episode in Jasper opened up large tracts of land basically unsuitable for the styles of management and production practiced upon them. After the environmental disasters of the '20's and '30's, much of this land reverted to range, and was subsequently taken over by the government as community pasture, or otherwise reverted to livestock production. The most desirable conservationist program for the Jasper region would be to exclude all farming from the driest areas and from the slopes of the Hills, and concentrate it in a few belts of heavy soils and level topography, leaving the higher elevations and the drier areas for livestock production. This program, in the form of a gradual economic change, is actually under way in Jasper, as we shall note below.

ADAPTIVE PROCESSES

In Chapter 1 we defined "adaptive processes" as the generalizations the observer might make of the outcomes of the adaptive strategies used by people in their efforts to cope with the problems created by their effort to use resources productively. Adaptive processes thus can be found in operation in any dimension: demography, social organization, economy, technology, cultural values. They will be conditioned not only by the objective needs and the rational procedures devised to satisfy them, but also by the pre-existing institutional frameworks. Jasper's adaptive processes were ordered by the conditions of settlement, patterns of land tenure and the economic system, and the differing cultural styles of the settlers.

These processes were, in the main, the results of a series of trial-and-error practices, and not the result of consciously planned operations—although the latter are beginning to be more evident in the contemporary period. The rancher had to learn how to raise cows on a particular microhabitat; the homesteading event, and its laws, was a gigantic trial-and-error experiment in which politicians and businessmen said to the nation: "We will open the land for settlement on a small-farm basis and let's see what will happen!" Throughout the period of farm settlement there have been countless little experiments with new varieties of grain, machinery, cattle, sheep, cultivating methods, feeding methods, and so on. Farmers had to approach the problem of credit cautiously—going into debt a little at a time, to see how easily they might pay it off. Often poor land was bought without knowing quite what could be done with it —but with the general feeling that 'something will work out eventually.'

We emphasize trial-and-error adaptation not only because it has been a dominant style for Jasperites, but also because we wish to point out that the role of agricultural extension in Jasper, as in other parts of the Great Plains, has been a recent one, and perhaps not as significant a role as some of its advocates like to suggest. It is understandable that extension officials will seek to enhance the value of their profession, since they must get funds from legislatures in order to maintain it. Often enough, however, the style and approach of extension work is geared to profitable farming under conditions of resource abundance; the marginality and unpredictability of the Jasper regime is difficult to reduce to principles or rules, and the farmer and rancher have been thrown back on their own resources, so to speak, to discover what would work. Their own experiments and errors probably were as effective as expert help and information.

Consequently the adaptive processes characterizing agriculture and stock raising in Jasper are summations of complex sequences of trial-and-error activities on the part of farmers and ranchers and townspeople, and based on information procured from all possible sources. Survival has been as important a goal as profit, and often the Jasper agriculturalists have forgone profit in order to survive. These processes are in continual operation: the search is not yet complete, the outcomes not yet final. It is in the nature of agriculture in a dynamic national economy to continually seek out new adaptive solutions, and the solutions at any one point in time contain their own problematic aspects, requiring further change.

Resources Specialization. The first process to be considered concerns the tendency for modes of production to seek out suitable resources, and locations where the costs of production can be more easily met. About 1915 the Jasper landscape was dotted with groups of ranchers in the Hills and the sandy areas, with small farmers everywhere else. This meant that farming was taking place on soils of bewildering variety and topography, and in very dry areas and in reasonably moist districts. The modes of production themselves were relatively unspecialized: range cattle ranching and small-scale grain farming with a few cows. Irrigation was confined to the ranches along the creeks, whose owners simply turned the spring flood into their hay meadows.

By the 1960's, after three generations of settlement, this pattern was still visible, but many changes had been made. As shown in Figure 2.2, new specialized enterprises had developed near the town to take advantage of transportation and marketing facilities, and, incidentally, more profitably utilize the saline and sandy soils in that district. Farming had withdrawn from the drier and rougher areas, and many of these had been developed as community pastures and grazing cooperatives. Water from the hills had been channeled into reservoirs and new irrigation plots, to grow cattle feed. While the small farms were rapidly disappearing, small enterprises of specialized types, like purebred cattle raising and cattle feed lots, were coming into existence, their profitability based on their intensive use of small amounts of specialized resources, properly developed.

These tendencies to allocate different resources to different specialized uses were produced by both local action and external aid. The local efforts were of two kinds: negative and positive. The negative adjustments were made by farmers who could not make a living and who subsequently abandoned their farms or sold out, leaving the land to be diverted to other uses. The positive adjustments were made by farmers, ranchers, and townsmen who perceived opportunities and took them, when capital was available. Local agricultural extension services helped in this effort since they provided information on new procedures and new and profitable modes of production. An example is the new methods of raising cultivated pasture grasses on submarginal soils formerly unusued or supporting failing farming enterprises.

The measures introduced from the outside have been described elsewhere. The new varieties of crops and livestock, the pastures and grazing co-ops, the irrigation programs, and various experimental measures to increase the productivity of certain resources all helped to reallocate productive activities into the highly specialized districts of the region.

In one sense the direction of resources specialization recapitulates, in a sedentary settlement, the basic pattern of adaptation of the Plains Indians. The Indians found it necessary to move from place to place on the Plains to find the resources and conditions they needed to perform various activities. The extreme variability of the distribution of resources and the marginality of some of the critical resources imposed a nomadic life on people with a low-level technology. The contemporary population has had to cope with this same variability, but on a sedentary base. This was bound to impose severe hardship until some recognition of resources variability was built into the technology and economy. Specialization of production, and specialized loci for these modes of production, become the sedentary response to the variability problem.

Cooperation and Competition. These strategies of interaction in the Jasper economy have been described in detail in the previous chapter. We define them as adaptive processes since they have facilitated the allocation, distribution, and utilization of resources. Some aspects of competition have, of course, impeded general solutions, and the regional culture has not yet found a balance between cooperation and competition. Both processes represent the results of Jasper agriculturalists working toward solutions to their problems in their own way, with various aids and impedences from government. The problems are the need for larger economic scale in order to reduce risk and to save money to use as capital; the need to redistribute resources so that they can be used more productively; and the need to level out agricultural prices.

Given an entrepreneurial frame for the economy, the Jasper operators found that the available natural and economic resources were inadequate for their survival or for desired income, hence they found ways of saving money by helping each other and leveling costs and prices. Bureaucratic regulations governing land and water allocation did not always work to the advantage of the more efficient operators, hence competitional means were developed to manipulate these regulations in order to ensure a supply that was both more suitable and less equitable. "More suitable" in the sense of political action designed to secure cooperative marketing and pasture and irrigation projects for the community; "less equitable" in the sense of benefits flowing to the energetic minority in the case of grazing leases and certain water facilities.

Competitive Replacement. This process was illustrated most dramatically by the influx of Hutterian Brethren, and of course the process is really a special phase of the preceding. It refers to the replacement of inefficient operators—that is, those who fail to develop their resources and enterprises in some manner—by those more efficient and with enterprises of larger scale. In a capitalistic economy the rewards go to those who can produce more at low costs—and also those whose opportunity costs remain low and therefore whose dedication to the locality and its resources is high. Ranchers share, with the Hutterites, the low opportunity costs and dedication to the locality, but their livestock production per unit of land is lower than both farmers and Hutterites. They are, in addition, a demographic minority, and lack the political skills of the farmers.

Another example of replacement is found in the emergence of the expansionistic type of operator called a "land grabber" by Jasper people. These were often (about one-third) relatively recent in-migrants, farmers whose expansion plans were frustrated in their home districts and who moved to Jasper to take advantage of the relatively cautious policies of its operators. Like the Hutterites, these people sought farms in poor resource locations, often in the hands of aging owners who are ready to sell. And like the Hutterites, the expansionistic farmers were prepared to pay bonus prices for land since they conceived of it as a commodity with development potential and speculative value, not as a fixed resource.

A similar process was under way in the area around Jasper town. This area was the site of a large number of small homestead farms whose owners often worked part-time at menial town jobs. In the 1960's, Jasper businessmen and a few larger farmers began buying these farms in order to convert them into house sites, cattle feeding enterprises, and other specialized enterprises.

Farmers were also showing signs of replacing ranchers—at least in certain localities where large ranch leases were vulnerable to criticism on the grounds of bad or excessively traditional management. Again the basic strategy was not only political intervention by farmers, but also the fact that farmers usually could raise more cattle on a given amount of land, and this argument was hard to refute. Modern governments are generally on the side of the producers. No one expected all the ranch leases to disappear, and no doubt the Hills proper would remain the home of a ranching industry for a long time to come. But farmers were unquestionably moving in on some of the other districts.

Behavioral Selection. This term is used to refer to the several linked processes leading toward conservative agricultural management. The first of these involved the demographic process of migration out of the community, and the partial replacement by new settlers. We noted that the initial settlement (particularly the homestead farmers) was heterogeneous: every conceivable type of individual and motive for settlement was present: get-rich-quick types, adventurers, drifters, serious farmers, bachelors, and family men. As environmental and economic difficulties drove people away, the attrition was especially severe among bachelors and those whose conception of farming did not include hard work, frustration, low productivity or indefinitely deferred gratification. Those who remained, and most of the replacements who came late, were the patient ones who either lacked the funds to start anew elsewhere, or who decided to accept the challenge of agriculture in this difficult region. These people had to "adapt or get out," in Carl Kraenzel's terms, and their adaptive response was a cautious, conservative, risk-avoiding strategy of farm management.

Another process involved in behavioral selection was learning. People who stayed but did not have the requisite skills were required to learn them. This they managed by watching their neighbors, or learning the strategies as farm or ranch hands and eventually buying a "place."

Similar processes were at work among ranchers, although the causes did not include migration. Ranching was always relatively secure and profitable, and these facts, as well as the kind of person attracted to ranching—the frontier type—were not inclined to "push" economically, as Jasper people put it. Many of them simply "coasted" on their relatively abundant resources.

Behavioral selection also operated in the educational process. A study of high school records suggests that the young men with the best academic records were also the most likely to migrate toward further education or urban jobs. The young men most likely to remain in the region from the 1920's through the 1950's were those with limited education and/or relatively poor academic records whose skills were concentrated on the practical aspects of agriculture. Their shortcomings in the spheres of business practices and accounting were often made up for by their wives, since the young women who remained in the region, or who married in, were likely to have more education than their husbands.

Thus in several related ways the ecological and economic conditions of the Jasper region tended to favor the survival of relatively cautious, consumption-deferring personalities. By the 1960's the processes of selection were beginning to work in the other direction: to favor the more innovative, daring, and sophisticated operators who knew the value of their investments and the need for higher productivity. If general economic conditions remain the same for an indefinite period, one may assume that this is the direction of adaptive behavior in the region for the future. Thus the economic and ecological situation lies behind such social phenomena as education, learning, succession to enterprises, or migration. This situation *does* constitute a form of determinism, but in acknowledging this, we do not offer a general theory applicable to all societies. Our observations are confined to agrarian contexts in which resources are variable and marginal, and where reliance on external economic supports is increasingly important.

Demographic Retention. This process is really an effect of all of the development measures described elsewhere. We refer to the tendency for Jasper township population curves to level out above the lowest point, reached in the 1940's at the end of the decade of drought and depression. We noted that where this occurred in farming districts there also were found community pastures, grazing cooperatives, and community irrigation projects. All of these measures introduced a degree of stability and raised or leveled off incomes. This in turn permitted a larger number of farms to remain as viable units, and therefore succeeded in halting—or at least delaying—population migration and the loss of farms.

This process is significant for reasons that transcend the circumstances of the Jasper region. The continual loss of population from rural areas in North America has had its undesirable consequences in the cities, which fill up with rural migrants seeking jobs. While some flow of population from country to urban areas is inevitable and desirable in industrial societies, the process can get out of hand, and some means must be found to hold people in rural areas. This requires adjustments in agriculture as well as the promotion of job opportunities through the decentralization of industry. Levels of living need to be adjusted so that the "social cost of space" and "status deficits" experienced by rural people are less apparent. Clearly there is a need for a reallocation of capital in North American society in order to control population changes that work hardships on certain sections of the society.

RECOMMENDATIONS FOR JASPER

Jasper will remain, for the foreseeable future, an agrarian society, because its resources and its distance from urban areas will prevent a major industrial growth. Consequently its future must be considered as a problem of agrarian development. But this does not mean that Jasper town cannot make good use of a few small-scale, light industries, both to provide locally needed commodities and to provide jobs for the young people of the town and country. Such industry will need subsidies. Jasper's one industry, a fence-post manufacturing and treating plant, survived for about five years in the 1960's, and then foundered due to lack of capital to provide sufficient expansion to achieve a profitable scale. Government would do well to select one or two such industries—a farm-machine assembly plant, a small-home prefabricating plant, a livestock by-products processing factory, perhaps a small oil refinery—and see them through their first decade or so of existence. The organized consumer cooperatives could help also—they already have, with distribution stations for agricultural commodities, a home-building service, and retail stores.

Jasper also needs further assistance in the reallocation of modes of production into areas with suitable resources. Too much farming is done in dry, light-soil areas that would be better shifted to livestock. More community pastures and grazing cooperatives will help. The system of private water rights needs changing to ensure a more equitable and predictable supply of water in certain districts. Cattle-feeding businesses need special subsidies. Sheep could be revived in certain districts with government-provided incentives and bonuses. The region needs more diversified agriculture, both to increase economic stability and also to provide more opportunities for the young men.

Informal cooperative mechanisms need strengthening. Jasper operators have already shown that they are willing to engage in these risk-spreading interactions—the custom should be formally acknowledged and built upon. The small scale of many Jasper farms can be enlarged to some extent by the large-scale measures already described, but Jasper agriculturalists themselves could be encouraged to engage in more cooperative interaction. There are probably too many powered farm machines in the region, and machine-owning cooperatives, relatively successful in other parts of Saskatchewan, should be encouraged in Jasper. Farmers and small ranchers could be given incentives to cooperate more on land use—aside from the formally organized grazing co-ops, cooperative use of pasture by neighbors could be encouraged and fostered. This would require considerable change in the present laws governing the use of pasture leased land, which is strictly reserved for the individual lease-holder.

Area redevelopment schemes, already beginning in some parts of western Canada under a federal government agency, are logical for Jasper. Large tracts of mixed and submarginal soils could be placed under joint management by government and local farmers and ranchers to begin its conversion to rational and mixed uses. A tie-in between forage-raising farmers and ranch-farm livestock raisers is the logical aim of such development projects. This would also serve the desirable economic objective of promoting cooperative specialization, the key to a more stable income.

More capital is needed for development purposes. There is no adequate means of financing new farm or ranch starts—young men without families, or with very poor families, have no suitable means for obtaining the money they need to buy and develop a new enterprise. The government loans tie up the entire farm as security and prevent the young man from obtaining short-term bank credit—although the regulations do benefit young men whose fathers help them take over the enterprise. A more cooperative approach to farm credit, in which the govern-

ment and all private sources, especially the banks, work together
to establish the credit risk position of young men would be a
desirable move. The special needs of the Jasper region—its high
risk agriculture—need to be carefully studied and exceptions
made in rules that were written with eastern Canadian farming
in mind.

The one theme running through all of these measures is outside intervention, especially government aid. In an individualistic culture devoted to individual success and self-help, these
measures need very careful planning. The difficulties of the
Community Pastures are a case in point: without some economic
stake in management of these pastures, farmers regard them
simply as resources to be exploited, not used cooperatively.
Spoon-feeding and bureaucratic paternalism do not work well
among people with traditions of entrepreneurial independence
and self-respect—yet clearly banks and governments must intervene. Imaginative procedures are needed; the safe bureaucratic
solutions do not work.

Most fundamentally, all agencies involved in intervention need
to consider the particular causes of the phenomena they seek to
remedy. Often the approach to agricultural development in
North America is viewed in strict economic terms—the fact that
many of the problems are sociological in nature is not grasped.
The family farm is viewed as a desirable ideal, and efforts are
made to preserve it by bureaucratic rule. However, many forces
affect the dissolution of the family farm: the general weakening
of kin ties in modern society; increasing educational exposure;
and the rising opportunity costs of farming work against it,
which means the city is in competition with the countryside.
The objective should be to make agriculture viable—however
agriculture is to be operated, by the family or by some other
means. Corporate structures are the future in Jasper as elsewhere—a family might continue to run the corporation, but
this will be and is a far cry from the idealized image of the
single nuclear kin group operating a neat little enterprise.

There is a disposition in government circles in both Canada
and the U.S. to consider rural phenomena as either unimportant,
or as subject to certain inevitable processes beyond human control. Flow of country population to the city is often considered

to be one of these processes; the decline of the small towns is another. There is no question that these processes are difficult to arrest or modify so long as they are regarded as automatic and beyond intervention. But the data on Jasper indicate that this is far from the case. The resource-development projects in the region have had an effect on population retention; the deliberate choice of towns for the location of new services (as in the case of Eldora for a high school, and Jasper for the hospital and some other facilities) contributed greatly to the population-retaining power of these towns and their commercial development, thus benefitting the surrounding population in many ways. Much more could be done to provide opportunities and services for local people in rural North America. While initial costs look large, the human capital they would create in time would surely be worth it, and the savings in terms of welfare costs in the cities would probably be even greater. Vision and daring is desperately needed.

Saskatchewan had, for a period of 15 years, a remarkably progressive government: the Cooperative Commonwealth Federation (CCF). Whatever its failings, this government and party had one policy regarded by this author as fundamentally correct: it perceived the continuing importance of the rural sector in Saskatchewan society and economy, and did many useful things to improve this sector and make life more interesting for its inhabitants. This era ended in 1964, when a Liberal government came to power. While the new government has not reversed the policies established by the CCF, it has not extended them, nor has it shown awareness of the need to foster and improve the agrarian basis of Saskatchewan life. Instead, it has chosen to focus on industrial development and urbanization. This is not all bad, but its ultimate value, in this land so far from markets, and so short of the resources needed for industrial production, is a matter of doubt.

Tourism will increase in Jasper—the town fathers in 1967 were working hard to develop a ski run and a winter carnival. They may succeed. The Provincial Park attracts a respectable number of outsiders, but it is obviously operated primarily for the benefit of local people, and there is nothing wrong with that. However, tourism income can be developed without serious injury to Jasper traditions by a more progressive approach by town merchants and politicians. The town lacks adequate stores and souvenir shops to part tourists from some of their loose dollars; the colorful Cypress Hills are only partly developed in terms of historical museums and trails.

Jasper's future is therefore both certain and uncertain. Like many backwaters in North America, it must remain agricultural in the main. But the direction this agriculture may take, and how it can be supplemented by other occupations, is not clear. One thing is certain: if outsiders do not help, it will remain pretty much as it was in the early 1960's—a half-developed region with considerable population outflow, and with few opportunities for its brightest youth. Surely it deserves better; surely Canada and the United States would benefit if the many Jaspers in each of them received a little more of their share of the national income.

POSTSCRIPT

Just before this book went to press, some of the recommendations seemed to be materializing: just west of the town, a large, automated cattle feeding enterprise was established, the first of these large-scale production ventures (small, manually fed feed lots had made their first appearance in the early 1960's). Thus Jasper received its initial example of industrial agriculture. The second development concerned the announcement by the Federal Government of the choice of the Jasper region and adjoining areas as pilot cases for tryout of the Regional Incentives Act passed by Parliament in 1969. This Act provides financing for small industrial plants in areas like Jasper having difficulty diversifying their economy and in need of subsidy.

BIBLIOGRAPHIC NOTES

The changes and processes of adaptation analyzed in this chapter are likely to be found in all agrarian societies, regardless of the level of their development. For example, when resources are specialized and unevenly distributed, the agrarian society will alter its settlement patterns in accordance with this distribution. Archeologists have provided a number of studies of instances of such adaptive specialization, since the archeologist can study change over longer periods of time. The pattern observed in the Valley of Oaxaca by Coe and Flannery is typical. In their study, hunting and food-collecting and very simple agricultural societies were found in a variety of microenvironments at different elevations on the valley sides and surrounding plateau. As intensive corn-bean-squash agriculture developed, however, settlement gradually became restricted to the watered valley floor proper. In this way the valleys of Mexico became the centers of city civilization. See K. V. Flannery and others, "Farming Systems and Political Growth in Ancient Oaxaca," *Science,* Vol. 158, No. 3800 (1967), pp. 445–54. For a comparable study for the Middle East, see Robert McAdams, "Agriculture and Urban Life in Early Southwestern Iran," *Science,* Vol. 136, No. 3511 (1962).

Differences between the raising of livestock and of crops lead to cultural differences, as we have shown in various chapters. The relationship is not a simple one, however, since at least some of the differences are based on cultural and social differences in the original settler populations or ranchers and farmers. In the anthropological studies of tribal pastoralists, certain provisional conclusions have been reached about the specific effects of livestock production on cultural and social organization. In purely pastoral societies, where no crops at all are raised, and where the society is wholly or partly nomadic, a number of traits have been identified as especially typical: emphasis on masculinity among the men, and a general cultural stress on the male role; a marked pattern of hospitality; ritual content suggesting the importance of mastery over animal species. For a discussion of these traits, see Walter Goldschmidt, "Theory and Strategy in the Study of Cultural Adaptability," *American Anthropologist,* Vol. 67 (1965), pp. 402–8.

The process of development of organized community life in Great Plains communities as a result of growing economic stability was first noticed by Earl H. Bell in *The Culture of a Contemporary Rural Community: Sublette, Kansas,* Bureau of Agricultural Economics, Rural Life Study No. 2. U.S. Department of Agriculture, 1942.

Anthropologists, as noted in the chapter, have tended to emphasize cultural factors in seeking explanations of the relative conservatism of peasant responses to innovation and change. Still, many peasant societies often show surprising interest in new ideas, and take up new ways as quickly as farmers, or even more quickly. Cultural factors often cannot provide the explanations for this receptivity to change, and the answers must be sought in technical and economic arrangements concerning risk-taking. A comprehensive survey of the literature on peasantry and the problem of change, including citations to studies that illustrate the peasant ability to change, is found in Joel M. Halpern and John Brode, "Peasant Society: Economic Changes and Revolutionary Transformations," in B. J. Siegel and Alan Beals, eds., *Biennial Review of Anthropology,* Stanford University Press, 1967. An article which is especially valuable for comparing change and development among farmers and peasants, is Charles J. Erasmus, "Upper Limits of Peasantry and Agrarian Reform: Bolivia, Venezuela, and Mexico Compared," *Ethnology,* Vol. 6 (1967), pp. 349–80. Erasmus' "upper limits" of peasant ability to innovate overlaps with the "lower limit" of our farmers and ranchers. An illuminating study of management decision-making, and change in peasant agriculture is Michael Moerman, *Agricultural Change and Peasant Choice in a Thai Village,* University of California Press, 1968.

A classic and controversial work on the general patterns of economic growth, with emphasis on the concept of "take-off" as representing the stage reached by a society when rapid economic development becomes possible, is W. W. Rostow, *The Stages of Economic Growth,* Cambridge University Press, 1960. A consideration of development in the agricultural context is included in Max Millikan and David Hapgood, *No Easy Harvest: The Dilemma of Agriculture in Underdeveloped Countries,* Little, Brown, 1967. This book is relatively pessimistic concerning the possibilities of change. An approach to agrarian development which is in some respects the opposite of the former, since it emphasizes that peasant agriculture contains the resources for orderly and rapid change, providing this is acknowledged and respected by the technical aid missions, is Ester Boserup, *The Conditions of Agricultural Growth: The Economics of Agrarian Change under Population Pressure,* Aldine, 1965.

Index